To Sue,

best regards

David Hughes

28.5.2014

Acknowledgements and References

Diageo
Sincere thanks for giving me permission to use the Benson and Gilroy images, Trade Marks etc, and for giving me a licence to publish this book. The Guinness archive supplied many original artwork images. Grateful thanks go to Eibhlin Roche and Heather Malcolm for their support.

Rob Niederman
Huge thanks go to Rob for invaluable support, ideas, encouragement and images.

History of Advertising Trust
Thanks to the History of Advertising Trust for supplying images and for help.

Museum of London
Thanks to the Museum of London for supplying images and help.

The Gilroy Family
This book includes a biography of John Gilroy, thanks to the significant contribution of his family. It was always the wish of his son John (who sadly died in 2012 after a long illness) to publish a biography, but it fell to his grandson Jim and his daughter-in-law Fiona and step-daughter Jenefer to provide much of the new material on his life. Jim Gilroy now runs his own advertising agency and his company kindly did some of the book design work. Jim's mother Fiona supplied *JTY Gilroy's Life and Times* written by Tony Thwaite, Jim Gilroy's brother-in-law. Fiona Gilroy and Jenefer Tatham provided many family photos and Jenefer provided great details of his life from 1960 to his death in 1985. [3]

Brian Sibley [4]
Wrote the first book on Guinness Advertising and knew Gilroy in the final years of his life. He supplied several images of Gilroy artwork.

Steve Tedds
Steve's discovery of the Benson's artwork in the USA in 2012 provided early inspiration for this book.

Michael Dukes Constantinides [1]
Worked for Benson from 1956 and was on the Guinness account after the Gilroy era. He knew Alan Wood very well and they moved the Benson advertising style away from the Gilroy imagery towards a more realistic everyday style. He left Benson when they were sold to Ogilvy to form his own business in 1971.

Hugh de Quetteville [5]
He worked for Benson as Guinness Account Manager from 1954 to 1963. He worked with Tommy Marks and Alan Wood of Guinness.

Edward Guinness CVO [2]
A member of the brewing family, he joined Guinness in London in 1945 as a Brewer and held senior positions in Personnel, Regional Sales and latterly as Chairman of Harp Lager and as a main Board Director during the Ernest Saunders era. Edward was the editor of the Guinness Time in-house magazine for many years and commissioned many Gilroy images.

Nicola Hobbs
Nicola is the widow of Bruce Hobbs, who was the Creative Art Director at Benson. She and Bruce cleared the poster stockroom in Kingsway in 1971 when the building was sold, but they did not come across the artwork archive at the time.

Liberties Press
My patient and encouraging publisher.

Doug Winter
Doug is ex-Guinness and supplied several images of Gilroy artwork.

John Hughes
A friend of Gilroy, he photographed many of Gilroy's portraits during the commission process, during the last five years of his life.

Alan Wood
Guinness Advertising Manager after Tommy Marks through the 1960s.

Robert Lloyd
Robert offered great help with canvas images, both sold and unsold.

Rory and Edward Guinness
Many thanks for the encouragement to produce a third book on Guinness and its colourful history.

Andrew Vogel
Who helped with canvas images.

Contents

Author's Note	5
Introduction – The Hon. Rory Guinness	6
Foreword by Jim Gilroy	7
Chapter 1 John Gilroy's Biography	9
Chapter 2 The Portraits	25
Chapter 3 Benson, Ogilvy & Mather and Guinness	39
Chapter 4 Guinness for Strength	65
Chapter 5 The Zoo and other exotic animals	85
Chapter 6 Show cards, lobsters, whales and fish	115
Chapter 7 Toucans	127
Chapter 8 Classic Cars	135
Chapter 9 London, the Olympics and Coronation	159
Chapter 10 Foreign Countries and War Time	167
Chapter 11 Watercolours and Roughs	197
Chapter 12 The Smiling Glass, Guinness Time and Christmas	209
Chapter 13 Golf courses and Knights in armour, Hastings 1066	217
Chapter 14 Early Black and White Adverts	225
Chapter 15 Conclusion	243
Appendix 1 Catalogue of Canvases	246

Author's Note

A large amount of newly discovered original artwork by John Gilroy for Guinness has turned up in the USA, which originated from the S. H. Benson Advertising Agency Archive. These works date from 1930 to the mid-1960s and they are all oil on canvas paintings. Many canvases (I know of about three hundred Guinness related canvases but I believe there were originally as many as seven hundred pieces) are advert or poster proofs, some are finished work, others unfinished. Many were never adopted for commercial use and have never been viewed since Gilroy's day. This amount and type of commercial artwork had not been seen on the market before and there is even considerable duplication of images. This is a huge art discovery bringing with it the detective story of how and when and to whom the Benson Archive was sold. This artwork is currently valued by the market at north of $2million. This book has been produced just in time before the art is distributed for all time across numerous private collections in the USA, Russia and Europe. Because this art is now scattering, I must apologise for the quality of some images but in many cases these grainy pictures were the only access I have had to many canvases. Some canvases have not aged well and have darkened or taken on a colour cast.

It could be argued that John Gilroy's portraiture work was the most important art he produced, as he painted Royalty, the Pope, the Guinness family, Military personnel and celebrities? For example in 1942 he painted Churchill in the London Bunker. The picture was allegedly given to Joseph Stalin at the Yalta Conference. However there is no place in this book for more than a few of his portraits, as I would argue his early commercial work on the Guinness account (1930-1962) in tandem with the S. H. Benson Advertising Agency, will be his lasting testimonial. It is what everyone will now, and in the future, remember him for. The artist had a foot in many different camps; being exhibited at the Royal Academy, hung in the National Portrait Gallery, and regularly appearing as a humorous commercial artist on the back page of the *Daily Express* or on poster hoardings across British cities. Gilroy and Guinness were the dream ticket!

John Gilroy was responsible for some of the best-loved, most remembered, iconic advertising poster images of the last hundred years, that will be forever remembered as the pinnacle of Guinness imagery. John Gilroy was credited with inventing 'visual silence' in advertising and that simplicity is what has made his work iconic. Was John Gilroy not one of the most famous British artists to come out of the Newcastle area?

The objective of this book is to display much of this unseen, unpublished, commercial artwork for Guinness, and to tell the unique story of Gilroy, his relationship with Benson and with Guinness.

Brian Sibley wrote a wonderful book on Guinness Advertising in 1985, that covers much of the commercially used Gilroy material. It is not my intention to replicate that seminal work, but rather to add a postscript about Gilroy's contribution and to complete this amazing story. Gilroy was never officially honoured for his work, but I hope now we can see him for the great influence he had as a popular artist of the 20th Century. The purists in the Art World looked down their noses at the commercial artists, hence he was never elected to the Royal Academy, but they in their elitist view denied the reach of Gilroy's art into nearly every home in this country. A multi-million pound industry has sprung up using his images. Few if any artists can claim this level of appreciation by the general public.

Gilroy led a full and rich life with good health, interesting friends and close family. He achieved great acclaim and recognition in his lifetime. Like many artists he was casual with money, spending as he earned. He lived in the present, making little provision for the future. Reward for his art was acceptable but of course never enough. In writing about the Artist's life, I have come to appreciate just how widely travelled he was and what a life rich in human experience he led. He was a smallish man but of giant stature, wit and humanity. I have come to greatly admire him and wish I had met him. Those who knew 'Jack' Gilroy (as John was often known), loved him for his personality. I do hope he would have appreciated this book.

David Hughes

Introduction by The Hon. Rory Guinness

When I was growing up at Farmleigh, a large house in the Phoenix Park in Dublin, I didn't know what my father did. I knew that he went to the brewery every day, and I knew that sometimes lots of important people would come from the brewery to meet my parents. I didn't understand that he was Chairman of Guinness.

However I did understand the posters of the zookeeper and various unruly animals that were hung on the walls of our nursery, and that they were a key part of brewery life. I was very happy thinking that my father was going to work with them.

It was in 1929 that my great-grandfather, Rupert Guinness, 2nd Earl of Iveagh, saw sales of Guinness flagging and decided that the time had come for the company to completely revitalise its marketing. Until then Guinness had been sold as a health-giving tonic. The S. H. Benson Advertising Agency was employed to add some vivacity and colour to the company's rather clinical promotional material. A young man called John Thomas Young Gilroy was put in charge of the artwork.

S. H. Benson must have created an amazing team of artists, writers and managers that looked after Guinness's account. But it was Gilroy's work that corralled together all the mechanics of advertising, the words and the pictures, to create the iconic Guinness advertising that I came to love.

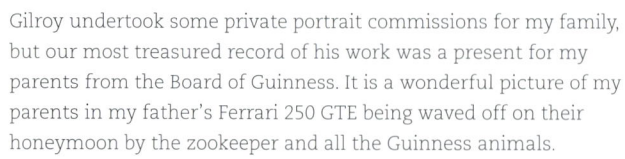

Gilroy undertook some private portrait commissions for my family, but our most treasured record of his work was a present for my parents from the Board of Guinness. It is a wonderful picture of my parents in my father's Ferrari 250 GTE being waved off on their honeymoon by the zookeeper and all the Guinness animals.

Looking back at the Gilroy advertising today, it still remains so fresh and fun, and yet it is so simple. This is not unlike brewing, so perhaps that is why Gilroy and Guinness made such a good partnership.

I am delighted to welcome you to this wonderful, and much needed, catalogue of John Gilroy and his amazing talent.

Rory Guinness

Disclaimer

This book contains historical product claims that are not now endorsed by GUINNESS®. In illustrating these advertisements it is not the Author's or Guinness's intention to promote benefits of drinking but to show GUINNESS® stout advertising over more than 80 years. Adults who choose to drink should do so responsibly.

Foreword

To me, my grandfather 'Pop' was the embodiment of his art. Loveable charm and cheeky humour flowed from him as it did from his paintbrush. He was an entertainer - on and off canvas.

As a child in the 70s, every visit to his Holland Park studio was memorable. It was a cavernous place filled with the heady smell of oils from the drying canvases of his celebrated sitters.

In amongst it all beamed Pop, sporting his favourite green velvet jacket, a jaunty bow tie and smoking a cigar. As our games became unruly he would whisper, 'Shhh, don't wake the baby.' Hours of fruitless searching for this elusive infant would follow as he quietly chuckled to himself.

My father inherited Pop's talent as a draftsman. On one occasion, shortly after graduating as an engineer, he noticed an early sketch of a new Guinness campaign and commented that the huge girder on the worker's head was balanced at the wrong point. After some discussion, Pop redrafted the ad and as a flourish adjusted the worker's features to resemble those of my father.

Pop and his son were both hugely proud of each other; it's sad that my father just missed out on seeing this book published.

David Hughes's passion for Guinness history has led him to unearth a wealth of previously unpublished work. Just as I was inspired to follow a career in advertising, I hope this collection will help inspire future generations of illustrators and artists.

John Gilroy's lasting contribution to the world of advertising is further cemented by this book, so too is the legacy of mischievous humour he instilled in those of us lucky enough to have known him as 'Pop'.

Jim Gilroy

1
John Gilroy's Biography

John Thomas Young Gilroy,
MA, ARCA, FRSA

Biography

John Thomas Young Gilroy (1898-1985) was a superb natural draughtsman and a versatile illustrator and artist, who produced classic advertising material, royal portraits, landscapes, murals and greeting cards. He was a prolific artist and much original artwork survives. The dominant feature of his art was the draughtsmanship and accuracy of dimension and form, embodying character and atmosphere. His poster philosophy was simple: 'make it bold, make it clear, make it vigorous. If you're designing a poster, then design it so that it can be read by the pedestrian, the car driver and the passenger on the upper deck of a bus. Complicated, intricate, fussy designs are, literally, a waste of space.'

'Make it memorable. Make it funny - or, if you don't want to be funny, then make it intriguing. Tease the observer. Make them laugh, make them think but, most of all, make them *like* it - even *love* it'. This is precisely what John Gilroy did.

Born on 30 May 1898 at Whitley Bay, Newcastle upon Tyne, he was the third child of a family of eight (five boys and three girls), born to John William Gilroy and his wife Elizabeth. Elizabeth was a skilled book binder and John William Gilroy was a technical draughtsman in a marine boiler works. He later became a well-known marine artist and photographic colourist, and it was obvious from an early age that John Jr was going to follow in his father's footsteps. In 1898 John William Gilroy had two pictures exhibited at the Royal Academy. Gilroy Sr was a natural humorist and Concert Party enthusiast. John Jr learned much from his parents and always remembered his father's words that 'it takes seven years to learn to draw and seven days to learn to paint' - and from then on became obsessed with the art of drawing. The young John practised copying cartoons from *Punch* and took on all kinds of work to pay for drawing materials. From the age of fifteen he was a paid freelance cartoonist for the *Newcastle Illustrated Chronicle*, commissioned to produce daily cartoons of well-known entertainers who played the Newcastle Theatres. There he drew amongst others, George Robey, Harry Houdini, George Formby, Vesta Tilley, the Terry Sisters and Sir John Lytham. For his cartoons he earned seven shillings and six pence a week.

John Sr, a portrait by John T. Y. Gilroy.

John attended Sandyford School where he came under the influence of A. K. Lawrence (five years his senior but already acclaimed by the teachers as a genius) followed in 1909 by Heaton Park Road Upper School. Vacations were spent on a farm where he learned to ride horses. John later admitted that his formal education suffered at the expense of drawing. At this date his family was living at 25 Kingsley Place and he was apprenticed to a designer of stained glass, studying drawing in the evenings. In June 1912, he left Heaton Park and, having attained his drawing certificate, at age sixteen he won the Christie Scholarship to attend Armstrong College Art School, Durham University to study full-time under Professor K.G. Hatten.

The First World War interrupted Gilroy's studies as, too young to enlist; he took a clerical post at Fenham Barracks, the depot of the Royal Northumberland Fusiliers, before he joined the London Scottish in 1917. From there, he transferred to the Royal Field Artillery, serving in France, Italy and then Palestine with Allenby's forces. Wounded, he was sent home on Christmas Day 1918. In 1919 he resumed his studies at Armstrong College. Another scholarship sent him to the Royal College of Art, Kensington, London (the RCA).

During his time there he produced illustrations for the college student magazine and occasionally played in goal for the college football team. In 1920 he attained his Board of Education certificate and the RCA Diploma in Decorative Painting. His work was also rewarded through scholarships and prizes, winning the Lord Northbourne Prize for landscape composition which gave him a

BIOGRAPHY

John on his horse in the Royal Field Artillery, 1917.

"We are here for an indefinite period . . ."

Gilroy's drawings for the RCA Students Magazine, 1923.

Gilroy's drawings for the RCA Students Magazine, 1923.

month at the Louvre in Paris, and in 1921, the college drawing prize and the British Institute Scholarship for decorative painting. The RCA had a strong presence from the North Country with A. K. Lawrence, Henry Moore, Barbara Hepworth, Henry Carr and Vivien Pitchforth. John also enjoyed the social side of the Royal College of Art, taking acting parts in revues and plays as well as playing football and ping pong.

In 1922 Gilroy was thinking of leaving the RCA to gain work experience but was persuaded by Prof Gerald Moira, the Chief Instructor, to stay on and sit the Diploma. In 1922 Gilroy had been made an Associate of the RCA, and fourteen years later he was elected a Fellow of the Royal Society of Arts. As a very young ARCA he won an RCA Travelling Scholarship in mural painting, and went to Europe for six months, and missed the Prix de Rome by only one vote. He visited Paris and Italy to study the Great Masters. In Rome he and some other students were presented to King Emmanuel and Mussolini, who Gilroy found to be 'short, squat and heavy of jaw'. Victor Emmanuel he found 'warmer, pathetically short, with a crumpled face and padded uniform - when he stood to attention his uniform was still at ease'.

Gilroy graduated from the RCA in July 1924 but stayed on there until 1925 as a teacher. From 1924 to 1926 he also taught Drawing of the Figure in the evenings at the Camberwell School of Art. He found he enjoyed teaching as an occupation and he was now earning enough to consider matrimony.

Whilst at the RCA he had met fellow student Gwendoline Peri Short (b1903). She was an attractive dark-haired girl studying pottery and cotton print design and on 6 September 1924, at St Helen's Church, Kensington, he married her. The couple had one son three years later, John Morritt (b. 1927). Gwen was a talented flower and landscape artist in her own right and would prove a wise critic of Gilroy's work.

The Gilroys were a talented family, his father and wife artists and his brother a concert pianist. John Gilroy had great love and admiration for his son. He named him John Morritt Gilroy, after his friend Colonel Harry Morritt, who was the child's Godfather. In later life he was to extend that great love to his three grandchildren, all of whom have a talent for the arts and design.

Joining the
Benson Agency

To improve his earnings Gilroy now looked for employment in the commercial sector. In 1925 he embarked on his long association with the advertising agency S. H. Benson Ltd (Benson). His contract was for three days a week at £500 per annum, twice his teaching salary. Although Benson was the first advertising agency for whom Gilroy worked as an in-house artist, he had already proven himself in the commercial art sphere. His earliest known piece of commercial art, dating from 1920 when he was still a student, was for a promotional leaflet for the Mangnall-Irving Thrust-Borer commissioned by the Hydraulic Engineering Co.

At Benson, his first assignment involved monotonous reproduction and lettering which soon led to him resigning. However the day he resigned, he met Dorothy L. Sayers who asked him to illustrate a booklet called 'The recipe book of the Mustard Club' for J & J Coleman.

Portrait of Gwendoline hung at the RA.

That night he sketched some pages which he handed to Miss Sayers the next day. Impressed, she went to Philip Benson who offered Gilroy full-time work, five and a half days per week at double the salary. John accepted as he could now do individual work. Working on accounts such as Coleman, Bovril, Johnnie Walker, and Imperial Tobacco, his work grew in scope and he was soon offered a free hand to bring out his inherent sense of humour. He worked on campaigns for Skipper Sardines, Sunlight Soap, Marmite, Austin Cars, Virol, Macleans and Monk & Glass Custard. But his first significant assignment was the Mustard Club campaign for Coleman's of Norwich, on which he worked with fellow artist William Brearley and the copywriters Oswald Greene and Dorothy L Sayers. Between 1926 and 1933 the pens of Gilroy and Brearley brought eccentric characters like Baron de Beef, Signor Spaghetti and Miss Di Gester to life on bill boards and in magazines everywhere.

His work on posters sprang up everywhere and had the quality of carrying the message clearly and convincingly without unnecessary force. His presentation was just enough rather than too much. In 1929 Benson won the Guinness advertising account and Gilroy became involved with the product with which his work is most closely associated. His first Guinness illustrations were black and white line drawings for use in National newspapers and magazines (see the last chapter).

His first known and signed Guinness poster was 'George and the Dragon', produced in 1929. Working with copywriters like Ronald Barton, Stanley Penn and Robert Bevan, Gilroy's art was at the heart

Gilroy about twenty-five years old, photo portrait.

BIOGRAPHY

of one hundred press advertisements and nearly fifty poster designs for Guinness over a span of thirty-five years. He actually produced many more ideas and images that were never seen by the public. He is perhaps best remembered for his posters featuring the girder carrier and the wood cutter from the *Guinness for Strength* campaigns of the early 1930s and for the Guinness animals. The animals, including the lion, toucan, pelican, tortoise, sea lion, ostrich and kangaroo, appeared with their long-suffering zookeeper on posters, press advertisements, show cards and waiter trays from the 1930s to the 1960s.

Gilroy continued to produce Guinness advertisements well into the 1960s even though he had left Benson's employment as an in-house artist in the early 1940s to continue his freelance work. Indeed once a freelance, Gilroy developed a direct relationship with the Guinness Advertising Managers in London and Dublin.

During the 1920s and succeeding decades, commercial art was not Gilroy's sole occupation; he began to build his reputation as a painter, both of portraits and landscapes. One of his earliest portrait commissions was to paint the Prince of Wales, the future Edward Vlll, for the Royal Mid-Surrey Golf Club, of which Gilroy was a member and the Prince was patron. Gilroy was later to paint Edward VIII as King, the only artist to do so, according to Gilroy.

In 1930, while the family was living at The Cottage, Hyde Park Road, Kew Gardens, Gilroy had his first painting, *Gwen*, a simple drawing of his beautiful wife, exhibited at the Royal Academy.

Gilroy's work was exhibited at the Royal Academy in 1930, '33, '35, '39, 1940, '41, '42, '44, '45, '46, '47, '48, '49, '51 and '53, and his adverts appeared on advertising hoardings, in newspapers and even in the Radio Times. In 1941, with the onset of the Blitz, the artist moved to Rasehill, Chorleywood Road, Rickmansworth. His wife and son moved to Cheltenham in order that his son could attend Cheltenham College. In that same year, he held a one-man exhibition of his work, which then travelled to Sunderland Public Art Gallery.

Throughout the war years, Gilroy's work continued to be exhibited at the Royal Academy while his commercial art talents were employed by the Ministry of Information in campaigns such as *Make-do-and-mend, Keep it under your hat* and *We want your kitchen waste*. He produced both pre-war and war propaganda posters plus Armed Forces posters to stimulate morale. He improved RAF morale by painting murals at various Royal Air Force bases as well as drawing the heroic flyers. Later he produced a series of drawings-in-one-line of contemporary political and military figures, called 'Headlines', which appeared in the *Star* newspaper. In all he presented fifty pictures to hospitals, nursing homes and barracks, for which he was thanked by the Prime Minister Churchill.

By 1945, when his painting 'Diamond Setting' was exhibited at the Royal Academy, the artist's address was given as 6 Avenue Studios, Sydney Close, London SW3. A year later he produced more murals, this time in the bar of the Morritt Arms Hotel near Greta Bridge on the estate of his close friend Major Morritt. The work at the Morritt Arms began on the 1 February 1946 and was completed within ten days. When Gilroy and his assistant proudly displayed the walls of the bar decorated with Dickensian figures, closer inspection revealed them to be caricatures of local

Painting the Morritt Arms walls with Dickensian murals.

BIOGRAPHY

people and staff from the hotel.

With the war over he returned to his Chelsea studio but the pressures of war had taken their toll. He was exhausted, lonely, tired, frustrated and ill. Luckily a doctor friend saw him and ordered him to bed before the inevitable physical and mental breakdown occurred. His eldest sister Polly came down from the North East to look after him and stayed on after his recovery, helping him in the studio to catch up on his workload.

Marriage to Elizabeth in 1950.

Post war, Gilroy wished to become freelance so he approached Benson, who, in order to retain his services on behalf of Guinness and provide continuity, offered him a retaining fee. Gilroy then undertook work for other agencies, but it was becoming too overwhelming and interfering with his portrait work so much that he decided to cut out all the agency work including Benson. Guinness was most unwilling to lose its most popular artist and made a direct arrangement with him to continue designing posters on a retainer of £1,250 a year. Now Gilroy was free of commitment to the agencies, and could pursue his serious art. He still did occasional work for Guinness, but it was already diminishing in volume. He had his own direct access to the Guinness people, to whom he used to float poster ideas.

In 1949 Esme Jeudwine, a former pupil and portrait subject, introduced Gilroy to the Royle family and another long and successful association began. Gilroy produced five greeting card designs for Royle Publications Ltd (Royles) in that year with another 464 published designs over the next thirty-five years. By 1966, Gilroy was acting Art Director for Royles.

The greeting card printing company, Royles, had started reproducing Gilroy's landscape work as prints. Several Directors of Royles had visited Gilroy's Holland Park studio and were very taken with his work, especially the snow scenes. They signed a royalty deal to reproduce his art as greeting cards. The print of a Japanese girl in a Kimono, called Kiku, became 'Print of the Year' in 1963 and was to become a big earner for Gilroy. Gilroy prints were starting to sell well on a regular basis, so they expanded the themes to humorous cartoons of other pursuits such as golf, shooting, fishing and hunting. By 1960 he was producing about fifty cards a year and his relationship with the Royle family grew to become very friendly.

A typical humorous Royle card.

When his first marriage broke down it must have caused some bitterness, but he had to put that away to continue his work. For several years he did not see his son, who had stayed with Gwendoline until he left school. His son then served a short time in the Royal Engineers and went overseas, before returning home independent and self-sufficient. From that point he started to get to know his father once more. Gilroy looked up to his only son and enjoyed becoming paternal again.

Gilroy remarries

By 1950, he had been separated from Gwendoline for the statutory three years, and his divorce became absolute. Now nearly penniless, he married Elizabeth Bramley, previously married to a Harley Street doctor. He had known her since 1937. The very beautiful Elizabeth Margaret Outram Bramley (nee Thwaite), hailed from Durham in the North East (b 23 April 1917). Elizabeth was nineteen years Gilroy's junior. As a girl, Elizabeth was educated at Casterton Boarding school in the Lake District, however she caught pneumonia and upon recovery was taught with Patience Welfare, by a Governess in Sleepers Hill, Winchester. The Governess became a life-long friend and godmother to her daughter Jenefer. John and Elizabeth had known each other since 1937 through a mutual friend, but she had married very young, to Dr Roland Bramley. In 1937, Elizabeth had acting pretentions and was given a one line part ('Thanks pal') in the Will Hay film *Convict 99*. They spent the war in Sidmouth, Devon where he was a GP and when the NHS was formed he decided to go private and

Gilroy in his huge studio with paintings of Mountbatten on the easel.

bought a property in Sunningdale for the family to live in and another in Devonshire Place, Belgravia, to practise from and for him to live in during the week. He commuted from one to the other but the marriage failed as he was a very difficult man and a poor father.

At the time of her remarriage in 1950, Elizabeth's two children, Jenefer ten, and Robin seven, were both at difficult and impressionable ages for such a family upheaval. They all moved into the 17 Queen's Gate, Kensington flat which Elizabeth loved, despite it being small. The children grew up not really knowing John Morritt, his son by first wife Gwendoline, who was an adult and so much older.

They had rented out the Chelsea studio and moved to Queens Gate. The house was delightful but not big enough for them and Elizabeth's two children Jenefer and Robin.

Both children were at boarding school but during the holidays they came back to Queens Gate and tried not to make too much noise and to keep things tidy. They at first called John, 'Mr Gilroy' rather than 'Uncle', until he told them to call him 'Jack'. They endearingly refer to him today as 'Pop' as he was a better father than the good Doctor.

John's humour kept them amused but he would occasionally 'blow his top' and Elizabeth would have to stand up for them until calm resumed. They all got over the change of lifestyle quite well with Elizabeth spending most of her time with the children during the holiday breaks from school. The children recall life being very eventful, such as John chasing a burglar down the street with a golf club.

They converted the basement into a studio but it was still too small. As luck would have it, a friend, Bill Gillie had seen a large studio in a house in Kensington which was owned by Sir Bernard Partridge, the famous black and white cartoonist for *Punch* Magazine, who was a particular favourite artist of Gilroy. He had always greatly admired Sir Bernard's penmanship, whose cartoons Gilroy had copied from *Punch* as a child. It had three huge studio type rooms which Elizabeth converted into comfortable living accommodation but it was not an ideal sleeping space for the whole family. Gilroy was delighted with the studio arrangement.

Jenefer tells the story- 'the basement studio proved to be far too small and the light was no good; coming in from a single skylight high up one wall'. So when a year later in 1951, No.10 Holland Park Road W14 came to their attention, they moved into one of the loveliest homes an artist could boast. 'Sir Bernard had died and his widow Lady Partridge, a huge, big busted "Victorian" lady who would stand with hands clasped across her stomach, put the upstairs flat with a local estate agent'. Despite Lady Partridge not wanting children in the other half of the house, she was persuaded to let the top part of the house at 10 Holland Park Road. Jenefer continues, 'The Estate Agent was a lovely man who wore a red wig, and was called Mr Furlonger. He told Mummy about this studio flat but said "no children". Well off she went with us in tow in our best outfits, and we saw this amazing

BIOGRAPHY

place, quite stunning!' The Grand Dame eventually said, 'I quite like the boy but not the girl' referring to Robin and Jenefer. She relented over the children and they all moved in.

This was a very substantial Victorian house, with a stone fountain and imposing frontage that could not be glimpsed from the road. There were two studios, one was a huge forty seven feet square room with a twenty foot square Great North picture window and dark green walls, which was originally the studio of Sir James Shannon. At the right side was a grandiose ornate carved staircase with gilded doorway giving access to a second gallery studio with a Venetian ceiling covered in gold leaf that became their bedroom. The bedroom possessed a Venetian balcony that overlooked the leafy garden, all protected by tall trees and a high perimeter wall. The property needed a lot of work done but they were penniless. They adapted it as well as they could and would redecorate when the money was available. The magnificent studio at Holland Park Road saw the creation of advertising work and was regularly visited by members of the Royal Family, Politicians, Actors and many others who came to have their portraits painted. In 1955, Gilroy won the first prize for a Guinness 48 sheet poster at the National Outdoor Award of the Poster Industry.

Elizabeth by Gilroy in 1949.

The Holland Park studio was the setting for many drinks parties he organised for his friends from the Garrick Club. Jenefer said that it was an extraordinary house for two children to grow up in, even though it had no central heating and 'Jack' would wear a bobble hat in the studio in winter.

Jenefer aged twelve.

In 1957 Gilroy held another one-man exhibition this time at Leighton House Gallery and two years later produced a series of landscapes of McGill University, Montreal, to illustrate a book *McGill, The Story of a University*, edited by Hugh MacLennan. In 1970 Gilroy held a retrospective exhibition at Upper Grosvenor Galleries and three years later an exhibition of his humorous designs for Royles was held at the London headquarters of Austin Reed Ltd.

In 1958 Gilroy bought Myrtle Cottage in Stedham near Midhurst, as a country residence but it didn't work out and was sold when his stepdaughter Jenefer married and stepson Robin had left Harrow to become a stockbroker.

Elizabeth loved swimming and sun bathing but John was the opposite,

Freeman Gilroy and supporters in the City of London, 1981.

leaving her left side paralysed. John had to take on basic household duties such as darning his own socks and sewing on his buttons, which he did without complaint. Most of Elizabeth's mobility eventually returned, except for a slight limp. Gilroy was never a gardener, though he loved roses and sweet peas. He read few books but loved to watch TV, especially wrestling, musicals and thrillers, whilst Elizabeth favoured the theatre, opera, and the ballet, so they each had a TV set.

In his later years 'Jack' Gilroy (as he was often known) was a longstanding and much-loved member of the Garrick Club where he was made Chairman of the Works of Art Committee and where a number of his portraits now hang. In 1975 Gilroy was awarded an honorary MA by Newcastle University, and in 1981, by then living at 6 Ryecroft Street, Fulham, he was appointed as Freeman of the City of London.

Gwendoline lived in the Kew Gardens house after the divorce once John Morritt had left home. She was a woman with broad interests and ran an antiques shop for a time in Barnes. She was a gifted flower painter as well as someone who enjoyed other handicrafts and moved to Cresswell Gardens in Central London where she had an artist's studio. John Morritt found her a charming little house in the middle of Cirencester, to be close to his family and the grandchildren. She kept up her passion for golf until her later years, she was well travelled and loved to be with the children. Later, when her health deteriorated she moved in to share John and Fiona's house, but after eighteen months she went into a home. She died at a good age in her mid-nineties.

in fact he could not swim. Once in Ischia, Southern Italy, where they went for treatment for Elizabeth's rheumatism, she tried to teach him to swim but was reduced to tears on failure. Whilst she lay near naked, lapping up the sun's warmth and curative rays, he would lie beneath a huge parasol, dressed in shirt, trousers and hat as his skin burned easily. One day he left his feet in the sun and blistered them so badly that he could not wear socks or shoes to walk the following day. As a good footballer, horseman and golfer it surprised her that he could not swim as well. As for driving, when first married he would insist on taking the wheel, but later in life when he started bumping curbs, she began to share the driving duties.

Elizabeth had a serious stroke on New Year's Eve in 1967, aged fifty,

BIOGRAPHY

The Garrick Club

Prince Philip, Duke of Edinburgh pencil drawing hanging in the Garrick Club.

Gilroy became a member of the Garrick Club in 1955 and served as chairman of the Works of Art Sub-Committee from 1970 to 1975. Gilroy undertook to clean the club's portrait collection in 1969. The Garrick has a large and prestigious art collection and Gilroy was responsible for its storage, display, cleaning and expansion. He was a regular user of the Club and was made an Honorary Life Member at eighty, up until his death in 1985. Bobby Bevan was also a member.

The Garrick retains a number of Gilroy portraits of members and other notables, with this excellent 1979 study of Prince Phillip being amongst them. Gilroy loved to hear the latest gossip of the day at the Garrick Club, where many arty, TV types, journalists and commentators would meet. He was great friends with Donald Sinden, Kenneth Moore, Trevor Fenwick and Robin Day and was a good storyteller himself.

He was a quick painter with a good memory for a face, as was proved when the Garrick Club held a party at the Derby. When he got home late that night he went to his studio and sketched the whole scene. On the final canvas he captured the faces of club members, cooks, waiters, gypsies and even gate-crashers.

The Garrick club on Derby Day, June 1967, oil painting by Gilroy.

BIOGRAPHY

John Morritt going up to Cambridge University to take a postgraduate degree in Civil Engineering, oil painting by Gilroy.

The golfer in plus fours.

H M The Queen Elizabeth in watercolour, 1979.

John was a very keen golfer, as was his son John and first wife Gwendoline. He was a member at the Royal Mid-Surrey Golf Course.

Gilroy painted the Queen's portrait several times. In 1982 at the age of eighty-three, he was in the yellow drawing room of Buckingham Palace, all set up to paint Her Majesty. The Queen came in with several corgis and as he got up to greet Her Majesty, somehow his foot caught the easel, making everything collapse and sending everyone to the floor to pick it all up. He called it a great icebreaking moment!

Gilroy claimed the friendship of Lord Alexander of Tunis, Air Chief Marshal Sir Hugh Constantine and Lord Mountbatten. He painted them all more than once. Lord Mountbatten was pleased and appreciative of his first portrait and suggested that he should paint Prince Charles. Prince Charles's portrait was unveiled by Prince Michael of Kent and for a while the two portraits were hanging at the entrance to the Painted Hall at Greenwich. Lord Mountbatten's portrait later went to the Royal Marines in Plymouth. Fiona remembers friendly letters from Mountbatten to 'Jack' about what to wear for his sittings. Regrettably these letters were sold at auction many years ago. Mountbatten had the Potters at Wedgewood make a small porcelain bust of himself. Of the 750 that were made; one went to Prince Charles and one to John Gilroy (they were numbered on the underside, his was fifty-two. This testifies to the good relationship between the two men. The family still retain that bust. Mountbatten went to the Holland Park house studio (as did Princess Anne, painted in her WREN uniform) for the sitting. Gilroy's was the last portrait painted of Lord Mountbatten, as not long after he tragically died at the hands of the IRA.

In 1966 his son John married Fiona Keville, daughter of Sir Errington Keville, a prominent figure in the shipping industry in the 1960s, (he was president of the Chamber of Shipping). They lived for a time in London and then moved to Bath. The family grew when three grandchildren came along who were to bring Jack much joy. He and Elizabeth were regular visitors to their home near Bath during the years that followed and again later when the family moved to Gloucestershire with their daughter and two sons. John Gilroy and his son John Morritt were very close but Morritt still felt the depressive effect that the divorce had on his mother.

Lady Partridge died in 1959 and the Gilroys were offered and took the lease on the entire Holland Park property. As they got older the

BIOGRAPHY

Fiona sketched by Gilroy.

house suited them less and Jenefer had found out that a house which also had a studio and was very close to theirs, was up for sale. With just fourteen years left on the lease they sold 10 Holland Park for a good price. The Gilroys moved in 1979 from Holland Park which they had rented, to 6 Ryecroft Street, Fulham (which they bought freehold) and even had a little residual money in the bank. The Holland Park house was huge, and proved impractical to keep as they got older, being draughty and cold with high ceilings. In Fulham he was only a few doors away from his step-daughter Jenefer and her husband David, at number twenty. They spent most Sunday lunch times at Jenefer's house and shared the enormous half-acre back garden that David had created from the land at the centre of their triangle of houses.

Two portraits of Lord Mountbatten.

In Old Age

Jenefer and David, were wonderfully caring of John and Elizabeth during their final years and John was able to keep working until his death. The top fourth floor studio in Fulham was very compact compared to Holland Park and he had far fewer sitters. He was commissioned to design posters for the Lord Mayor's Show in 1982 and 1983. In 1984 he was diagnosed with motor neurone disease, which progressed quickly, especially in the last six weeks. Elizabeth later became bedridden in her Ryecroft first floor bedroom that looked out onto the garden. She would suffer from shingles and other neurological disorders, having carers to support her until her death there in 1999.

Edward Guinness was telephoned one day in 1985 by Lady Constantine, whose husband was Air Marshall Hugh Constantine, to be told that Gilroy was terminally ill in hospital and that he was very upset because a man had died very noisily in the next bed. Gilroy had made no provision for private medical insurance to afford better surroundings. Lady Constantine advised that he couldn't die happily in peace in such a place. Edward put Gilroy's plight to the Guinness Board, led at the time by Ernest Saunders. An Irish Director, Professor Kennedy stated that Gilroy was owed a debt of gratitude by the company and that Guinness must help him. As a result, funding for a move to a private nursing home was agreed for three months, with a review at that point. Unfortunately Gilroy died soon after moving into the private nursing home.

John Gilroy died in Guildford on the 11th April 1985, aged eighty-six, and is buried at Ampney St Peter in Gloucestershire. His son was subsequently buried next to him. A memorial service was held in St Paul's Church, Covent Garden (known as the 'Actor's Church'). The service was organised and paid for by the Garrick Club. It was a very well-attended service, Elizabeth his second wife though almost an invalid, was there with Robin and Jenefer, John and Fiona. Also attending was a large Guinness contingent, and former Benson Advertising people, Garrick friends and other relatives. Following the service, a wake was held at the Garrick Club in the upstairs room.

In the memorial speech it was said, 'all of us who knew him for what he was, knew he was a man with a great gift for friendship. His contribution to advertising must be the most recognisable made in our lifetime. No one has done more in this field than did Jack. In portraiture, his sitters must have enjoyed being painted by Jack as much as he enjoyed painting them. We give thanks for having known him and we will miss him'.

Although his will showed probate of £70,000 in that October, a not inconsiderable sum, Elizabeth had no form of income except the state pension.

Following his death, the contents of his studio were put up for sale by Elizabeth at Christie's. Before the sale, John Morritt had the pick of his art, but the sale was needed to provide money for Elizabeth's old age. On 15 May 1986, the sale of two hundred lots beat its estimate, fetching £23,000. Unfortunately, a few early family portraits were sold off which was later regretted. His son John felt 'the family silver had been sold'. Looking back, much of the art went quite cheaply in bundled lots. Guinness related material was low grade and constituted about twenty five lots, there were some fifty portrait lots and the rest were landscapes or greeting card scenes. Gilroy was a generous man and had already given much artwork away to those he met like Martin Pick and Brian Sibley. However, Gilroy was such a prolific artist that pieces of his artwork abound in various collections, archives, museums, and with family and friends. How wonderful to own an original Gilroy! Many people do and I happen to be one of them.

Christie's Auction Sale catalogue, May 1986.

A centenary exhibition of his work was held in 1998 in both London and Newcastle galleries, sponsored by Guinness and organised by the History of Advertising Trust. Anna Morgan, who was working at the time for Guinness in Park Royal, catalogued his known work, which identified 155 portraits, over 140 published Guinness press adverts and some 55 Guinness posters.

Since 1998, the Benson's Artwork Archive has been discovered, which contained hundreds of original oil on canvas examples of Gilroy's artwork including a lot of new material, unknown even to the current Guinness Archivists. The Benson archive contained numerous examples of campaigns planned for many countries of the world that for various reasons did not proceed, and these campaigns were forgotten. The canvases were stored rolled up and many of them had to be separated, cleaned of dirt and mildew and then reconditioned before they could be sold. Over a third of the material was in such a state of dilapidation that it was rendered unfit for hanging. I have catalogued as much as I can of this new Guinness artwork in the Appendix. Note that it is not exclusively all by Gilroy.

In Memoria
Some further recollections from friends and family

His Grandson Jim remembers Jack when older, going off into Central London with dark glasses and a white painted walking stick. He would fake being a blind man to gain a seat on the tube or bus. He was often spotted by his friends walking along with his white stick.

At the age of seventy he was described by his nephew Tony Thwaite as 'being round and ruddy faced, somewhat cherubic with sparkling eyes. His North Country accented chatter was amusing and witty. He had a continuous line in patter that would be the envy of any comic scriptwriter. He was quick on his feet, agile and well muscled for his age'. As a man he had more than his full share of blessings, the greatest of which was good health. 'To ask his opinion on modern art would elicit a non-stop thirty minute diatribe on the works of the classical artists Michelangelo and da Vinci, expressed in a beautiful prose that left the Picasso School spinning in their graves with burning ears. He exuded energy as he talked, ate, or painted. Despite his rugged exterior, he possessed an appreciative soul for great beauty that is more akin to that of a poet. Those tough strong hands of an artisan can paint and draw softness and can strip naked the false veneer that people cultivate to improve their image'.

Fiona his daughter-in-law remembers him as 'very good company, close to his family, tweedy in dress with comfortable shoes, coloured shirts with a bow tie, round glasses, a G&T and cigar in hand. He was lovable, entertaining and could always be expected to cheer you up. He favoured wearing a green velvet jacket and a blue smock if in the studio'.

Tony Thwaite writes that 'at age seventy, he had achieved an orderly disciplined regime. He rises at 7.30am, plans his day by selecting the work that best suits his mood. Over breakfast, sometimes eaten standing up, he reads the papers, pouring forth invective at beards, mini-skirts, politicians and modern art. He puts on his bulldog face with jutting bottom lip in a sort of Churchillian disgust, but really due to the fact that he had worn his teeth down from grinding them. He rushes around like a man going over a waterfall in a barrel. In the studio he works at a terrific pace, no tea or coffee breaks until the 1 o'clock news pre-lunch. Sometimes he took a short lie down after lunch before resuming work, a tea break if he has

BIOGRAPHY

'Jack' about eighty years old, photo.

a sitter, and then working on until 7pm depending on the light. His sitters are all treated to a discourse of prodigious entertainment. Lunch must never interfere with the news, so it is served at 13.10 or 13.15. He eats small portions and demands a pudding of egg custard, rice pudding or the like. He still possesses tastes and habits from the North Country. He has stamina and endurance but does not subject his body to over-eating or excess.'

Thwaite goes on, 'He never did appreciate the smutty joke, especially involving women. He could remember and would occasionally sing the ribald ballads, sung as Army marching songs, and swore only for the fun of it or to emphasise his feelings on a point. As a small man he did not have the customary chip on his shoulder, rather he gave off a presence and was immensely strong and agile. When occasionally ill, and he detested all ill health, he would shun pills and he became monosyllabic and morose such that everyone was only too aware of his physical state. As for drinking, he made a little go a long way and was moderate in habit. Politically he was a 'Whig', no Royalist, but he had admiration for some of the Royal Family and was outstandingly critical of others. With any government in power he would castigate any legislation that led to the betterment of rich or poor if he could relate the consequence to his own pocket or freedom of action.

Domestically, and as far as repair of furniture and maintaining the house went, John was a 'bodger', content to use sticking plaster or paint over damage. His washing up was usually half completed but Elizabeth found him uncomplaining and easy to feed with his love of simple foods, milk puddings and custards, meat and two veg. Elizabeth after eighteen years married to John said of the man 'Oh! He always makes me laugh - in fact he sometimes makes me just roar - not every day, but every day he makes me laugh. It's not just what he does so much as the way he does it- his facial expressions, his walk and his patter'. She also claimed he had a good voice, sang well and she loved to dance with him as he had rhythm. As for entertaining he was a popular guest as well as an enthusiastic host. He was great fun and could monopolise conversation at the table but Elizabeth worked out a way to balance this when needed,' said Tony.

John had terrible obsessions; for instance tidiness, 'he cannot stand anything out of place, yet he is the tidiest "untidy" person one can meet. He has obsessions over money and really worries when people don't pay their bills, and I can't stand seeing him short of money. He enjoys drink but is much more abstemious than he was when he was younger. He has a great many bees in his bonnet so it takes me great tolerance to see them through without causing too many upsets,' said Elizabeth.

He hated to be kept waiting, getting edgy and fidgety so Elizabeth had to be an excellent timekeeper. He thought artists should have no time for temperament, yet he suffered from it as much as anyone. Elizabeth also tried incessantly to spruce him up, but failed miserably. He would pick up and wear cast-off hats, scarves, ties or jackets for the most inappropriate occasion. His wardrobe was a real 'junk shop'.

Money was often short in the Gilroy household. When he married Elizabeth they had just £25 to their name. Like many artists money arrived in dribs and drabs so there was occasional drought and flood. In the 1930s he was on a good salary with Benson, and by the end of the war he went freelance which made his earnings irregular. His work for Guinness declined but was replaced by earnings from Royle Cards. By the 1970s he was quite reliant on portraiture. He was a very generous man and often gave away his art or failed to charge enough for his portraits. In later life his Guinness bursary kept them afloat but when he died Elizabeth only had her State Pension and the support of her children.

Watercolour, humorous card for Royles of a fashionable lady and her dog shopping.

BIOGRAPHY

He did not indulge in expensive hobbies except the Garrick Club, but he and Elizabeth did enjoy foreign holidays and luckily their many wealthy friends offered them use of their villas or they paid for trips, many of which had a work content attached.

A great regret in his life was non-acceptance by the Royal Academy. When he did get a picture accepted for hanging, he would dash around the house in great delight at the forthcoming exhibition. He loved 'varnishing day', the day prior to the opening, when all the artists turned up and great fun was had by everyone. If he ever got a picture 'on the line' then he was in rapture. Too often his efforts ended in failure. In truth he was just too well-known as a great commercial artist for the 'serious' art community to recognise him.

'John was born with great gifts, his artistic eye and his sense of humour and warm humanity. These gifts served him well.' Such were the words spoken by The Duke of Northumberland at his Honorary MA degree ceremony in Newcastle University in 1975. Now he was able to call himself Professor Gilroy.

Photo of Gilroy in the Holland Park studio with the portrait of his wife Elizabeth, c 1956.

The Holland Park house - access to the false gallery via a grand carved wood 18th century staircase that came from Lincoln's Inn.

Inset is the Italian doorway to the bedroom.

BIOGRAPHY

Two self-portrait drawings of the artist in his studio.

Two photographs of the artist at work in Holland Park. He seems too well dressed for painting - posing! In later life he would get his portraits photographed during the painting process, to send to his patron for approval.

2
The Portraits

The Portraits

When his work for Guinness was in less demand, Gilroy turned increasingly to portraiture to earn his living, still producing them until his mid-eighties. The *Evening Standard* wrote an article about John Gilroy and his portraits on 26 November 1976, in which he is quoted as saying 'I never do anything I don't want to do. At one time I would paint anybody. Now by the grace of God, I pick and choose. I'd rather do a funny Christmas card than paint someone I don't like.'

'I'm a speedy worker. I believe in painting right off and if it's wrong, off with it! I talk all the time, I never stop and I like them to talk to me. If you lose the animation you may as well get a photograph.' As for his subjects he claimed Lord Hailsham was his worst sitter, 'with all respect to a wonderful personality'.

In 1923 John was proposed by Dyson Smith the Sculptor, supported by the painters Munnings and Orpen, to join the Chelsea Arts Club. Bohemian in nature, it was frequented by famous London artists of the day. CAC was renowned for their Chelsea Arts Ball on New Year's Eve at the Royal Albert Hall. Gilroy got involved painting huge back-drops and tableaux for the Ball, together with Munnings and A. R. Thompson. Tommy Thompson was a gifted artist and deaf but Gilroy had learned sign language and they became great friends. Gilroy attended the club on Monday evenings to play ping pong and watch Charles Cundall and Alexander Fleming play billiards.

He was also made an Honorary member of the Green Room Club for Actors in Dover Street, as a result of his 1947 portrait of Sir C Aubrey Smith at the age of eighty-four. Aubrey Smith said of it 'that it was the first really satisfying picture of "yours humbly" which has been done'.

In 1927 the year of his son's birth, they moved to a pleasant house in Kew, on the Thames. Proposed by Frank Reynolds and seconded by Major Morritt, he joined Royal Mid-Surrey Golf Club in Richmond. Golf was the only other sport he enjoyed playing. Here he met many influential people who were to help him in later life. A while later, Gwen his first wife, would become Lady Captain. Sir Stanley Jackson was men's captain and five times Open winner J. H. Taylor was the professional. Gilroy took to the game and was soon playing off a handicap of ten. In 1926, the Duke of Windsor, then the Prince of Wales was made Captain of the Club and Gilroy was asked to paint his portrait. It was a difficult task as the Duke would not sit for him.

Pencil drawing of a boy soldier next to his father.

When she saw the portrait, his mother, Queen Mary, disapproved of it saying 'that's not my David!' Gilroy retouched the canvas 'to make him look a pretty brass-haired boy'. Gilroy hated the picture after that as it did not represent the Prince's true character and pathos. Tragically all the club portraiture and memorabilia were destroyed when the clubhouse burnt down in 2001. This included the portrait of the Prince.

He also played golf with the then Chairman of P&O, who asked him to do them a poster. Gilroy asked Benson for permission which was granted. So in 1928, a black and white poster appeared with two seagulls sitting on a ship's mast - one despondent, the other happy and self-satisfied. The happy bird says to the other 'I always travel P&O'. It received great acclaim and as a reward Gilroy was offered travel on future Summer P&O Cruises at a nominal cost. He greatly enjoyed several of these cruises, visiting Cyprus, Greece, Italy and Palestine. It was in Haifa that his career nearly ended when a hire-car driver shut his hand in the car door.

These Mid-Surrey days were mostly happy, but though his wife Gwendoline played golf, a deepening rift of incompatibility was becoming more evident. In 1942 when they separated, Gilroy resigned from the Club, leaving his wife and son as members. The Club had given him all he required from an institution - exercise, social contacts and stimulus. However, the rift within the family and the War would prevent him from enjoying the benefits.

Since 1926, Gilroy had been a regular guest of Harry Morritt at the Garrick Club. He longed to join and in 1955 a vacancy arose and his name was proposed by Morritt and seconded by A. G. Bryant, who had been best man at his wedding to Elizabeth in 1950. The lunches and dinners at the Garrick were interesting affairs, the flavour of which can be gauged by the following: Sir Alfred Munnings sat at the head of

PORTRAITS

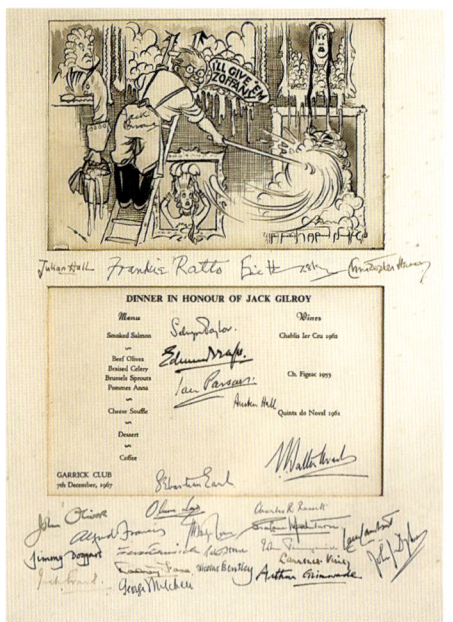

The 1967 Garrick menu signed by members.

the top table and often gave thunderous discourse. Gilroy sat on Morritt's table with Carpenter, the boxer, A. E. Mason, the writer and Sir Seymour Hicks, the actor. At this particular meal, 'Munnings sat with his admirers and others flanking him. There he would recite his famous Café Royal ballads, holding forth, and giving expression with voice, hands and face to his clever composition - brooking no interruption, and woe betide anyone who did not lend ear enraptured - whether they were enjoying the poetry or not, for they would be severely castigated and duly stung by Munnings whiplash tongue'.

On the death of Sir James Gunn RA, Gilroy was elected to the Picture Committee and then the General Committee. By now, several of Gilroy's pictures of members hung on the Club walls. During the closure of the Club in 1967 for staff holidays, Gilroy cleaned many of the old pictures that hung in the dining room. Years of London grime and cigar smoke disappeared to reveal the works for what they were. In appreciation, the Club held a dinner in his honour attended by the Council Committee and other members.

Thursday evenings were men only nights and Gilroy dined there with his friends Trevor Fenwick, Sebastian Earle, Sir Lionel Heald, Dr. Breen, Oliver Law and John Dykes, the lawyer.

Morritt

In 1922, Gilroy was introduced to Major Harry Morritt, a wealthy North Yorkshire landowner who was a keen amateur painter. He had served in the Boer War and the First World War in the Tank Corps. Morritt wanted tutoring to improve his style and technique. Gilroy was teaching art at the time. They met in London and then at Rokeby Hall, near Barnard Castle on the Tees. Gilroy so admired the wonderful scenery around Greta Bridge, the setting for Morritt's brown stone Georgian mansion, that he painted it many times. He was greeted by Harry's wife, Grace, an American born girl who loved golf. Harry was a big man at six foot two inches, an excellent shot, fisherman and golfer. A fervent Tees-sider, he entertained well and introduced Gilroy to the life of a country gentleman who lived for the seasons and their different sports, as well as fine food and wine.

The house was full of pictures, clocks, dogs and guests. Morritt possessed two Reynolds, *The Rokeby Venus* by Velazquez, (now in the

Gilroy and chums at the Garrick.

National Gallery) and a Rembrandt drawing. Dogs had the run of the house including their own reserved chairs. Clocks were wound weekly by an old clockmaker from the town who was referred to as 'The Penguin'. He carried a large bunch of keys reminiscent of a jailer at the Tower of London. Interesting guests at Rokeby included Sir Harold Gillies the surgeon, Frank Reynolds the editor of *Punch* Magazine, The Lord and Lady Millbanks, the Baker-Baker girls, Arthur Ransome and Murrough Wilson, Chairman of LNER.

Gilroy was to visit Rokeby Hall for the next forty years, as he and Morritt became firm friends. Morritt could spare little time for being tutored in art as it got in the way of his other favourite pursuits, but Gilroy was to meet many new patrons for his services on these visits. In fact Morritt's right hand was injured and missing a finger, which prevented him attaining great detail in his art. They were very distinctive when seen out together due to their difference in stature but both possessed the same wicked sense of humour.

After the War, Gilroy and the Major were sitting in the 'Morritt Arms', a famous hotel in the village of Greta Bridge, that was owned by the Major. Morritt asked Jack how to refurbish the pub after the restrictions of the War. The hotel was duly closed for two weeks, emergency repairs carried out, walls were replastered and then Gilroy set about painting Dickensian murals across all the walls of the bar. Charles Dickens had stayed there in 1838, so now it became known as the 'Dickens Bar'.

Gilroy's first love of humour in commercial art killed his chances of recognition in the portrait field by the Art Establishment. And now with the passing of his supporters, Munnings, Augustus John, Orpen and Gunn, Gilroy's chance of being elected a member of the Royal Academy was lost. In 1935 having proven himself in commercial art, he gave an exhibition of his landscapes and portraits at the Fine Art Society in Bond Street, in the hope it would gain him the serious recognition that he believed he deserved. The Scotsman on 23 April reported, 'John Gilroy has academic ambitions. He is well known as the comic artist who celebrates the strength-giving qualities of a certain stout. Half the hoardings in the British Isles display Gilroy's skill as a commercial designer, so that it is hard to imagine him sitting down to serious work. He is like Charlie Chaplin aspiring to play Hamlet. His ambitious work "Sic Itres ad Astra", in the tradition of the British school at Rome, is let down by a number of facile and unpretentious drawings'. However the Times on the same day said 'the portrait is a striking and brilliant work, however the public associate him with 'strength', though not as yet a serious portrait painter'.

In 1938 Gilroy and Gwendoline travelled to America on the Queen Mary but she had to return immediately on arrival as her mother had become seriously ill. That left Gilroy, who was hosted by the Attorney for Western Electric, in the clutches of the Greenwich Village artists, who plied him with alcohol and taught him their style of painting.

On his return he met Tommy Thompson and his German wife, who worked for the BBC as an interpreter and she was in constant touch with what was happening in Hitler's Germany. All the reports were of looming war.

Returning to S. H. Benson, he contributed poster designs for the Ministry of Information as well as doing work for the Guinness account, such as 'What the situation demands' and 'Dig for Victory' in 1942, which were taking the tone of supporting the war effort. It was then that his Kew house was bombed and unfit to live in. The blast injured his housekeeper and her daughter, so Gilroy had his wife and son evacuated to Cheltenham, together with her ailing mother. He moved to the Avenue studio in Chelsea, which he shared with Flora Line, Frank Hodge, Dyson Smith and Lord Brabazon (who used the space to layout his model trains).

Work continued for a while at Benson until the Benson studio roof was blown off, so the agency relocated to Rickmansworth, Herts. Gilroy moved into the Rickmansworth house of his friend Donald Gillies, who was also working for his family agency, 'Graham and Gillies' on Ministry of Information work. The house was shared with Gillies' manservant, Dod Osbourne, who had been an adventurer and gun-runner before the war, and a French woman who owned the house and ended up getting arrested for menacing behaviour. They were quite a mix of personalities. Gilroy toured the RAF bases and painted murals of views, Dickens scenes, and aviaries of exotic birds and animals on the drab Nissen hut walls, to cheer up the airmen. He was aided in this by another artist friend Esme Jeuduine and some Prisoners of War. This work came to the attention of Sir Archibald Sinclair, the Minister of Aviation, who commissioned more similar work. The idea caught on in a big way. At a meeting with Brendan Bracken he was asked to prepare posters depicting Winston Churchill with cigar in hand. Gilroy did several of these Churchill posters for various purposes, plus posters of other leaders of the War Cabinet. He produced a series of cartoons of eminent people for the *Evening Star* newspaper, drawn as a single unbroken line, and they became a regular feature.

Letter from Clementine Churchill, 1942.

Following the war, Gilroy wished to become freelance so he approached Benson, who, in order to retain his services on behalf of Guinness and provide continuity, offered him a retaining fee. Gilroy then undertook work for other agencies, but it was becoming too much and interfering with his portrait work so much, that he decided to cut out all the agency work including Benson. Guinness was most unwilling to lose its most popular artist and made a direct arrangement with him to continue designing posters on a retainer of £1,250 a year. Now Gilroy was free of commitment to the agencies, and could pursue his serious art. He still did occasional work for

Elizabeth Gilroy in portrait pose, c 1956.

Guinness, but it was already diminishing in volume. He had his own direct access to the Guinness people, to whom he used to float poster ideas.

On New Year's Eve, 1956 Gilroy was introduced to Mrs Lois Maclean, sister of the Canadian tycoon and Philanthropist Henry Birks. He was subsequently invited to Montreal where several commissions were organised. He sailed on the last voyage of the Empress of Scotland, and whilst on board he met Dr. Cyril James, the Principal of T. E. McGill University. He painted commissions for three months, returning to the UK richer in experience and dollars (which for good reason he left there). He returned to Canada in 1957, sponsored by Cyril James. He presented to the University a portrait of Lord Alexander of Tunis who had been governor-general of Canada from 1952-56. The University gave him a special 'hanging lunch' to which other well-connected people were invited. Dr James organised for Gilroy a four and a half day trip by train across Canada through Winnipeg, across the prairies, to Moose Jaw, Calgary, Banff, Lake Louise and over the Rockies to Vancouver. He set up a studio in the George Hotel for his sitters, where he was interviewed by CBS TV. This exposure got him another commission, from the Molson Brewing family.

In 1962, he visited Calgary as the guest of Col Harvey QC, a Canadian who had become a millionaire when oil was found on his land. He was a patron of the arts and spent a fortune supporting young aspiring artists. The Colonel commissioned Gilroy to paint his

Lord Alexander of Tunis portrait.

and his wife's portrait, which so pleased them that Gilroy was invited to spend some time at their ranch in Alberta. He had a free hand to paint whatever he saw, which included the Calgary Stampede. He was presented to the crowd by the Colonel's wife, dressed in cowboy rig including Stetson and tooled leather boots and proceeded to sketch the Chuck Wagon Race plus numerous other pictures of horses, bison, moose, native Indians, ranchers and cowboys. On return to the UK over the next year he painted forty-eight canvases which he sent back to Colonel Harvey in Canada.

Gilroy made an arrangement through Dr Thomen of the Agency of the Ambassador of the Dominion Republic to paint Pope John XXIII in the Vatican whilst he was giving a public audience. The Pope made his entrance; 'a short squat man with a very saintly aura' was how Gilroy described him. Gilroy was positioned near the front of the audience and painted for ninety minutes whilst the Pope sat still and leaned forward on his seat, as if he was standing. Gilroy had to restrain himself from chatting as he painted, but managed it. He was then conducted to a place where the Papal uniform was displayed so it could be copied in detail. He returned to his hotel and set about his work for the next two days. On the third day he was admitted to another audience lasting two hours this time. He noted certain qualities and colours in his sitter that had not been previously apparent. He was then led to the papal throne for a blessing in French. He returned to England and completed the portrait, but by that time the Pope was very ill. Gilroy sent photographs of the work to the Vatican and he received a message back to say the Pope liked it very much but although the Vatican did not want it, they had no objection to it being exhibited. After the Pope's death, the picture was altered and was presented to a charity. Gilroy did not want to sell the painting and gain from such a wonderful experience; he preferred to donate it for a good cause.

His artist friends

Sir Alfred Munnings was President of the RA in 1956 when Gilroy attended a dinner at Burlington House. Munnings was an outspoken, old school, cantankerous man, who would have nothing to do with the 'modern' painters, calling them 'charlatans'. Munnings publicly embarrassed Gilroy in front of his fellow artists, when he loudly singled Gilroy out for praise of his posters, saying 'I would prefer to hang the horse and cart poster rather than the monstrosities that are disfiguring our walls'. Gilroy's admiration for Munnings was genuine and sincere, and both disliked the modern trend, favouring craftsmanship and 'good art'. They had both started out the same way, doing poster work commercially. Munnings was twelve years older and had a passion for horses, owning and riding them, attending the races, and riding to hounds. His painting of horses has few equals even today. When Munnings retired, Gilroy knew his chances of becoming a Royal Academician were over as his work would be considered 'too conventional and lacking gimmicks'.

Gilroy met Augustus John through Tommy Thompson, as he was a supporter of the Chelsea Arts Club and they often met in the 'Pheasantry Club' in the Kings Road. Though never the best of friends, they admired each other's skill as draughtsmen. One of John's comments on art that stuck with Gilroy concerned painting and painters as compared to drawing – 'one could either draw or could not draw, and one's ability left no room for dubious consideration. This is not true of painters'.

Pencil drawing of John from 1961.

Augustus John had a reputation amongst those who did not really know him, for being untidy, bad tempered, and outrageous - a bearded monster! John was a great supporter of Gilroy's humorous work but not of his serious art. He loved Jack's wit but never discussed his art. Gilroy did not want to become involved with the artist, whom he called 'notorious'.

Nevertheless one day in the late 1940s, Gilroy had taken his sister Dorothy and husband Dr Tilley to the 'Pheasantry Club' to show them his way of life and meet his friends. In walked an annoyed looking Augustus John, who asked if he could sit with them, which concerned Gilroy but his party thought it was wonderful. Gilroy enquired as to what had upset him and he recounted that he had just left Winston Churchill's house, where he had been trying to make a character drawing, 'but the great man was in one of his moods and he held to an expression like an Atlantic storm'. Augustus John was forced to pack up and leave, suggesting to Mrs Churchill that 'they would be better to spend 7/6d and get fifty Polly photos'. Augustus John spoke with deliberation and quiet charm in a relaxed tone of voice, and they found him to be an excellent lunch companion, not the roaring fearsome man he was alleged to be. Gilroy noted that Augustus John, in later life, had become more dignified and meticulous in his dress and appearance, his eagle eyes glinting out from under shaggy eyebrows.

The famous artist Illingworth was at the RA as a student at the same time as Gilroy and they were friends until Illingworth gave up academic life and became a cartoonist of great repute. Gilroy disapproved of his abandoning his serious art. Gilroy also admired the cartoonist, Cummings' work. In addition, they shared political affiliations and were both Garrick members. David Jagger was a Garrick member, admired by Gilroy for his wonderfully accurate portrait painting. Jack commissioned Jagger to paint his family members. They were both originally members of the Chelsea Art Club. David only seemed to paint when he needed money to finance his horse racing bets. He would appear at the Club with the racing papers and his form book, content and happy until circumstances forced him to return to the studio.

In the flat above their rooms in Queens Gate, lived the Joffeys an entertaining family, who made the ideal neighbours. Gilroy discovered that Mrs Joffey was the daughter of Epstein, the great sculptor. The Gilroys met him and became frequent visitors to Epstein's studio, opposite Churchill's at Hyde Park Gate. When they moved to Holland Park the Joffeys and Epstein were frequent visitors. Epstein admired Elizabeth for her beauty and offered to sculpt her. Unfortunately, Epstein's charges were too high for the Gilroy's funds, which were at a low ebb, so the work was never done. At the Epstein studio they met a nice young man who wanted to paint Elizabeth but it did not progress when he found out Gilroy was an artist. Shortly afterwards they met again at the RA where Jack wanted to buy his exhibit *The Monk* for £100, but it was already sold. Later the young man, who was called Annigoni, achieved great fame with his portrait of the young Queen Elizabeth. They had come so near to owning an Epstein and an Annigoni.

As an artist, Gilroy admired the talent of Field Marshall The Lord Alexander, whom he described as 'a sound painter who plans and executes his work most carefully'. Gilroy painted him on at least three occasions. Gilroy liked and admired the Field Marshall, finding him 'most charming of manner and a wonderfully dignified person, not because of what he is, for he is gracious without being pompous, a good attentive listener, able to cast off the aura of fame and to talk of mundane things sensibly'. Alexander would walk around the Holland Park studio, putting Gilroy at ease, making constructive and useful comment on the picture, and talking about his favourite subject: pictures, painting and painters. Due to the need to paint Alexander in robes, the Field Marshall had carried 'The Sword of London' wrapped up on the underground. The Office of the Order of the Garter had supplied the robes and feathered hat. The two artists met each other several times a year, usually at the Canada Club dinner and got on well.

FM Alexander in Army uniform, oil by Gilroy.

Gilroy presented to Scotland Yard, three historical police paintings of – *a policeman, the first woman police constable and an original peeler*. They were unveiled by the Home Secretary Lord Brooke.

Princess Margaret's picture was commissioned to commemorate the presentation of the new colours to the 15th/19th Kings Royal Hussars at Tidworth Barracks by their Colonel in Chief, Princess Margaret. Gilroy flew back from Portugal to attend the parade which he sketched, made notes on and took some snaps of the formation. Also in attendance were the Queen Mother and General Younger, the commanding Officer Colonel Hugh Davies, the Chaplain and Colour Party.

Colonel Davies saw the canvas in production and so liked it he suggested painting the Queen Mother. Arrangements were later made at Clarence House where he set up his easel and waited. He heard a swish-swish of satin gown; she was five minutes late but made a stunning entrance, radiant, smiling, hand outstretched in greeting. Her dress was rose pink which surprised Gilroy. She read his expression and said if he didn't like it, she could change but Gilroy assured her how lovely her dress was.

Pink was admirable; he could not remember having seen a picture of her in it. He made a colour match and a layout on a small canvas then got to work on the large canvas. As he worked they talked of many things and so full of grace and radiant charm was the Queen Mother, he felt completely at ease. The sitting lasted ninety minutes. Lord Gordon, the Comptroller of the Queens Household looked at the canvas and approved. Her Majesty approved and said she thought that he had made her look 'benign'.

Princess Margaret then wanted her own portrait and so it was arranged for her to visit the Holland Park studio. Dressed informally, she brought with her a Norman Hartnell dress and a tiara to be painted later. She had a fringed hair style so in the picture he changed it to suit the tiara and altered the neck line of the dress. The Princess approved and thought the picture better than the original. She proved to be like her mother; an excellent sitter and chatty, with views on art influenced by her husband. Gilroy was enthralled by her brilliant blue eyes when facing the light.

It was how he saw the sitter's face and character that Gilroy aimed to capture on canvas, for this was where he spent most of his painting time. He was an orthodox portrait painter by choice and achieved a decent level of recognition through his work. His wife, Elizabeth, thought him a superb artist but was a little sceptical about some of his portraits, which she found inconsistent. She believed he did too much touching up of the canvas as an after-thought, which could spoil the final result, often telling him to leave it alone. She was his hardest critic but they were very compatible and he valued her opinion.

Sir Hugh Beaver was managing director of Guinness and due to poor health, was about to retire in 1961. The Board required a portrait painted and Gilroy got the commission. Beaver came to his studio to sit and they got chatting on all sorts of subjects. The two men found they were kindred spirits and shared a dislike of advertising agents. Gilroy by now believed the agencies to be pedlars of 'humbug', trying to please clients with whatever it took, irrespective of their own convictions, so as not to prejudice their 12.5% commission. The two men became friendly, usually meeting up in London.

A few years earlier Gilroy had drawn a Guinness poster design of a beaver gnawing through a tree trunk with the slogan 'Guinness for Strength'. Though novel and beautifully designed it was turned down in case some might interpret it as Sir Hugh bringing down the House of Guinness.

On the 14 September 1967, John Gilroy had on his easel an unfinished portrait of Lord Iveagh, one of six he had painted of the Guinness Chairman. It was on that same day that Lord Iveagh died.

Sir Hugh Beaver portrait.

He found Lord Iveagh to be an interesting and entertaining sitter. He painted Lady Iveagh as well, whom he described as a great beauty, gracious, and a versatile conversationalist. He loved to listen to her fund of political anecdotes. Often on arriving at the studio, Iveagh would greet Gilroy with words like 'Good morning my little friend, thanks to you we sold a few extra pints yesterday'. The portrait of Rupert Iveagh in Garter Robes was especially difficult due to his sparkling white hair. Once finished and on show at the Royal Portrait Society, Gilroy won several important commissions including the Belgian Banker Baron Janssen.

Gilroy was invited to the Baron's Chateau to paint him, and his allocated studio room already contained great works of art, including works by Rembrandt, El Greco, Cezanne, Lautrec and a small Rubens nude. With the Baron's portrait finished, he then painted the Baroness holding a shot gun in the grounds. Then he painted the Baron's favourite horse. Gilroy and the Baron - known as Charley to his friends, was a humorous and energetic host. They would eat together and then sit up till late telling stories and drinking fine Cognac. Charley had served in the RAF during the War. Gilroy also painted the Baron's cousin, the Finance Minister, in his regalia for the Bank board room. The next year Gilroy returned to the Chateaux with his second wife Elizabeth for a brief holiday. They moved on to the Baron's shooting lodge in the Ardennes which contained a Salvador Dali painting of 'a hunt'. The Baron organised a boar hunt for his guests but Gilroy did not ride due to his age and was driven around in a jeep by the Baron's chauffeur. The tour ended in Brussels where they met the head of the great advertising agency Eperco. Gilroy was invited to produce some posters for their Benelux clients, but his design for Ginger Ale was so similar to his Guinness themes that Guinness politely asked him to refrain from working for competitor products, to which he readily agreed.

PORTRAITS

A Gilroy portrait of Churchill was accepted by Sir John Cockcroft and hangs in Churchill College Cambridge. A Lord Mountbatten portrait was given to the Royal Marines and another to the Greenwich Naval College, which hangs with his portrait of Prince Charles in Naval uniform.

A pencil sketch of the Guinness for Strength *beaver poster c 1960.*

Gilroy in studio painting with failing eyesight, rough sketch.

PORTRAITS

Edward Heath.

Prince Charles.

Probably Gilroy's best portraits were of Earl Alexander of Tunis in Garter robes; Lord Iveagh, the Guinness Chairman in Garter robes 1951; Winston Churchill in 1942, and The Queen Mother 1960. These canvases capture not just the look but something of the personality of the sitter.

I could not ignore Gilroy's portraits in this book on Guinness. I have reproduced a number here to show the quality and range. Fiona thinks his men are better than his women. You decide. His favourite subject was certainly Elizabeth, of whom over a dozen exist.

PORTRAITS

PORTRAITS

35

PORTRAITS

36

PORTRAITS

3
Benson, Ogilvy & Mather and Guinness

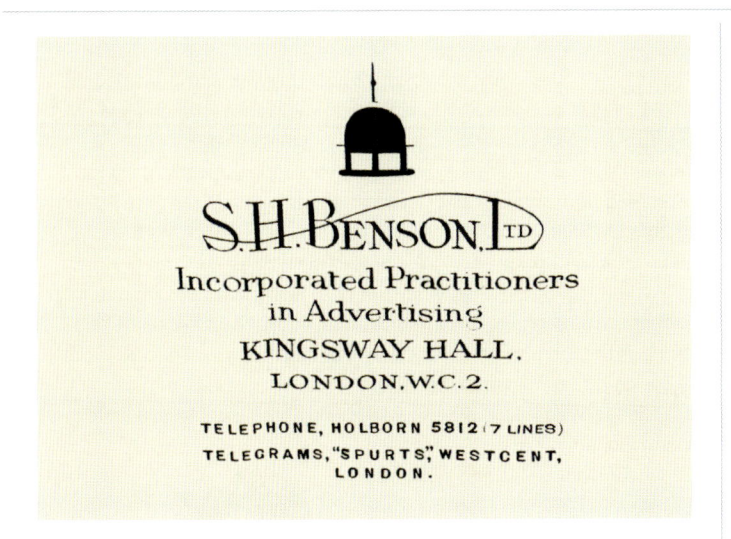

S. H. Benson Ltd Advertising Agency

S. H. Benson was one of the oldest and most prestigious Advertising Agencies in London in the first half of the 20th Century. Founded in 1893 by Samuel Herbert Benson, the Agency's reputation was quickly made with a striking campaign for Bovril as their first account. Samuel Benson had worked with Bovril prior to starting out on his own. In 1914 upon Samuel's death, the firm was taken over by the founder's son, Phillip de Gylpyn Benson, who after being invalided out of the Navy in 1916, had visited America to study new methods of psychological marketing and scientific advertising. Phillip Benson was an authoritarian who ran a regimented style of business.

The firm operated from premises in Kingsway Hall, Kingsway, at that time the centre of the advertising trade in London because of its nearness to Fleet Street's newspaper offices. Benson undertook all types of advertising, producing everything from small adverts in magazines to large outdoor posters. During the 1920s, it created campaigns for many household names, such as Andrews' Liver Salts, Rowntree's Chocolate and Lipton's tea.

One of Benson's most famous campaigns was its 1926 campaign for Colman's Mustard, which invented a fictional Mustard Club with a cast of quaint characters. The purpose of The Baron de Beef, Lord Bacon, Miss Di Gester and so on was 'to inspect public sandwiches and report when they contained no mustard'. The firm's greatest success came in 1929 with the first advertising campaign for Guinness. Benson chose the old-fashioned approach of simply telling the public that 'Guinness is Good for You'.

Although Phillip Benson ran his agency along American lines, he was not altogether sympathetic to the 'scientific' approach that many American agencies adopted. At Benson, the copywriting department was called the 'Literary Department', and maintained something of a bohemian atmosphere, producing copy that was humorous, clever and elegant. Among Benson's copywriters in the 1920s was the young Dorothy L Sayers, whose novel *Murder must Advertise* is set in Pym's Publicity, a thinly disguised Benson. Benson's reputation was built on producing clever campaigns, fine artwork and punning copy that consumers remembered and responded to.

Upon the death in 1927 of the first Lord Iveagh, who had ruled the Guinness Board autocratically and was very much against advertising, the pressure to do something to stop the steady decline in Guinness sales since before WWI led to a Board directive that an advertising trial in Clydeside, Glasgow would be undertaken.

After Lord Iveagh's passing, the brewery came much more under the control of the senior managers rather than the family, and the one thing that everyone had an opinion on was advertising. In 1928, Guinness had held a beauty parade of potential advertising agencies, and Benson, being a famous name was prominent amongst them and selected for the trial.

Benson was however, already known to Guinness for their advertising because they had been working for many of the independent export bottling companies in Liverpool and London who bottled and exported Foreign Guinness around the world. Prior to 1929, these exporters paid for their own Guinness advertising material including posters, trade cards, newspaper adverts plus many forms of merchandising such as mirrors, ashtrays, waiter trays etc. E & J Burke of Dublin was the biggest seller of export Guinness, especially in the USA. Others were Machen & Hudson and J. S. Woodfield of Liverpool, Read Brothers, Probyn and Stone of London and Speakman of Melbourne. They all had their advertising designed by Benson. Examples of their posters or show card designs are illustrated a few pages forward.

The UK market was very important for Guinness's profitability and Scotland was chosen for the trial as it was a limited area that could be monitored; sales had fallen faster here than in England. The Scottish trial was a great success so Benson was appointed and Oswald Greene, a Director of Benson, was despatched to prepare copy for a pilot campaign. He worked closely with T. B. Case the Guinness managing director and Ben Newbold the deputy managing director. The people who were going to design and write the actual advertisements made a number of special visits to the Guinness St James's Gate Brewery in Dublin.

Bobby Bevan

With Mr Greene was a young copywriter called Bobby Bevan, who seventeen years later would become MD and Chairman of Benson. Bevan was a big man, extrovert, tallish, impressive and charismatic. He was good-looking with a wide face and hawkish nose with fair curly hair. He was also intelligent, vigorous and had wide interests in the arts. His father had been a famous artist.

He was born the son of Robert Polhill Bevan (1865-1925), Painter, and Stanislawa, daughter of Alexander de Karlowski. Bevan had been educated at the Hall School before entering Westminster School as a Kings scholar in 1913 at the early age of twelve. In 1919 he went up to Christ Church College, Oxford and read Greats obtaining seconds in Mods and in Finals. In 1923 he entered the advertising company of S. H. Benson as a junior copywriter, and went on to become, what former colleague R. D. Bloomfield described as, 'the personification of the greatest days of English advertising'.

It was in his time at Benson that some of the best known advertising campaigns of the 1920s and 1930s were produced. The products advertised included Guinness, Bovril, Johnnie Walker and Colman's. Bevan was personally handling most of these accounts, and he was still handling the Guinness account thirty years later in the 1950s when he commissioned John Nash to provide colour illustrations to Happy New Lear (1957). He was behind slogans such as 'Guinness is Good for You' and was the inspiration for Mr Ingleby in Dorothy L Sayers' 1933 thriller *Murder must Advertise*.

Bevan led the creative teams inside Benson on the Guinness account for thirty years. As a director he dominated and cowed his co-directors such that he got no challenge to his ideas. This eventually led to Benson having no trained successor in place when Bevan retired. Bevan became a friend of Sir Hugh Beaver and Phillips of Guinness, and fitted in as a part of the Guinness establishment.

Bobby Bevan was a member of London's 1930s literary set. A particular friend was the novelist Anthony Powell; who presented Bobby with copies of his first four novels, each fully dedicated with 'somewhat randy inscriptions'. He was a passionate sailor and member of the Royals Ocean Racing Club. In 1937 he and a friend, Harold Paton, commissioned a yacht Phryna, which was designed by B. Heckstall-Smith and Wm. McMeek, and built by J. Samuel White in Cowes. They had a very successful couple of years racing before the outbreak of the Second World War.

During the War he was a Staff Officer in the Royal Naval Reserve, and was posted to Washington in 1943 to liaise with US Naval Intelligence. He rose to the rank of Captain which was a great achievement.

For a short period during the war, Bevan was Director of General Production at the Ministry of Information. However, having joined the RNVR in 1937 he was soon on active service. After a spell on HMS Ellington he was posted as a liaison officer to the French Navy. Following the fall of France, Bevan prevented the scuttling of the 'Commandant Dominé' and forced the captain to join the Free French at gunpoint. He was appointed OBE for this act in March 1941. In 1944–45, as a Captain RNVR, Bevan was working as the Deputy Chief of Naval Information, in Washington DC. This was a post that not only exercised all his skills at communication, but gave him access to many of the top players in American Intelligence, which was to prove useful in his later advertising career.

Bobby Bevan had a difficult relationship with his father, which might explain why there is only one known portrait of the son by Robert Bevan, yet numerous portraits of his daughter, Halszka, survive. He also appears to have had problems in his relationship with women. He did marry on his return from the war in 1946, his bride being a vivacious, divorcee– Natalie Sieveking (née Ackenhausen), daughter of Court Denny. However, within a year he found himself in a well-publicised ménage à trois involving his wife and Randolph Churchill. This affair was to continue until the latter's death in 1968.

Bobbie Bevan photographed at Oxford, 1920.

Bevan was married but also gay, which suited both him and his wife. As a couple, they were glamorous, sociable and well off. They delighted in entertaining the upper classes and intellectuals at their flat in Lowndes Square, Belgravia, London or at their country house in Boxted, Suffolk.

The Bevans lived at Boxted House on the Essex/Suffolk border and had a flat in Knightsbridge, London. They entertained greatly and Boxted soon became a gathering place for artists, writers and gardeners. Weekend parties might consist of Maggi Hambling, Francis Bacon, A. P. Herbert, Ronald Blythe, Beth Chatto and John Gathorne-Hardy. Other friends included the artists John Armstrong and Frederick Gore, and others more closely associated with East Anglia, such as Cedric Morris, John Nash and the architect Raymond Erith. The composer Benjamin Britten and the tenor Peter Pears might be there as would the art dealer Anthony d'Offay, who once brought down the artists Gilbert & George.

BENSON, OGILVY & MATHER AND GUINNESS

Between 1954-64 he was Chairman of S. H. Benson Ltd, being appointed CBE in the Queen's Birthday Honours of 1963. Bobby Bevan was something of a mentor to the New York based advertising executive David Ogilvy who frequently stayed at Boxted during his trips to England. In 1948 Bevan had established Ogilvy as head of a new advertising agency in New York. This was to become Ogilvy, Benson and Mather. In 1964 it merged with David's brother Francis's agency to become Ogilvy and Mather International Inc. Ogilvy once said of Bevan 'I was in awe of him but Bevan never took notice of me!'

Mani Ayer, former CEO of Ogilvy & Mather (India) said of him:

'Bevan was not a man who would share his experience or knowledge with you. He was an intellectual and came from a well-known family of painters and he preferred to live like an aristocrat.' However, the artist, John Nash, who had known him since 1913, said of him, 'Robert Bevan was a significant figure and there was a bond between us. This was Bobby's 'cosy' side – he could be moody and at times rather formidable but beneath this one sensed always his intense loyalty to his real friends, mixed with an affection that his undemonstrative nature hardly allowed him to disclose. I like to think I partook of these latter qualities. He was a very private person, talking little about his personal deeds even less about his personal thoughts and worries. His sympathy to those in distress was almost feminine in its understanding.'

Gilroy's 'Said the moon to the earth I declare' advert, GE 675, 1937.

Guinness's Independent Export Bottlers

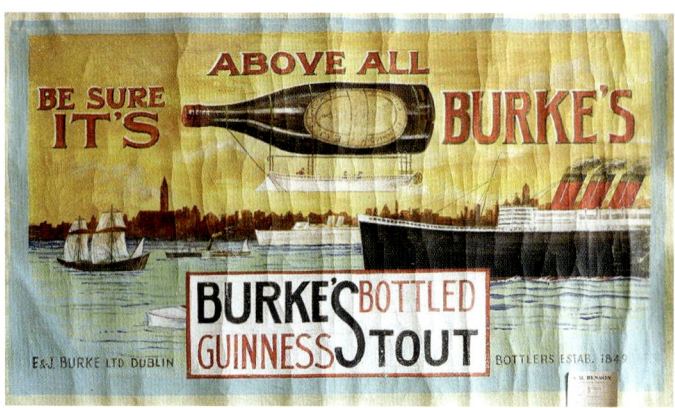

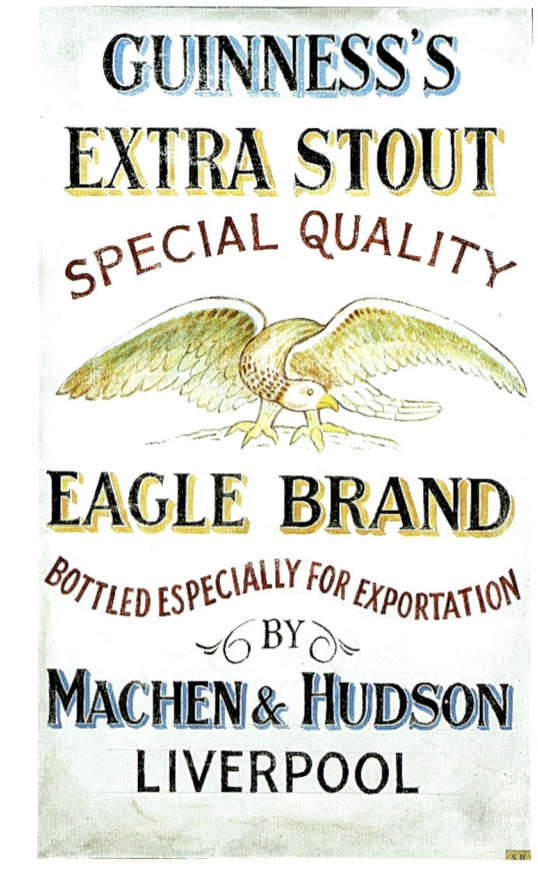

Poster and show card designs done by Benson.

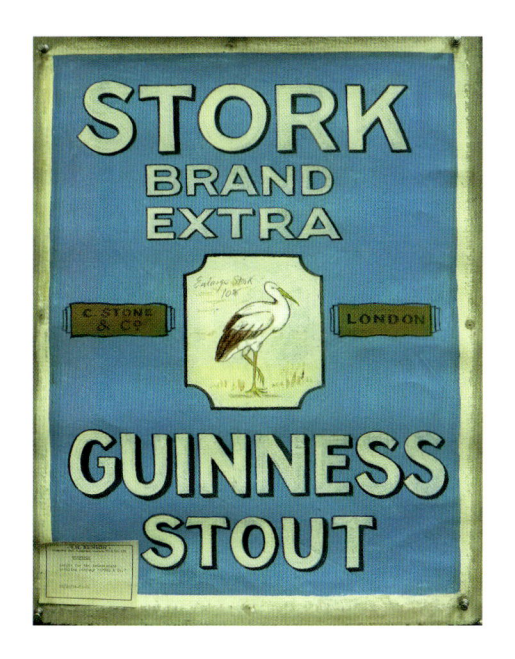

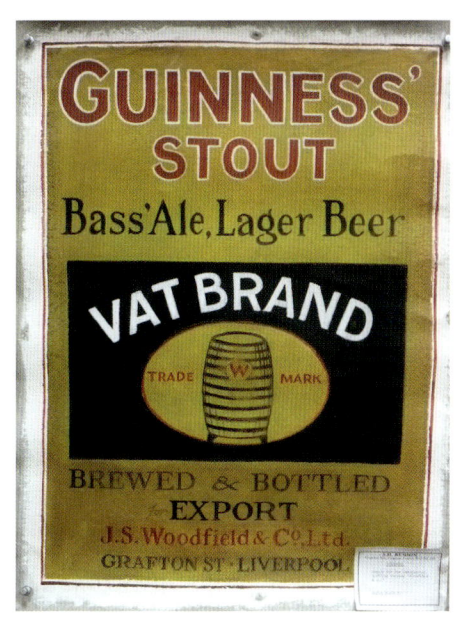

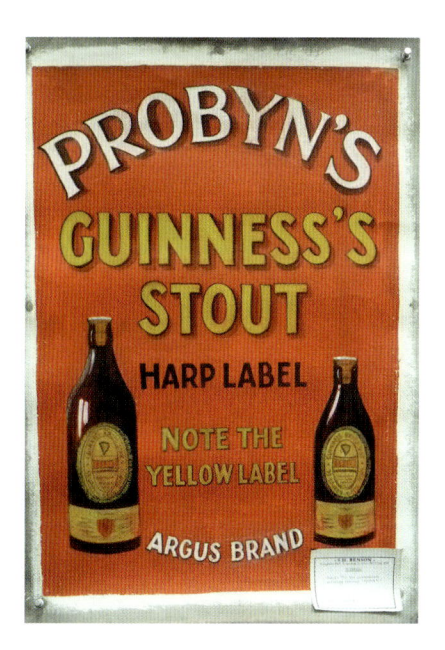

These pre-WWI to the 1920s oil on canvas paintings all have the Benson archive stickers attached.

Benson collected information not only about the brewing, but about every aspect of the production of Guinness right back even to the research and experiments made by Guinness in growing the best types of barley. What Benson saw during these visits of inspection was with the eyes of the advertising expert looking for things which can be made into interesting and convincing selling stories, and they had the advantage of long and helpful discussion in Dublin with publicans, Guinness drinkers, managing directors, brewers, staff and craftsmen.

One of the purposes of these talks was to select, among the hundreds of interesting things going on at a place like the Guinness Brewery, just those particular things that lend themselves to development into effective advertisements. The enduring slogan 'Guinness is good for you' came out of that research.

People, of all sorts and places, had long been in the habit of talking about Guinness as being 'good for you'. The phrase was almost a colloquialism. A first rate slogan, it was already half-famous! That seems obvious enough, but at the time that slogan was very nearly discarded for the precise reason that made it famous. Surely this was the kind of thing anyone might say it was, and in that apparent weakness lay its strength.

On February 2nd, 1929 and the days following, the first advertisement for Guinness ever to be published in a national newspaper appeared. It was all text except for two small glasses of Guinness at the bottom. The first poster in Spring 1929 showed a large pint of Guinness, brimful, in a straight glass with the 'GIGFY' ('Guinness is good for you') slogan in bold red capitals. This could well have been painted by Gilroy but they are unsigned. Early posters were sober, serious looking, no-nonsense with a glass of Guinness in central position. When Gilroy's influence started to come through, he introduced some humour and light-hearted relief. John Gilroy, the artist, interpreted and gave form and colour to so many humorous ideas for Guinness adverts and posters. Guinness posters were to dominate the hoarding sites in London and other major cities for years to come. Visitors to London were struck by how many times they saw Guinness advertising.

Apart from 'Guinness is good for you', the other classic banners adopted were 'Guinness for strength', 'Guinness Time', 'Have a Guinness when you're tired', and 'My Goodness my Guinness'. Gilroy's smiling glass, Guinness and oysters and Lewis Carroll's *Through the looking glass* and *Alice in Wonderland* themes followed. These led directly into the 'My Goodness My Guinness' Gilroy animals, the Zookeeper and the famous *Guinness for Strength* images of lifting girders and chopping trees. The 30s were the classic period for Gilroy imagery and the recognition they got from the public was huge. In 1932 the Strongman statue was used, 1933 the porter and

A 1929 Straight Glass advert, probably by Gilroy.

acquaintance'. The genius of Gilroy was the empathy the public had with his drawings.

Hugh de Quetteville gives an illuminating insight into what it was like to work at Benson in the 1950s and before; it attracted extrovert, literate, arty, creative and at times bohemian types. It was fun and quite well-paid. For those who preferred a more classless organisation than a City institution, they rewarded good performance and you could rise through the ranks quickly. It was a young industry that attracted lots of pretty girls to boot! Much drinking was done, the expense account lunch was an enormous affair with far too much rich food and booze at midday, leaving the afternoon a blur. Intellectuals and those that questioned the norms could thrive in this environment. It was a home for bright ideas, witty words and the visual arts.

The story is told that when Robert Bevan came for his interview, he deliberately wore a pair of spats and carried a copy of Balzac under his arm, advertising himself as an intellectual with style. He was always a sharp dresser. Working on the Guinness account was a high accolade at the agency. Because of the enormous range of periodicals and magazines used, that all required tailored ads, as well as the national posters, the press, show cards, bus sides and other promotional advertising, life was very busy and exciting.

column, 1934 the girder man, 1935 the sea lion and toucan, 1936 the ostrich and tortoise, 1937 the lion and wood chopper. Then WWII intervened. 1939 saw the pelican, 1941 the spitfire, 1943 the kangaroo. Postwar, we had the horse and cart in 1949, the kinkajou in 1952 and the bear up a pole in 1956. Despite this mass of advertising, Guinness sales in Great Britain fell, as did all beer consumption. Guinness sales never reached the level experienced in 1932 and kept falling, but declined at a lesser rate than other brewers' beers. These were the years of the Great Depression and things would have been much worse without Gilroy.

When Benson took charge of its public image, Guinness was already a household name. What Benson gave that name was character and personality; they made it a friend rather than just an

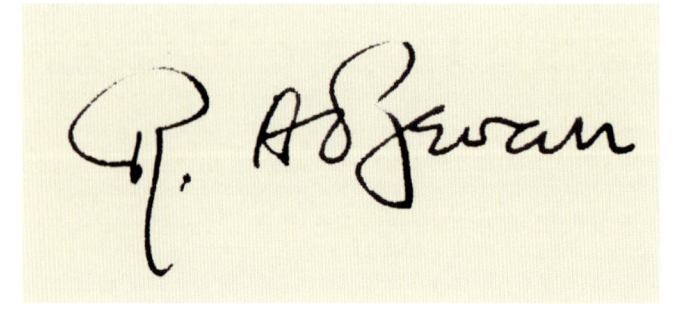

Bevan signature.

Ogilvy & Mather

David Ogilvy had worked for Gallup, the pollsters in the late 1930s. During the War he was posted to New York in Naval Intelligence liaising with American Intelligence, where he met Bevan. In 1948, after being out of advertising for ten years, David Ogilvy started his own agency in the USA. His brother Francis who was MD of Mather and Crowther Agency in London and a friend of Bobby Bevan, the MD of Benson, each made a generous investment to financially assist him get set up. S. H. Benson Ltd invested forty-five thousand dollars, but insisted that Ogilvy hire someone who knew how to run an agency. Ogilvy hired Anderson Hewitt away from J. Walter Thompson to be president, and appointed himself vice president in charge of Research. The business opened as Hewitt, Ogilvy, Benson & Mather. They became massively successful.

By 1960, Benson was almost two agencies in one. The traditional accounts were under Bobby Bevan and the newer accounts under Gilbert Hughes (Lever Brothers and Beechams), formed the other side. Both camps adopted different operating styles.

In 1964 OBM merged with Mather & Crowther to form Ogilvy & Mather International. Benson were originally based in the Kingsway Hall (the Methodist Centre) in Kingsway and by 1959 they were outgrowing their shabby offices. Bobby Bevan decided to move and with great good fortune had acquired in 1964 a long lease on a fabulous new property in central London, opposite Holborn Tube Station, 129 Kingsway. It was worth about six million pounds. In 1969 in order to raise money, S. H. Benson became a publicly quoted company. Prior to 1962, their only overseas offices were in India. Benson moved late to become an international agency with offices in Canada, Kenya, India and Australia. They also handled the Guinness export accounts for foreign markets such as Malaya. Some of these moves were a disaster financially, so the Bankers at Lazards were brought in to try to sort things out and they received a place on the Board.

However, profits were not adequate to give a decent return on assets, the share price dropped and they were subsequently bought out by Jacob Rothschild Investment Trust (RIT), who stripped off the valuable property in London and abroad, and resold the agency in October 1971 to Ogilvy & Mather. S. H. Benson now became part of Ogilvy, Benson, and Mather in London. In 1971 on their transfer to the Ogilvy offices, Benson had to clear out their stores and they donated eight hundred of their old printed posters to the London Museum and one hundred and seventy-five to the Victoria and Albert Museum. Eventually the Ogilvy Group was acquired by WPP in 1989.

The reason for the interest in who owned Benson and when, lies in how their Advertising Archive got sold off to an American buyer.

Benson sticker.

The Gilroy oil on canvas artwork was stored by being cut out of the wooden stretchers used for display at the presentation to Guinness, a sticker was placed on each canvas and they were rolled up for storage in the Artwork Room. The Gilroy Guinness collection formed the largest and most valuable part of that Archive.

Author's Note: Individual Guinness canvases were selling in early 2013 for up to fourteen thousand dollars each.

The Guinness element of the archive should probably never have been sold off, as many of the cardboard tubes that contained the rolled up canvases had 'Return to Guinness Park Royal' typed on them. At that time Guinness did not have its own archive although their marketing department did retain a lot of material. The archive appears never to have been offered to Guinness for purchase, not that at that time they would necessarily have bought it. Of course they may have taken the view that it was their intellectual property anyway. In truth I do not know exactly how the archive was sold so I have to speculate. The buyer wishes to remain secretive about himself and the transaction, which is his right.

Many years later, around 2009, the American owner of the archive came across a US dealer in silver, antiques and furniture, at an upmarket antiques fair. The antique dealer had on display an old beer sign, which is what attracted the owner to make contact. It came out in conversation that the owner had not just beer signs, but original Guinness material; oil on canvas pictures of adverts. At that stage they were stored in rolls and very dirty, with each canvas needing reconditioning before selling. A deal was agreed and the antiques dealer then started receiving restored canvases from the UK where they were kept, and began selling the canvases at the better US antique and art fairs, to US collectors. A few were sold and then a few more and eventually it became clear that this source had large numbers of original canvases, by various artists and across a number of accounts, not just Guinness. Champagne marques, Distillers whisky and Rum brands, Bells whisky, Pimms, Players cigarettes, and many more major brands were represented. With a ready market proven, in 2012, a second US dealer was being supplied.

What is curious is the forty year delay in bringing this art to market, because during that time in storage, maybe as much as a third of the canvases were spoiled, stuck together or covered in black mildew. It is my guess that the archive was sold to a private buyer around the time when Benson changed hands in 1971. I find it difficult to believe that either Benson or Ogilvy would have sold off the 'family silver' so to speak, but I have been unable to gain hard facts. It was a long time ago and few survive who would know. Others are being secretive.

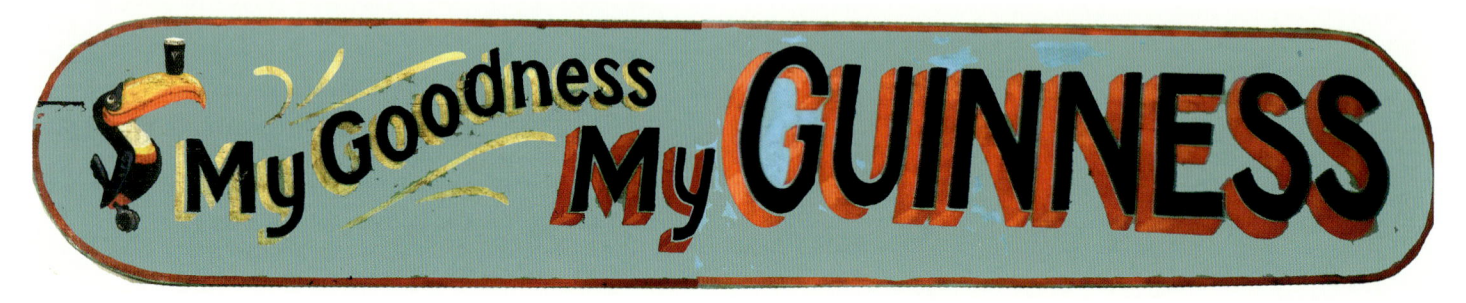

Antique wooden Guinness sign from Benson's archive.

The Art of creating a Guinness Poster

Posters are the biggest advertisements people see and their message needs to be bold and simple so that anyone on a bus or running past one may recognise and read it quickly. Where posters can be studied at closer quarters and with more leisure, such as on London's Underground system, the approach can be more intimate and more text can be used to convey a message. Gilroy perfected the use of the large poster medium. The boldness of the red type display and the expert use of white space to focus the eye on the subject matter, were the hallmarks of Guinness's classic posters. Gilroy kept his backgrounds to a minimum, often just white, so as not to distract the eye. Boldness and simplicity made the message easy to understand.

For the poster, let us take the familiar one of the man carrying an enormous girder on his head. This began its existence at Benson's as quite a rough pencil scribble by John Gilroy, a mere broad indication of the general idea.

From this were developed other sketches, equally simple, trying out the idea in a number of forms until the final size of the girder in proportion to the man, the angle at which he was to be walking, and a number of other details concerned with composition, balance and so on, had been decided. The next step was to make a rough coloured sketch with the lettering in place. The term 'rough' is used in a technical sense. Note Gilroy's use of geometric lines to ensure accuracy and perspective are correct.

Most people would regard such a sketch as a pretty careful painting and indeed a great deal of care went into it. The colour scheme, for instance, had to be arranged to give the best possible effect with the fewest colours, because if too many colours were used, the cost of printing the poster would be too high.

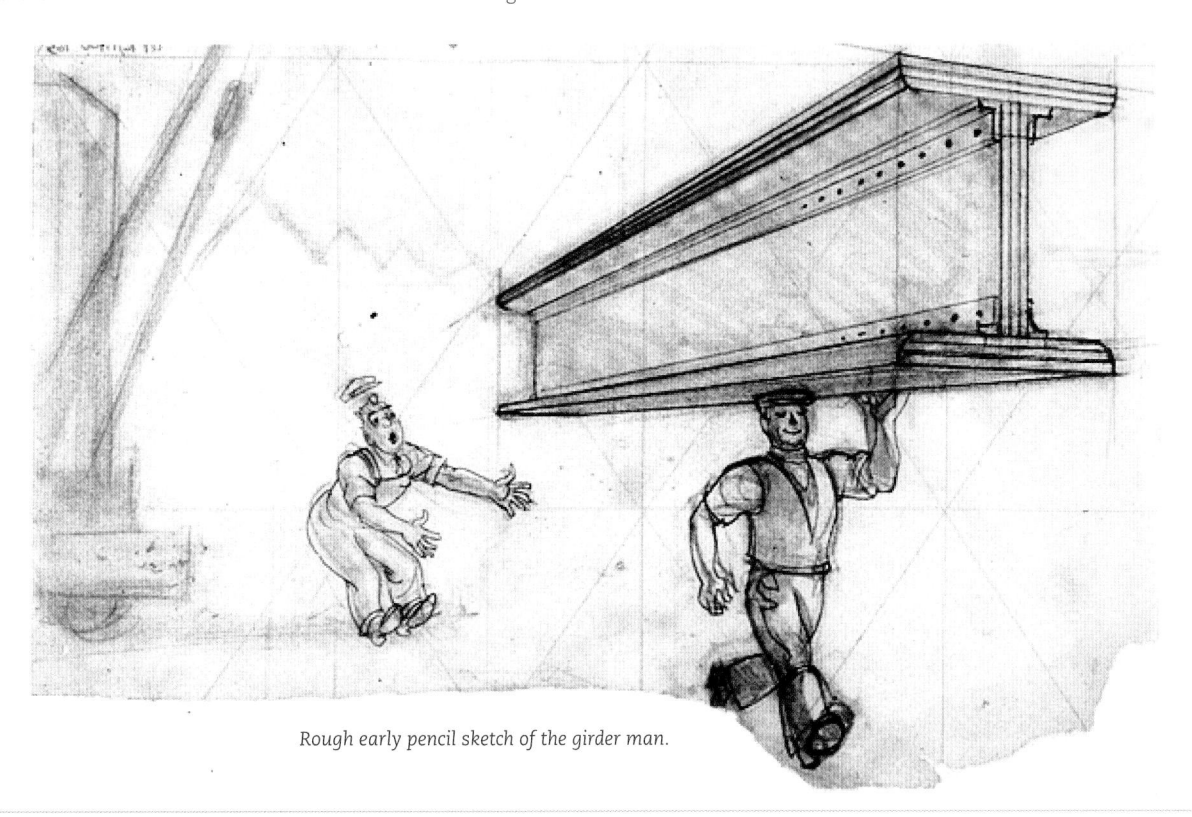

Rough early pencil sketch of the girder man.

Watercolour rough of the girder man.

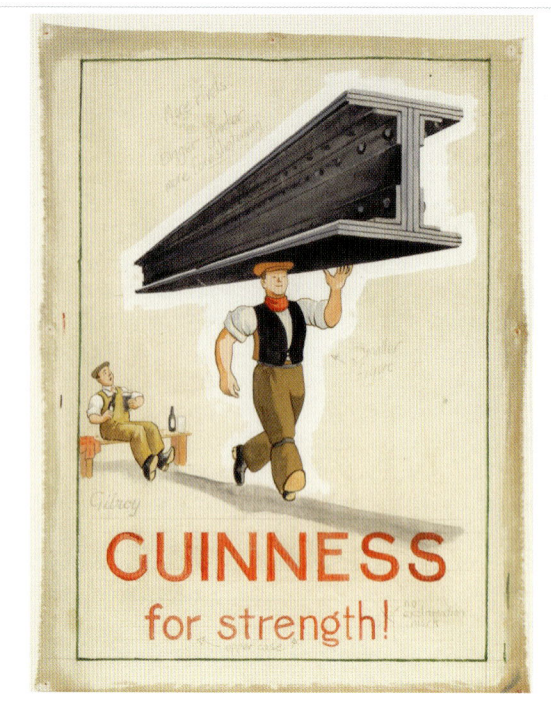

Benson canvas for the poster.

Gilroy's poster designs were deceptively simple: the colours strong, the palette sparse, the type bold, the background white, and the elements balanced but dramatically positioned to convey the product's two related themes of strength and goodness. Gilroy's tools were humour and hyperbole. His outrageous scenarios, especially the girder-carrier sequence from the early 1930s - in which a Guinness-drinking workman transports metalwork with ease - defy belief, except in the essential brand promise. Humour and fun enlivened the work of this energetic, versatile, and influential artist. Gilroy and Benson were to create a unique brand of imagery.

Once Benson's had approved the sketch and any necessary amendments were noted, a finished coloured painting was produced by the artist, from which the printer would work if approved by Guinness. It seems likely that Gilroy used Japan Drier as paint thinner and to aid fast drying. A thinned application of the oil paint would allow the canvases to be rolled without cracking for storage. This finished painting would probably not be the same size as the poster to be made from it, but would always be in the same proportions. Nearly all the Benson's archive paintings were made about 34 inches by 22 inches, though much larger ones, double the size, such as the toucans over the RAF base, toucans on the weathervane and the Knight's helmet were done as well. The final painting was the most expensive part of the poster production process. Paintings were all stored (even the rejected ones) in the Benson Artwork Room, and had to be signed in and out.

A first rough canvas of the Gnu - Original artwork from the Benson archive.

Next came the job of printing the poster, for which the Guinness Advertising Department Print Buyer was responsible. Just as the artist could not very well paint his picture full size, so the printer could not print such a gigantic picture all at once on a single sheet of paper. A poster, as you can see when it is being pasted up, is put together from a number of separate sheets of paper, each of which has to be individually printed from metal plates, as many as 64 of which may be required for the largest poster. On outside hoardings, Guinness used 16, 24, 48 and 64 sheet prints. Small single sheet or up to 4 sheet were used for internal purposes such as pubs, buses, the Underground, trains and stations. In the final process, the printed sheets were collated into poster bundles wrapped in brown paper, and sent out to the billposting firms to be pasted on the spaces already booked for them.

A later canvas of the Gnu - Original artwork from the Benson archive.

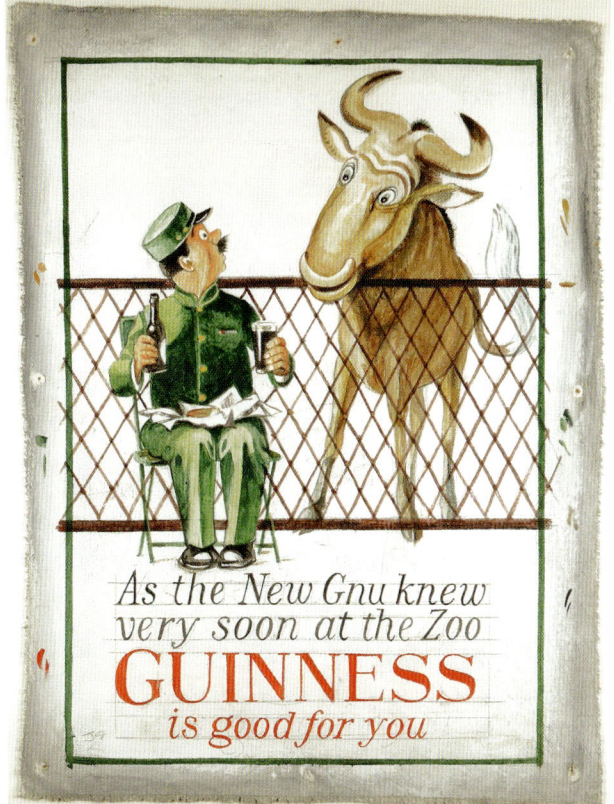

Two canvas versions of the Gnu. Original artwork from the Benson archive.

When we see the elaborate and highly technical nature of all the processes that go into the making of a Guinness poster, it is easy to see that the work must begin a long time before the poster is due to make its appearance. In fact; the design of Guinness posters displayed at Christmas time usually starts the previous summer.

Not one of Benson's best, it is a mismatch of verbal and visual ideas, lacking immediate understanding and simplicity of form.

The first humorous Gilroy Guinness advert, 1930.

The Poster Printing Process

It is said that Lithographic printing offers the best quality. The use of graduated tints and large solid blocks of colour tend to lead to Litho being selected as the preferred process. Litho is more suitable for longer print runs like posters. The earliest form, stone lithography, was popular with artists because it was the first printmaking medium to allow the artist to naturally 'paint' or 'draw' onto a flat stone to create an image. The artist creates the work directly and naturally. This process would not have been used by Gilroy in the 1930s, as he had no direct contact with or access to the printers.

Lithography is based on the elementary principle that oil and water do not mix. The main idea used in stone lithography is extremely simple:

1. **The artist draws/paints on the stone with a greasy substance.** For example, a litho crayon is a soft waxy/greasy crayon. There are also litho paints and pencils. The stone picks up this greasy substance and holds it.
2. **The stone is moistened with water.** The parts of the stone not protected by the greasy paint soak up the water.
3. **Oil-based ink is rolled onto the stone.** The greasy parts of the stone pick up the ink, while the wet parts do not.
4. **A piece of paper is pressed onto the stone,** and the ink transfers from the stone to the paper.

The drawback was that large slabs of limestone had to be used which were extremely heavy and bulky, consequently some of the major lithographers turned to using a lighter zinc plate instead of the limestone. By the late 1930s, another major change was the movement to offset presses, though the print output was distinguishable from that of the stone.

A more modern process used zinc or aluminium plates rather than stone, and photolithography to create the litho plates. This is how Gilroy's art was made into a printing plate. His final proof oil painting was photographed to create a negative.

The use of offset printing for posters was first undertaken in the 1930s. This process was more economical, and the offset plates were easier to handle and store. However, although some early examples were able to duplicate the full colour of stone lithography, posters gradually began to lose their colour depth and could not match the lushness of colour and tone subtleties as the offset printing process evolved.

Offset lithography is generally accomplished on a press with three cylinders. A lithographic plate of aluminium or zinc is wrapped around the first cylinder. The plate prints on a second cylinder that is covered by a rubber blanket. The impression on the rubber is then printed on the paper which is on the third cylinder. This third cylinder has steel fingers called grippers that hold the paper in position while it is squeezed against the rubber surface.

One major advantage of offset-lithography is that the soft rubber surface of the blanket creates a clear impression on a wide variety of paper surfaces and materials. Lithography printing is easily recognized by its smooth print, as well as by the lack of any impression or ring of ink or serrated edges that are characteristic of letterpress or gravure printing. Sheet-fed lithography is used for printing advertising, posters, packaging, coupons, and art reproduction.

For Guinness posters, the single and 4 sheet smaller posters were most often silk screen printed, usually by Mills and Rockley of Ipswich. S. C. Allen & Co Ltd, and The Dangerfield Printing Co, were also early screen printers. The larger 16, 24, 48 and 64 sheet posters were all litho printed in fourteen or more colours by either Sanders Phillips Ltd of London, Waterlow & Sons Ltd or John Waddington Ltd of Leeds. In order to fit the image into the various width formats of these posters, as many as three different designs of each poster were made. For instance if we take the 1957 crocodile, we have three basic poster designs, one in portrait and two in landscape, each with its mouth a little longer and less wide than the last. For the very long bus side poster, another design is needed this time with the mouth nearly closed. This meant the artist had to produce many variants of each approved design, which is what we see in the Benson archive record.

GA/2241-2246
Range of Posters in General Billposting Scheme from 1st June to end August, 1957

GA/P1/2241 Size 30 ins. x 20 ins.
GA/P4U/2242 Size 60 ins. x 40 ins.
GA/P16/2243 Size 120 ins. x 80 ins. 
(No Quad Crowns)
GA/P32/2244 Size 120 ins. x 160 ins. 
GA/P48/2245 120 ins. x 240 ins.
GA/P64/2246 120 ins. x 320 ins. 
See paragraph 3 below.

1. Printed in 11 colours.
2. D.C.'s and 4 sheets silk screened by Mills & Rockleys. 16 Sheets. Litho. Sanders Phillips & Co., Ltd. 32 sheets. Litho. Leonard Ripley & Co., Ltd. 48/64 sheets. Litho. Leonard Ripley & Co., Ltd. March 1957.
3. 64 Sht. layout is a 48 Sht. with additional buff sheets at each side.

January, 1957.

BUS SIDE STREAMERS   GA/2247
Dimensions: (Depth first)   ...   ...   21¼ ins. x 17 ft. 6 ins.
Posting period 1st June - end August.

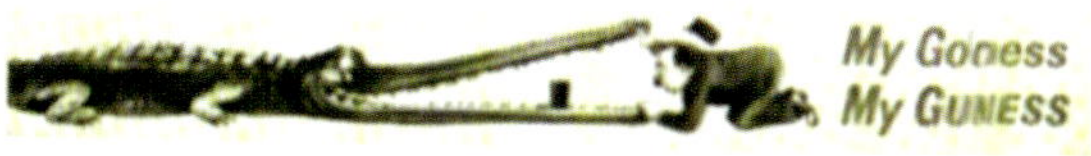

The Creation of a Guinness Print advertisement

Although posters were certainly one of the most important forms of advertising they were not by any means the only way of putting a message effectively before the public. That vast array of publications known as 'The Press', including the great national Daily and Sunday papers, the provincial newspapers, the weekly and monthly magazines as well as innumerable specialised publications, trade papers and technical papers, all offer the advertiser an efficient means of telling his story to one or more sections of the public. Many of the weekly and monthly publications too gave opportunities for the use of colour. Colour printing in the 1930s was expensive.

When a London daily newspaper began the experiment of printing in two colours, Guinness, always ready to help make life brighter, took a half-page for 'Tis the Voice of the Lobster' with the lobster printed in real lobster red.

The life story of a Guinness newspaper advertisement, also begins, like that of the poster, with a rough pencil sketch. But it is a different kind of sketch this time; for underneath the broadly roughed in picture are a number of ruled lines. The lines are a temporary 'stand-in' for the words to be printed there later on. Their purpose is to enable the artist to see how much of the space he can deploy to the picture, how much will be needed for the words, and how much for the slogan at the bottom of the advertisement. Compared to a poster which has to have immediate impact on the eye and memory, the paper advert can be read more slowly with more precision. The words become relatively more important.

Gilroy's oil on canvas artwork.

The words of a parody advert were often written first, then a rough sketch of the whole advertisement was made and this was down to the artist, who drew his finished picture the right shape and proportion for the space

'Tis the Voice of the Lobster,

I heard him declare,
"I am ready for dinner, if Guinness is there."
As a duck demands peas, so a lobster appeals
For a Guinness at dinner and other such meals.
It brings out the flavour, the epicures say,
(And who should know more about flavour
than they?)
A lobster's a good thing, but do not forget a
Lobster with Guinness is twenty times better.

GUINNESS and LOBSTER

Daily Express advert, June 28th GE167, 1931.

Launching a new campaign

The print advertisements were now ready and the means for printing them was in the hands of the newspapers and magazines where they would appear. The posters have been printed and sent to the billposters who were busy pasting them up on the hoardings. But still we have not come to the end of the long sequence of careful planning upon which a successful advertising campaign depended. A continuous check had to be made to ensure that the posters were displayed in the proper places and that they were kept clean and tidy. At the same time the sites themselves were under constant review. The development of new towns and suburbs made it necessary to follow the shifts in population while the building of any new and better sites offered opportunities for strengthening the display. For this purpose, a staff of inspectors was employed by Walter Hill who, under the control of the Guinness Advertising Department, kept in touch with poster contractors up and down the country and with the Guinness organisation, in all its Regional offices.

In due course the advertisements would appear in the papers, and they must appear on the right days and in the positions ordered. Benson receive one copy of each paper in which a Guinness advertisement had been booked to appear, and all these papers were gone through and each advertisement carefully checked.

allotted to it. Unlike the paintings or posters, the drawings for press advertisements are usually made bigger than they will eventually appear. This is particularly necessary with a drawing such as this one containing a lot of detail which would be difficult, if not impossible, to draw satisfactorily on such a small scale.

The drawing is first sent to a firm of printing block-makers, who prepare a metal plate or 'block' from which the picture will be printed. The wording is set up in type, and from type and block together a proof or rough print, is made of the complete advertisement. This is carefully read through, checked and corrected. Finally, a number of plates or stereotypes are cast of the complete thing and one of these 'stereos' is sent to each newspaper in which the advertisement is booked to appear.

Point of Sale

Up to now we have been concerned only with the Guinness advertising in the best known forms, in the press and on the hoardings, seen by the general public. But that was not by any means the only Guinness advertising.

There were over one hundred thousand licensed premises in the country in the 1930s; nearly all of them sold Guinness and many of them displayed or used Guinness advertising material of one sort or another. The list included beer mats and serviettes, trays, clocks, menus, playing cards, ashtrays, barometers and waistcoat buttons. Off Licences could call for special material for windows and counter displays. A Guinness display service equipped with vans covering the whole country delivered the material and arranged the window display in co-operation with the retailer. And so the whole complicated machinery behind the Guinness advertising was built up and set in motion.

BENSON, OGILVY & MATHER AND GUINNESS

Two finished wooden advertising menu boards for Irish pubs, from the Benson archive.

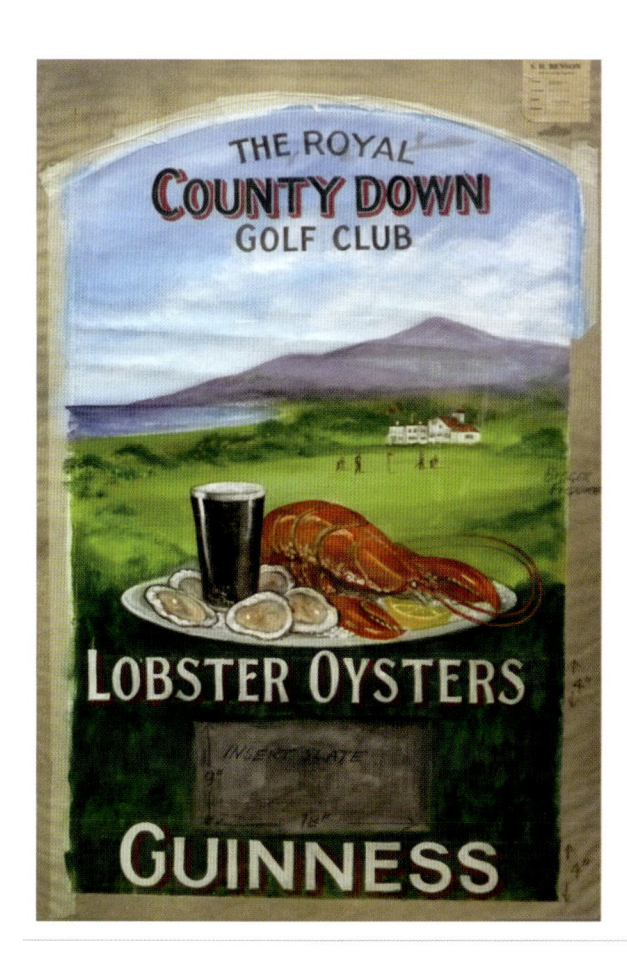

Two canvases of artwork for Irish pub menu boards, painted by Brearley, 1938.

53

How the Guinness advertising account was managed

From 1929 onwards, Guinness set up a function to manage the 'English Trade' and this would also cover advertising. The Board set a budget and designated Martin Pick to work with the agency to deliver the 'propaganda', as it was referred to in Dublin. It was not until much, much later in the 1960s that the advertising department was integrated with sales, as early on it was assumed that little or no real linkage existed between the two activities. Guinness were a long way away from the marketing concept we understand today of integrated sales/advertising/promotion.

Each year, Benson would plan a series of seasonal campaigns based on a theme (for example, a slogan such as 'Guinness Time') and the in-house artists would be put to work illustrating different scenarios to fit those themes. The winter press campaigns were the biggest. Guinness was always a cold weather drink and enjoyed a Christmas sales boost. Gilroy was one of a number of artists on salary, who originally worked on the Guinness account. The artists had the licence to be creative in their imagery but it would have to be approved by Bobby Bevan and the account manager at Benson prior to being shown to the client, Guinness. Guinness would then adopt the ideas, suggest modifications, or reject the work.

Gilroy usually, but not always, signed or put his 'JG' initials to each drawing, to establish recognition for his art. The other in-house artists sometimes did this as well. He also used some small recurring elements that became signature motifs, such as the use of a startled bird, the rising hat and a red polka dot handkerchief. See how many times you can spot these in his pictures. There is no doubt that Gilroy was not just an excellent illustrator, but he was creative and used his natural humour to make his images very appealing.

'Guinness for Christmas', GE66, Dec 1929.

The profusion of ideas he produced is amazing to see in the surviving artwork record. Later on, when Gilroy had become a freelance artist, he would approach the Guinness advertising manager (Mr Pick or Mr Marks) directly at the Park Royal Brewery or their London offices, with poster artwork ideas. He had open access to Guinness; this did little to enhance the relationship between Gilroy and Benson but it was the route that Gilroy used to get full recognition for his ideas. There is nothing an agency dislikes more than ideas coming from another source than themselves, but Benson were clever enough to accept this as a special situation and it worked well for all parties.

Gilroy had, over the early years, seen many of his images accepted by Guinness, only for Benson to employ another commercial artist to deliver the final copy. In that case, he got neither remuneration nor the kudos for the work. Here is an example of an original Gilroy idea being reworked in the finished advert by another commercial artist. The scenes are identical except for the vanishing glass of Guinness in the claws of the crab and the French slogan 'It's Guinness' becoming 'Where's the Guinness'.

One thing that became clear from these relationships was that if Guinness liked one of Gilroy's ideas for a non-advertising application, such as the *Guinness Time magazine*, it would not need to be put forward for approval by Benson. Guinness would directly commission the printing from the artwork. By 1950, work for Gilroy on the Benson Guinness account was already starting to dry up. By 1960, it had just about ceased. His last work dates to about 1964.

Once Benson had agreed with Pick or Marks that a specific image was suitable to use on the account in national advertising, it would be presented for approval to Will Phillips from the Guinness Board at the next quarterly meeting. Major campaign artwork was always shown to the full Guinness Park Royal Board for final approval. Agreement as to what was used in the mass of regional or specialist publications was between Pick and Benson. There were so many types of advert done that it was not practical to burden the Guinness Board with all of it.

The Board did reject ideas occasionally, but it was thought most were accepted. That conventional wisdom has been overturned by the finding of so many unused pictures. That was then the end of the process, with Benson handing over the artwork to the Guinness Print Buyer. Guinness directly placed all their own orders for printing of posters, display material, show cards, booklets, in-house magazines, bus side posters etc via a print buyer, who was Charlie Moore up to the early 1970s. The print buyer supplied the artwork to the printer from which they made the printing plates. Benson or any newly appointed agency was responsible for direct placement of newspaper and magazine advertising. Benson could do this easily due to their proximity to Fleet Street.

BENSON, OGILVY & MATHER AND GUINNESS

The relationship between Guinness - Martin Pick (and later Tommy Marks), and Benson - Bobby Bevan and Keith Egleston, was very close indeed. They became great friends. It was when Guinness began updating itself and Stan Darmon came in as marketing director that the relationship changed. Under Alan Wood as advertising manager, Benson lost the account. It was felt that Benson had held the account a long time and it was becoming rather institutionalised. The leadership problems after Bevan's retirement sealed their fate.

The direct relationship between Gilroy and Guinness grew stronger once Gilroy started to paint the portraits of the Guinness family. He first painted Lord Iveagh in 1951. Originally in 1929/30 Gilroy may not have been invited to the approval meetings with Guinness, but we can be certain that in the 1950s he was present as he made the written pencil comments on his own canvases. Nearly all of the Benson archive canvases so far found have been marked at the time of the presentation to Guinness with pencilled comments on the canvas about wording, typeface, size of images, colours, making

Gilroy oil canvas.

Gilroy poster canvas in French. Note the presence of a glass.

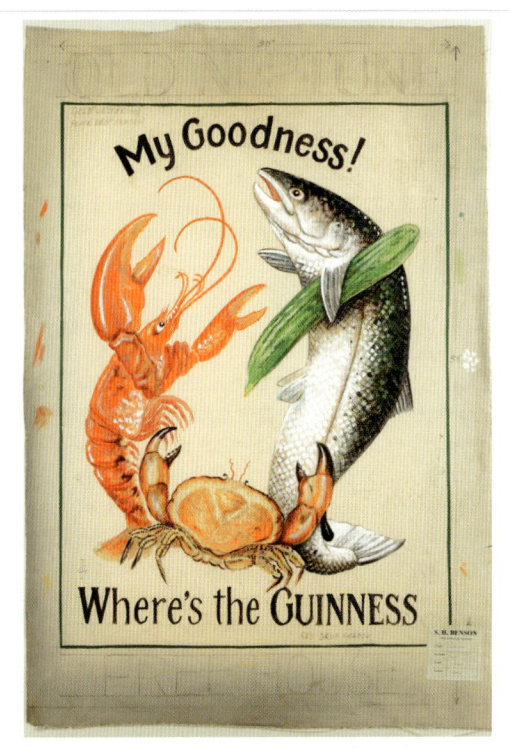

Advertisement GE1230 issued in 1946, using a different artist.

BENSON, OGILVY & MATHER AND GUINNESS

things bigger or smaller and so on.

Here we clearly see the draughtsmanship of Gilroy, who with a few deft lines has captured a workman at full tilt, digging a deep trench with a spade and a smile on his benign face. The movement is captured wonderfully. In this sequence we can see the progression from a basic humorous idea, through to a more filled in picture with colour schemes and people standing up top watching in amazement. This particular image did not get commercially used for reasons unknown, but it would have fitted into the family of *Guinness For Strength* images easily.

Benson's Archive contained many pictures on the same theme (i.e. the GFS fisherman catching a huge fish). Some were early proofs, some were done as mirror images, some are in different languages for different markets and yet others are done at different times and with small changes, which indicates how often many images were reused across the years. One example was the 'Kangaroo', issued in 1943, and again in 1948, 1950 and 1955. It is amazing to note how many times the same advert was painted by Gilroy and it is remarkable how faithfully he copied the original image – a tribute to his excellent draughtsmanship. Much of the archive material dates from the 1950s and there is little for the early 1930s and the war years as would be expected. There are worrying gaps in the archive record. From the pencil comments made by Gilroy ('Good luck!') we can see how he constructed this iconic bird's image.

Quick pencil sketch of the trench digger.

Right middle –'Shadow under the bill and from glasses', top – 'don't forget ruby gleam' pointing at the glasses, left middle- 'add feathers on larger drawings', bottom- 'two toes on front claw'. He also adds his

Two early Guinness for Strength 'man digging a trench', watercolour.

BENSON, OGILVY & MATHER AND GUINNESS

colour palette at the side.

This poster indicates the co-operation between artists on the Guinness account, from the fact that Gilroy would sanction other artists to reproduce his famous toucan in flight with two pints on its beak.

An instructional canvas from the Benson archive; Gilroy showing the other commercial artists in the drawing room at Benson, how to paint the toucan. There were a number of commercial artists employed at any time, and many just did copy work.

How was the Guinness account lost by Benson?

Gilroy had had a good run since 1929, but by the mid-50s Gilroy's relevance to Guinness advertising was waning with other artists being used in producing different styles. The launch of commercial TV in 1957, started to spell the end of the Gilroy era as his animal poster concept did not translate well to it. The first Guinness TV advert ran fourth on the first night of this new commercial medium. It featured a member of the Crazy Gang as the zookeeper, with a sea lion, which did not cooperate at all. By 1965, when Bobby Bevan came to retire, they had made little proper provision for his successor. Benson was family owned and a number of contenders for the chairmanship arose. Guinness were worried as to the future focus and ownership of the agency. There was little desire in Guinness to leave the agency as Benson were very capable of providing TV adverts as they employed excellent people already experienced in both real life film and animation.

The period after Bobby Bevan, was very uncomfortable for Guinness as they saw various people of differing quality come to the fore at Benson. Eventually a Banker called John Hatch from Lazards rose to the top and at a meeting in Upper Brook Street with Guinness chaired by the Guinness MD, Robert McNeile, Hatch stated that it was no good talking to him about advertising as he was a banker! McNeile exploded and thumped the table, saying 'well for God's sake give us someone to talk to us about our advertising', and that was the beginning of the end for Benson.

When Benson lost the account in 1969, the relationship with Gilroy ended and it was believed that Guinness owed him a 'debt of gratitude' for the work he had done and the huge impact it had had on the brand. Since he didn't work for Guinness, its pension scheme was not available to him. He was offered an annual honorarium of about two thousand pounds, which was funded by the Guinness advertising budget. He was very pleased with this gesture and it lasted all his life, but died with him.

Born 1898 kept alive by Guinness
Illustrated letter from the artist, in 1979, thanking Guinness for his annual honorarium. Gilroy notes his change of address, from the more expensive Holland Park to Fulham, 'due to inflation'.

1979 self-deprecating hand drawn card sent to Guinness Marketing Department announcing his change of address to Fulham. It shows the importance that he placed on his honorarium now that other income had declined.

The Guinness advertising people

Martin Pick

Martin was appointed in March 1928 to the post of Guinness advertising manager, a post he held until 1955. He was the brother of Frank Pick, the charismatic manager on London Underground advertising. He was a fair-haired man, about six foot tall, with bushy eyebrows. Not an easy person to get to know, he was an introverted, quite shy, Yorkshire man and a qualified engineer with a BSc. He was associated with the aircraft industry in WWI and subsequently the Wembley Empire Exhibition of 1920.

After training in Dublin, he opened his first Guinness offices in St Paul's Churchyard, London. He was a passionate believer in advertising and worked so hard he appeared not to take holidays. The early days were difficult as he met much resistance in Dublin to the concept of advertising. The culture was totally production led, from the chairman down. It was Col Ben Newbold who encouraged him and led the move into the modern world of visual brand imagery.

Pick brought flair and good taste to the job. He was held in high regard within Guinness and by Benson. With his engineering eye he oversaw the erection of the huge Guinness Time clock in Piccadilly and later the moving Gilroy animal Guinness Festival clocks that travelled around the seaside resorts in the 1950s and 60s.

Gilroy's influence on the Guinness Festival Clock was undisputed. If you ever visited the Festival Gardens in Battersea Park in 1951, you would certainly remember the mechanical Guinness Clock, signalling each quarter with a burst of frenzied activity. It was such a success that nine smaller travelling versions were made to tour the country. Many were situated at seaside resorts for the summer. At each quarter, the ZooKeeper emerges under an umbrella and looks about him; the Ostrich pokes his head out of the chimney; the Mad Hatter hauls a diminishing series of fish from the well; the doors open, revealing toucans chasing each other round a tree; and the cone on top opens up into a round-about of spinning figures, all of course, to music.

When the woodcutter poster came out, there was a flood of letters saying the man was holding the axe the wrong way round. Gilroy acknowledges he made a mistake, however Pick started keeping an axe in his office to demonstrate that it was the right way round. He encouraged the argument as 'Good for Guinness'.

In an extract from a conversation between W. E. Phillips and Pick in 1949, we can gauge the importance of Gilroy. It was stated by Pick 'the horse and cart poster by Gilroy had been such a success that Benson would probably have to employ Gilroy again, but there was difficulty as Gilroy had parted with Benson due to a dispute (he was freelance). Benson's present poster artist's work was not up to Gilroy's standard. The 1950 poster campaign featuring a glass in two periods (by Pierce) was using the glass too frequently possibly because of their inability to find a really good artist'.

Pick attracted into the Advertising Department a number of very good-looking ladies who came to be known as 'Pick's peaches'. They were young, sporty and rare beauties that soon established their reputation in the Brewery, not that Pick would have noticed; he was far too busy and serious-minded.

Tommy Marks

Tommy Marks came into Guinness from BEA in 1955 where he had been the advertising manager. He had had a 'good War', being awarded a Military Cross. Marks was a very upright man, tall, intelligent, a shy introverted type and very precise, a people-person but not sporty. As was the case in all departments of the Brewery, there was a brewer in charge of advertising who was nominally overseeing it. In this case it was Ted Kidd, but Tommy Marks would have none of it and he ploughed on regardless, and without hesitation. Early on he moved the advertising offices out of Park Royal to Baker Street to be near the Agency so they could work 'hand in glove'. He was a very good organiser with a well-drilled and motivated staff of considerable size. Another member of the Garrick Club, he had a good circle of friends.

He loved the Gilroy style of posters and imagery. He did not like the new psychological profiling based on consumer research, preferring the reliance on tried and tested methodology. However it was under his watch in the late 1950s that the National Stout Survey was carried out by Public Attitude Surveys PAS, a Guinness subsidiary company run by George Wrigglesworth.

PAS worked in tandem with the Benson Research Director James Cameron. The National Stout Survey was designed to look at drinking trends and opinions covering all stouts (though mainly Guinness and Mackeson). By talking to consumer groups around the country they discovered some very worrying things. They found that:

- Guinness drinkers were unlikely to ever drink Mackeson.
- From 1930 to 1950, Guinness had been drunk as a restorative or reparative beer, a tonic. During this period Guinness were increasing their UK distribution which drove the sales.
- The Gilroy adverts of this period were very well recalled, appealed to the public and were brilliantly supportive of the advertising themes (Guinness For Strength, Guinness Is Good For You, My Goodness My Guinness). Brand recognition was very high.

- By 1955, Guinness drinkers were drinking less per head, and they were aging as a group - sales were under pressure. Since the distribution of Guinness across the UK was saturated, there was nothing to drive sales upwards. Drinkers were still drinking Guinness as a restorative.
- Advertising in the 1950s was misdirected and failing by not working to change the demographic and recruit younger drinkers. It also failed to move Guinness drinking towards being refreshing and pleasurable rather than for vigour and health. The 'Guinness with food' campaign was aimed at this but had limited success.
- Guinness had achieved a classless appeal due to the use of a very wide range of magazine ads that targeted all social classes and pursuits. The Guinness drinkers were on average older than beer drinkers.
- It pointed towards Guinness advertising becoming narcissistic.

In 1959 Tommy was moved to head up the Harp Lager Company as MD and Alan Wood was brought in to replace him. Alan Wood and Tommy were friends before he joined Guinness.

Alan Wood

Alan wood was recruited from Rank Hovis McDougall marketing into the Guinness advertising job. He was an experienced TV advertiser and an extrovert, urbane, witty and courteous man. He suited the Guinness management style exactly. He was ready to make changes to Guinness advertising and with Brendan Nolan, the Benson account manager, he did. TV started to become the dominant advertising medium although posters and newspaper adverts still had their place in the mix. He brought a more up to date style to the Guinness brand, making it more realistic, less frivolous and more responsive to market research. He was also a long time member of the Garrick Club.

Charlie Moore

He was responsible early on for bill posting (poster sites) and rose to become advertising manager after Alan Wood.

Tony Anthony

He was until the mid-70s, the Print Buyer for Guinness. Sometimes a tough man to deal with, he was witty and very quality focused. He was also a great Gilroy advert fan.

Gilroy in a self-portrait with his beloved animals around him.

Guinness Time magazine

Guinness Time, the in-house magazine for Park Royal Brewery, began life in 1947 after Edward Guinness, who was living in the Bodiam Staff House in the Park Royal Brewery, had commented to Norman Smiley (the MD who was also resident in the house at that time) that 'it was an awful pity the sporting prowess of the London Brewery was not trumpeted or recorded in some way'. Smiley sat upright at dinner and said that he had been looking for someone to start up a Guinness Staff magazine for a while, and would he (Edward) take it on?

A small editorial team was formed that included Martin Pick. Pick set up a lunch meeting with John Gilroy and Edward to discuss the front cover designs. After the meal, Gilroy produced some charcoal from a pocket and, to the horror of the serving staff, set about drawing across the table cloth. Various animals were sketched and Gilroy decided that a pantomime scene featuring the Alice characters was appropriate for the first Christmas time cover. He also drew a very amusing snake and zookeeper image but said 'it could not be used as his animals had to be lovable by the public and snakes did not fit into that category'.

Many covers of Guinness Time were drawn by Gilroy, who by now was a freelance artist and not working via Benson on such

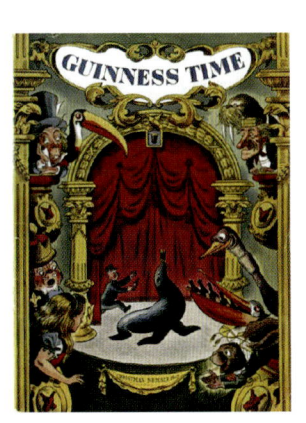

Xmas '47

Summer '48

Spring '49

Xmas '49

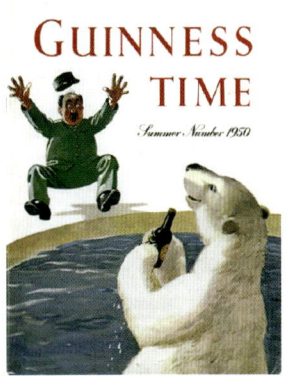

Summer '50

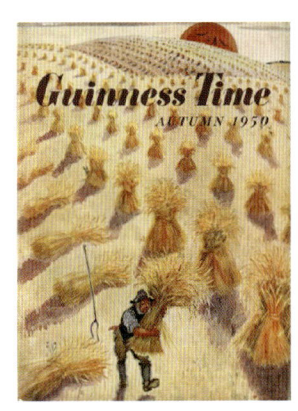

Autumn '50

Autumn '51

Xmas '51

A rough Gilroy watercolour with the snake theme, rejected for use.

BENSON, OGILVY & MATHER AND GUINNESS

commissions. Many images were unique to the magazine and were never used in commercial advertising. Maybe some had been proposed but rejected. Some, like the spring 1963 Wedding of the Chairman, Lord Iveagh, were special commissions (the original artwork for this was given to the Countess Miranda Iveagh).

The *Guinness Time* magazine ran a four page article on Gilroy in their publication of Spring 1952.

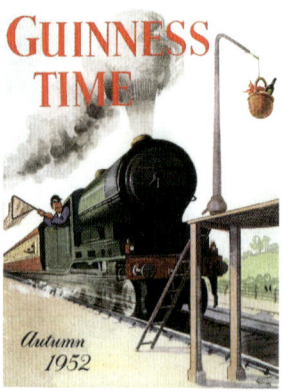

Autumn '52

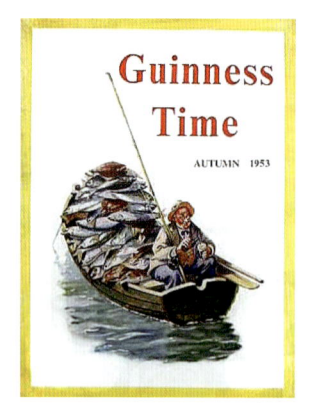

Autumn '53

Xmas '53

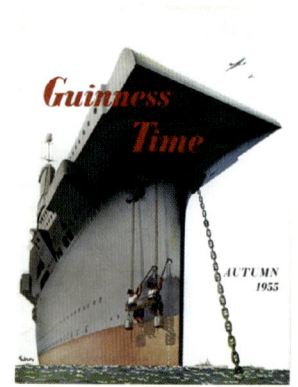

Autumn '55

Xmas '55

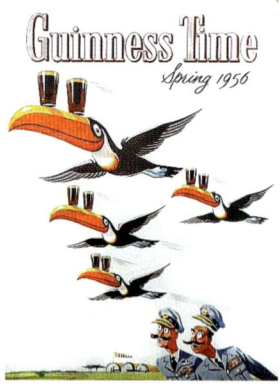

Spring '56

Autumn '56

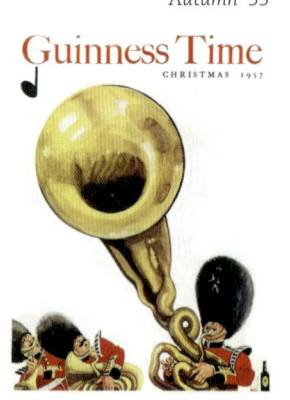

Xmas '57

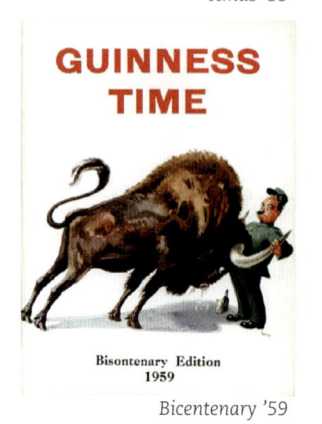

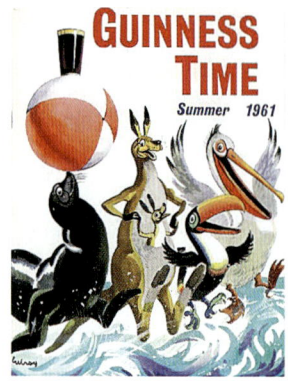

Bicentenary '59

Summer '61

Xmas '62

Spring '63

62

Harp magazine

The Harp magazine was the in-house staff magazine for the St James's Gate Brewery in Dublin, and it too featured John Gilroy on its covers. The zoo animals were the feature in various brewery situations.

Bicentenary Autumn '59

Spring '59

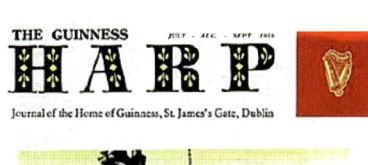

Summer '59

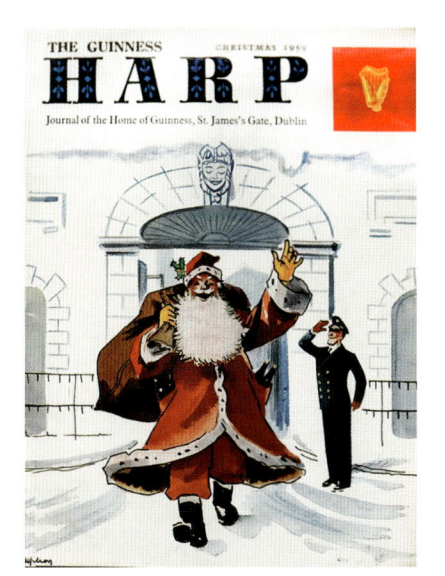

Christmas '59

Xmas '60

A rough watercolour cover for *Guinness Time* magazine Spring 1958, with the wonderful lines 'Spring is sprung, the grass is riz, I wonder where my Guinnessiz'. Ascribed to Gilroy but not signed, from the Benson Archive.

4
Guinness for Strength

Guinness for Strength

The *Guinness for Strength* campaign was one of the earliest conceived and longest running in the history of Guinness advertising. John Gilroy was its principal artist, devising myriad exaggerated ideas, some of which are now in the Guinness Poster Hall of Fame.

The first Gilroy colour poster Guinness for Strength design from 1930, rejected by Guinness and never used. It was replaced in 1930 by 'George and the dragon'.

Two Gilroy watercolour versions of the porter with heavy cases - 'I feel I need a Guinness', 1933 and the later 'Guinness for Strength'.

Cart and Horse

Originally the image of the carthorse and farmer pulling the cart was proposed to Guinness pre-WWII but was turned down. It was later used in 1949. That year, when Gilroy entered the Garrick Club, he received a standing ovation from the people in the bar in recognition for the poster. At an exhibition of his work in Central London, his friend from the Garrick, Kenneth Moore the actor (whom he painted several times), paid glowing tribute to his art.

In 1981 Gilroy was quoted by James Blackmore who printed a signed limited edition set of six of his best posters, as saying 'When I drew this poster for Guinness, it drew a testimonial from an unexpected source. The late Sir Alfred James Munnings RA is reported to have said I'm supposed to be a great painter of horses. Another man, greater than I, can make horses happy and lovable, while mine are powerful and polished. I would love to see that man's (Gilroy's) horses hanging in the Royal Academy. My carthorse never did, but it was a very kind thought, Sir Alfred. You won't know, but I'll tell you, that the Zookeeper is actually a caricature of myself. And the horse bears a remarkable resemblance to my father.'

Rough pencil line drawing of the carthorse sequence.

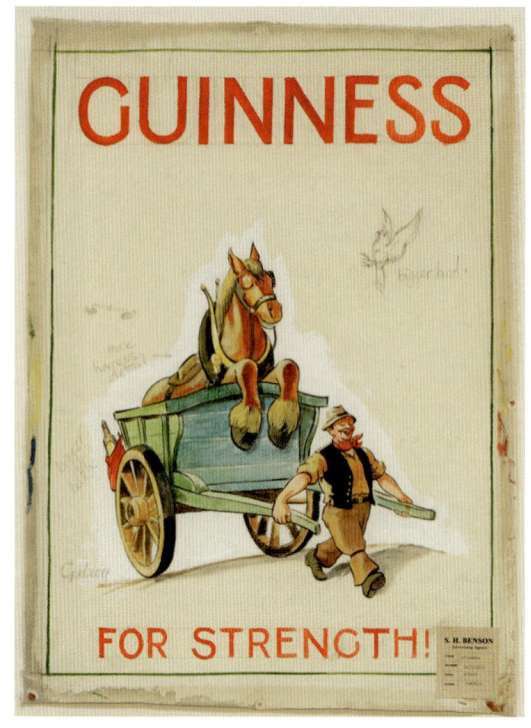

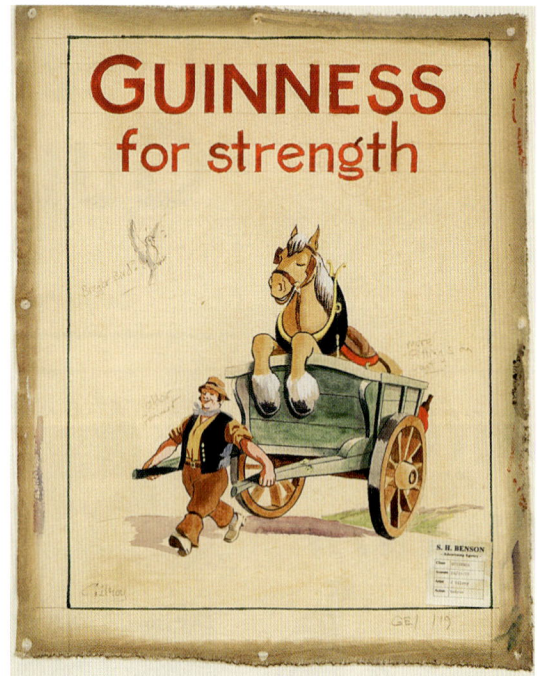

Two carthorse canvases from the Benson archive. Note the pencilled bird and words 'bigger bird'.

Bandsman

Whilst Gilroy was painting the portrait of FM Lord Alexander, he hit on the idea for a *Guinness for Strength* poster with a guardsman blowing his tuba so hard that it untwists. None of the rough watercolour on paper versions here were used commercially.

The finished poster had a turquoise blue border as below.

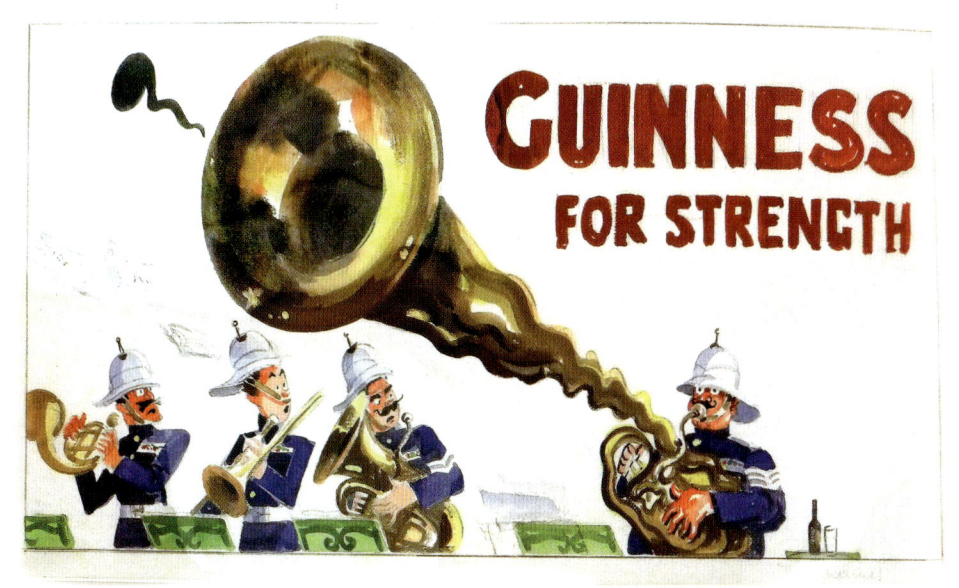

GUINNESS FOR STRENGTH

Steamroller

The final version and this canvas of a steamroller poster was painted in 1951 by Wilkinson (Wilks), one of Benson's commercial artists. However the idea came from Gilroy as can be seen in the watercolour on paper rough below.

A number of these Gilroy steamroller canvases exist for Greece, Russia and Israel and date from 1952.

Gilroy rough drawing of 'Guinness for Strength', a man lifting a sewer grate under a steamroller.

68

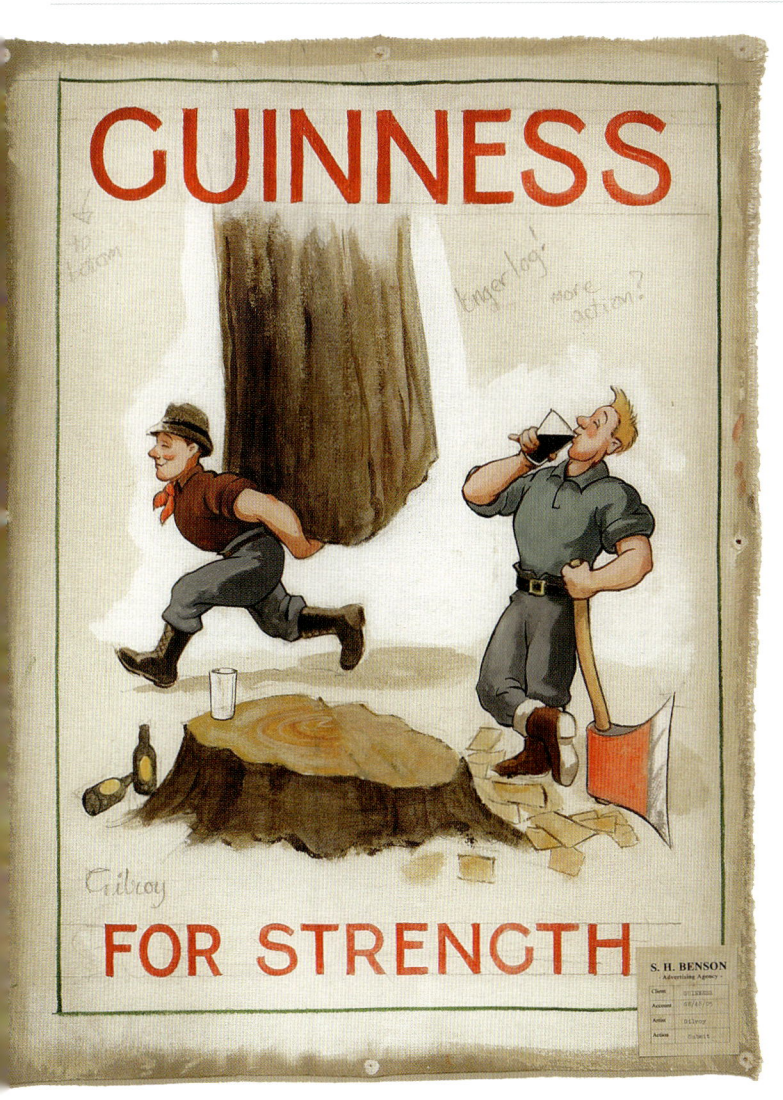

GUINNESS FOR STRENGTH

Woodcutter

A different version of the woodcutter by Gilroy; a great image but never used commercially. The same theme of the man carrying a fir tree was used on a Christmas poster.

The commercially used woodcutter poster below, has the distinction of being drawn with the axe head the wrong way round. This caused much public debate which only added to the celebrity of the poster.

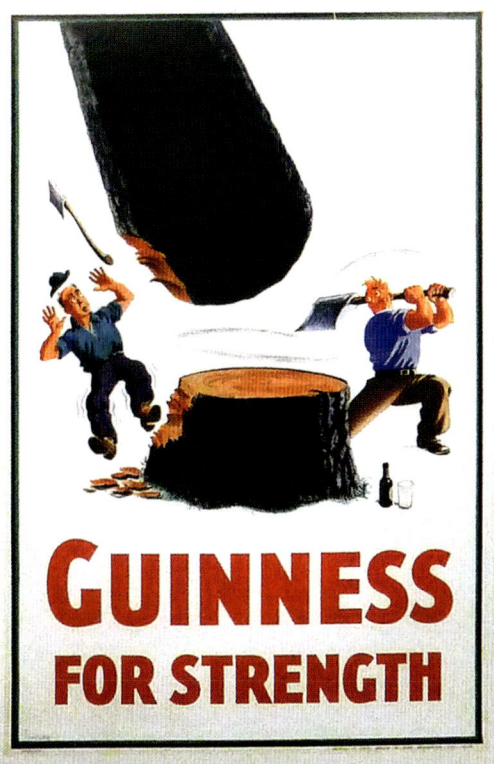

Rough sketch of man lifting the tree.

Canvas of man lifting a tree, 1948.

The woodcutter felling a tree with a single swing after drinking his Guinness. A great visual joke.

GUINNESS FOR STRENGTH

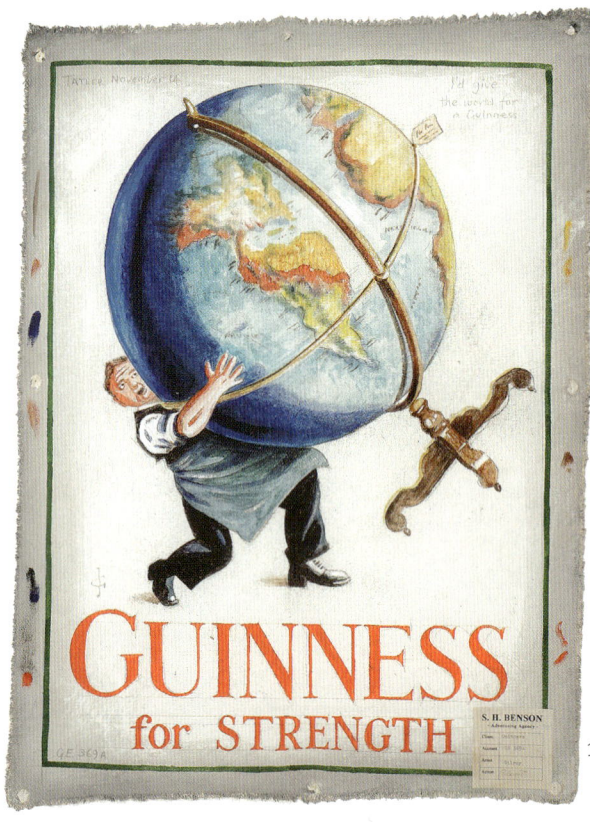

Canvas of a man lifting a giant globe, never a poster but a 1934 GE394 advert for Tatler magazine.

Italian Canvas - The Roman Forum.

Waterloo Bridge is coming down. 'Guinness for Strength' partially completed watercolour artwork from 1934.

Pencil writing at base 'don't get blue too dark'. Clearly this borrows its theme from the porter leaning on the column. Used as a poster in 1, 4 and 16 sheets for sites around London during the bridge removal in 1934.

Guinness for Strength Sketches

A series of visual jokes as watercolour sketches, never used commercially. These sketches all come from the Guinness archive in Menstrie.

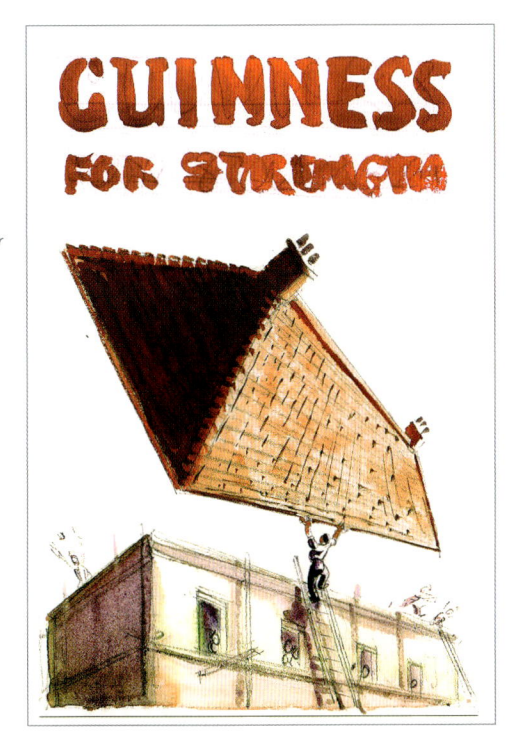

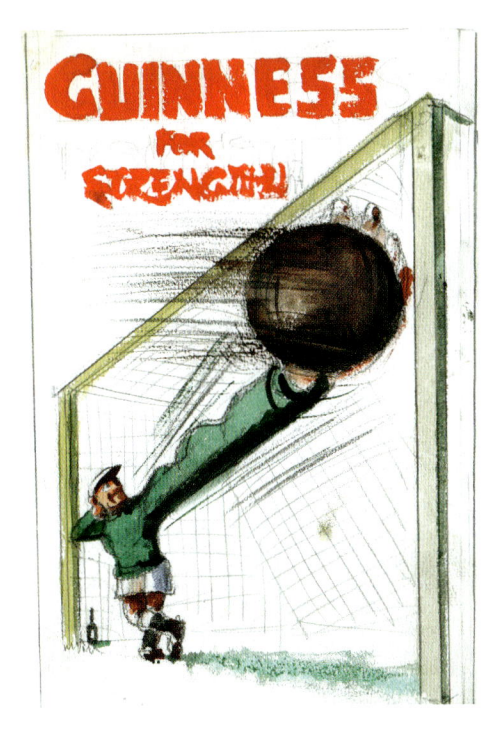

GUINNESS FOR STRENGTH

More visual jokes in sketch form, never used commercially. These sketches all come from the Guinness archive in Menstrie.

72

GUINNESS FOR STRENGTH

Three amusing concepts in rough water-colour format for Guinness for Strength. Never commercially used.

GUINNESS FOR STRENGTH

Motor Mechanic

Final 1948 poster, note the differences in the car.

Benson canvas, 1948. Note the bonnet is open here but not on the printed version. The car is similar to that used by Churchill during the war.

Earlier watercolour with a different car, a passenger and ducks instead of the startled workman.

GUINNESS FOR STRENGTH

Farmer with Giant Scythe

Rough watercolour sketch of the farmer with a giant scythe, bottle at its tip.

1952 canvas with the sun setting and long shadows.

Benson Archive painting of the same concept, with a cornfield and the pint in his pocket, oil on canvas, 1952.

Pencil writing on the canvas, top right corner - 'Bigger blade'.

75

GUINNESS FOR STRENGTH

1952 Export Posters

Dear John,
Park Royal are having a big export drive this summer. They are bringing over a handful of influential buyers and want to show them what we can do.

I would suggest that you dig out some successful English advertisements and adapt them for the foreign market. Sales in France and the Netherlands are stable so concentrate on their new markets which are the Soviet Union, Greece and Israel. I have yet to track down a reliable translating service so do your best. As always time is of the essence, please use one of the drawing office juniors if you need help.
Bevan.

Bevan to Gilroy letter 4 April, 1952.

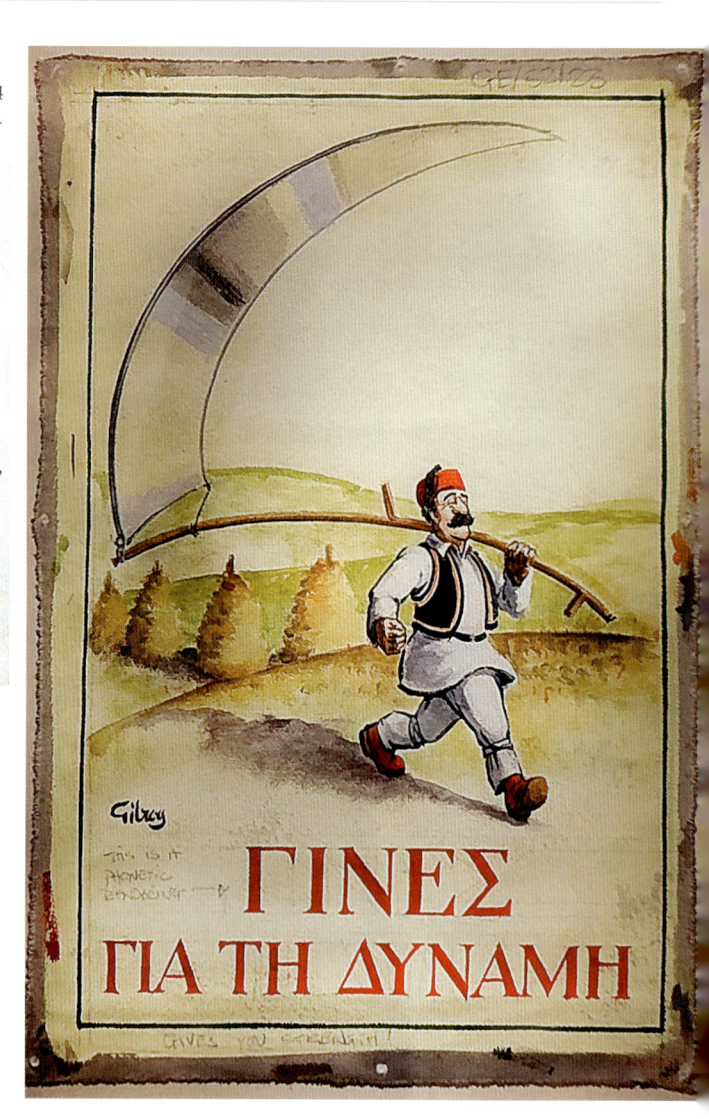

Greek above, Israeli and Russian canvases left

76

Dig for Victory

Dig for Victory poster 1942, 'Guinness for Strength' slogan.

This is an incomplete design. Note at top margin - 'Dig for Victory' is written in pencil. This was to be added as a strapline across the top. Used on wartime poster and Underground sites.
It was again used as a poster in 1948, to encourage post-war productivity, this time with the strapline at the top -'My Goodness' and at the bottom -'Let's all get growing'.

The same theme with Hebrew writing for the Israeli market. Note the clothing of the man and fruit in the basket is changed.

Note in pencil top right corner - 'What do they harvest in Israel?'

Over page are very similar paintings done for the Russian and Greek market.

GUINNESS FOR STRENGTH

1952 Export canvases.

The Russian canvas reads in pencil - in top right corner-'make steamroller red and star yellow'. The Greek canvas reads in pencil in right corner -'substitute a Hellenic symbol centaur' pointing to the nameplate.

78

GUINNESS FOR STRENGTH

Greek, 1952.

In pencil, left top - 'no bird'. Lower left -'this is a phonetic rendering -> please check'.

Israel, 1952.

In pencil, top margin- 'My Goodness'; donkey in hat, oranges in cart, man in local garb.

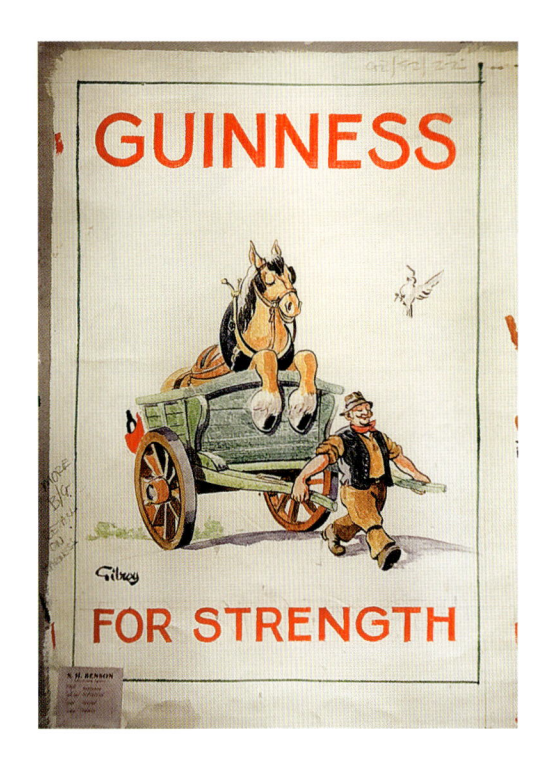

Russia, 1952.

UK, 1952.

In pencil, lower left margin -'more B/G detail on harness'.

79

The Cellist

This image is a similar concept to the bandsman blowing his tuba straight. The cellist is sawing so hard with his bow, he cuts his instrument in two.

The mad cellist sawing his instrument in half, Benson canvas, 1946.

Pencil writing top centre - 'Framing?'

The commercially used poster and advert.

Five Million Guinness

Five million Guinness sold every day, Gilroy canvas, 1960.

Pencil writing on the canvas top left margin 'more detail in girder'.

Left mid-margin: 'move bottle/glass to the right'.

Bottom left margin: 'change wording to Guinness for strength every day'.

This poster is of course derived from the Guinness for Strength *girder man. Here the man has managed to bend the steel girder into the figure 5 representing the five million glasses of Guinness drunk daily by 1960.*

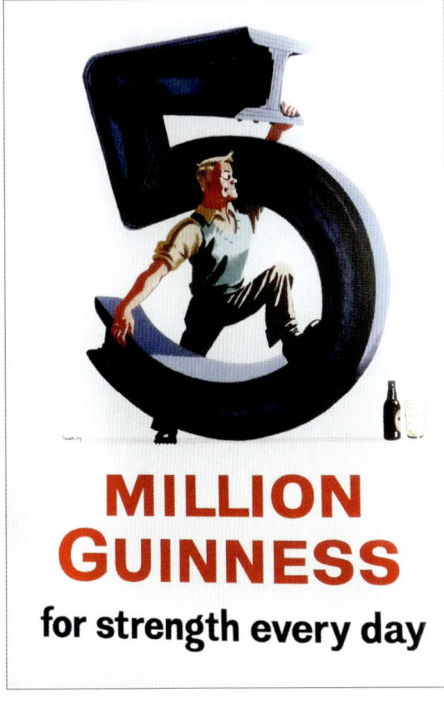

Commercial poster, 1960. Different caption in the final version and the bottle has moved.

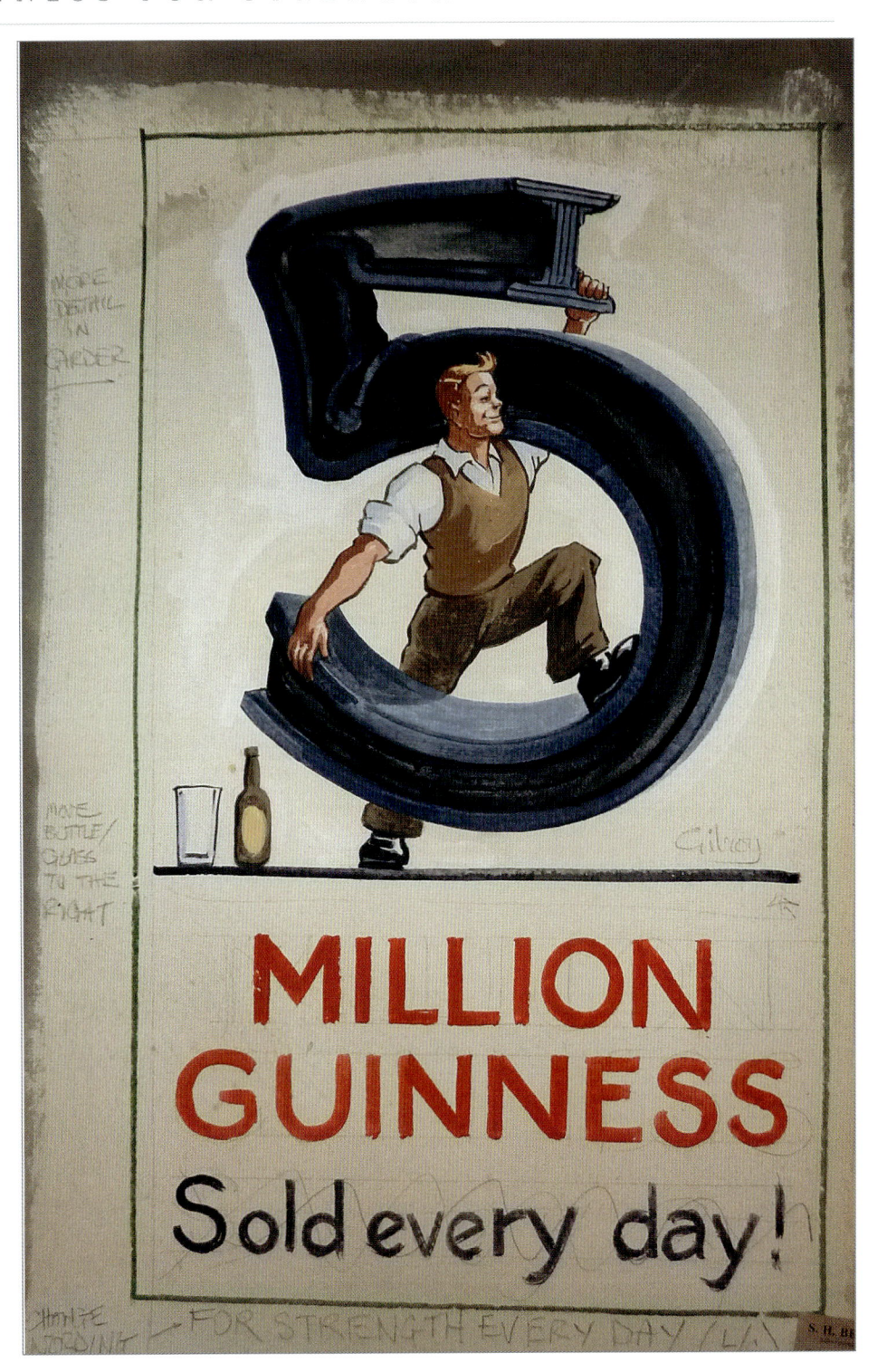

The Girder Man poster

1932 canvas 'for strength' in upper case.

In pencil on right side - 'lengthen girder by 5 inches, add rivets to girder, for strength in U/C'.

1934 canvas, lower case 'for strength'.

GUINNESS FOR STRENGTH

Sketch of a giant bottle of Guinness as a bridge support. These two sketches come from the Guinness archive in Menstrie.

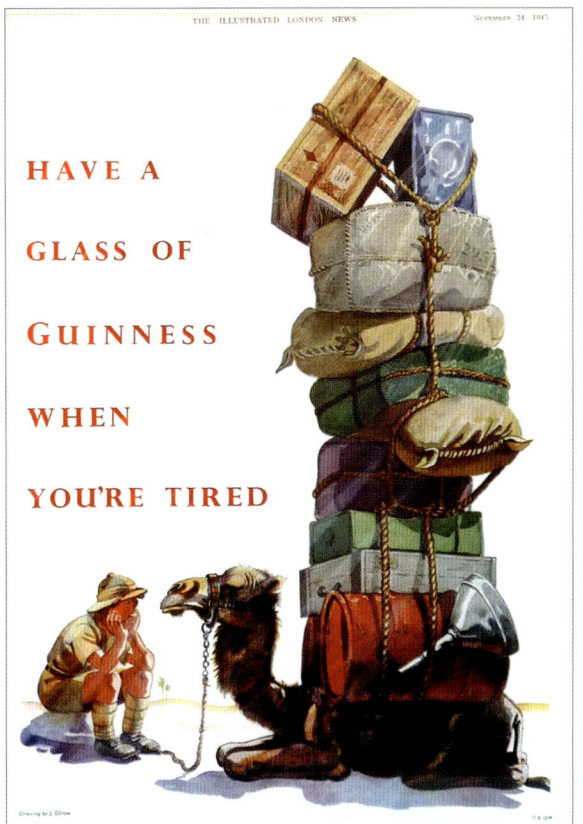

A rare 1945 'Have a glass of Guinness when you're tired' advert from the Illustrated London News GE1238.

A very humorous grossly overloaded camel, refusing to move. The goods are tied on in the most outlandish manner.

Sketch of a man launching a ship single-handedly.

83

5
The Zoo and other exotic animals

The Zoo and other exotic animals

The use of zoo animals began in the early 1930s with the 'Lovely day for a Guinness' two seals in 1934 and the 'My Goodness My Guinness' running sea lion in 1935. They were followed quickly by the toucan, ostrich, tortoise and the lion, to name but a few. Thus began the Golden age of Guinness advertising under the slogan 'My Goodness My Guinness'. This campaign of using these animals ran for the next twenty-seven years and is likely to be the longest running campaign in World Advertising History. The secret to their success was how they were drawn. To make them friendly to the public, Gilroy created visual jokes around them. Usually they were getting the best of the zookeeper by stealing his beer. He also drew them with a kind eye and a smile on their faces.

An early exception to this rule was this 1936 serious depiction of the lion and the unicorn fist-fighting. The drawing is excellent but without the humour and smiles, it is less famous than its brethren. It was used in Underground posters in 1938 and in a 1930s 'Alice' Doctors Book.

Watercolour artwork for 'Bottle Royal' poster, 1938.

'I'm sometimes asked about the origin of the whole animals campaign for Guinness. At the time, they had spent what seemed an enormous sum of money on famous artists from around the world, from Japan to Germany anyway, to create a real, human family for Guinness.

Everyone who was involved in deciding on the posters hated someone in the 'Guinness family for being too handsome, or too ugly. So, I invented the animals, whom everyone loves and no-one can hate. Even the only human present in this series of posters -the zookeeper is a caricature of myself, so, for Guinness, I was the only human who could not give offence.' said Gilroy in 1981.

A pencil sketch of the menagerie, showing the use of geometry in his art.

A rough crocodile.

A rough kangaroo.

86

The 'Gilroy' Zookeeper in classic startled pose, his hat flying off.

1959 Menagerie at the Brewery Bicentenary.

The original and most famous animals in typical pose walking line abreast.

Elephant and zookeeper under the My Goodness My Guinness banner.

'Guinness for Strength' elephant and zookeeper.

'Guinness for Strength' elephant and zookeeper.

'Guinness Time'.

Koala bear with a bottle, watercolour, unused.

Woodpecker, 'Have a glass of Guinness when you're tired - Guinness for Strength'.

Zookeeper riding a camel, chasing a bottle on a stick - 'Guinness is so refreshing', watercolour, unused.

The Crocodile
My Goodness My Guinness, 1957

Both Russian and Hebrew versions of the crocodile were produced, facing the other way.

Watercolour artwork, 1957. Smaller teeth than the final version.

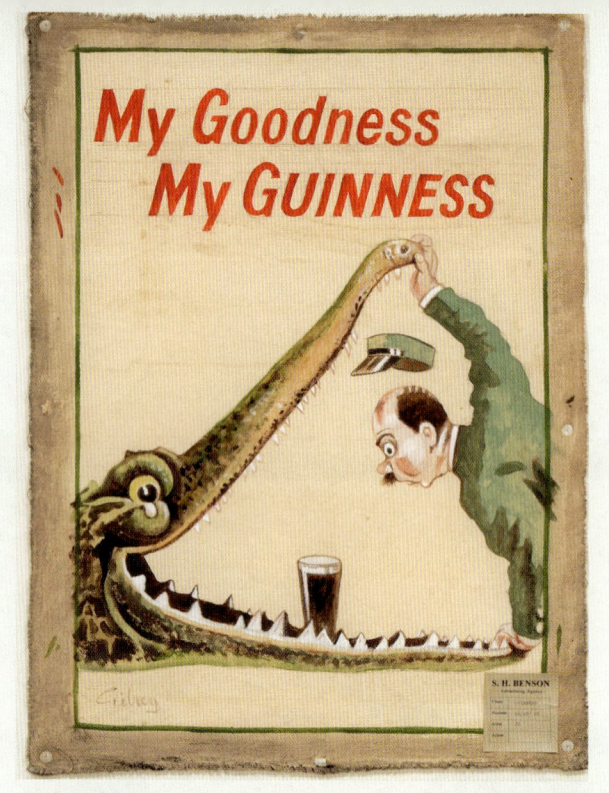

Benson canvas, 1957.

Display artwork, Johnson, 1953.

Dancing ostrich and zookeeper canvas, never used.

Stork - 'Have a glass of Guinness when you're tired', watercolour.

92

Guinness for Strength, man carrying a whale, rough crayon drawing.

Elephant and zookeeper canvas, never used, 1939.

In pencil in middle with an arrow to the zookeeper, the poster reads 'make fatter, uniform greener'. At bottom right corner it reads add 'no bottle？' Notated in pencil in left margin 'make elephant bigger' is written in pencil. This elephant canvas was also done in Russian in mirror image, with a fatter zookeeper in 1950.

Two canvases from 1939, the gorilla and the orangutan in the zoo series. Never used commercially.
Canvases also exist with the apes in a mirror image of the above, both from 1948.

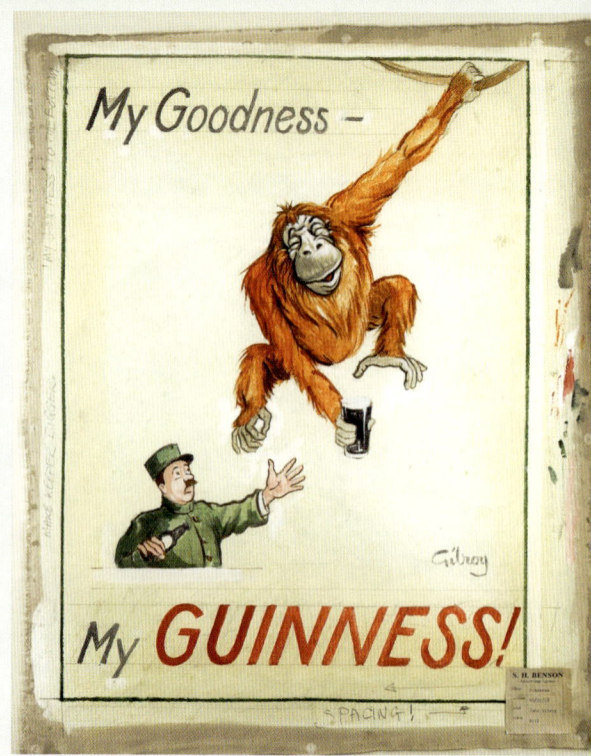

My Goodness – that's My GUINNESS!

My Goodness – My GUINNESS!

"GUINNESS IS SO GOOD FOR YOU" BECAUSE IT ISN'T SWEETENED

The antelope and the hippo. This watercolour uses unusual straplines: 'Guinness is so good for you' and 'because it isn't sweetened', never used.

This poster proof employs a very unusual strapline 'because it isn't sweetened' which I have never seen used again.

The Sea Lion
1935

'By 1935, I was well into the idea of Guinness animals. We'd done the Ostrich and the Toucan. I was at Olympia in London as usual, to see the Bertram Mills Circus. I went every year and I saw the sea lion doing its tricks and it clicked. Later on, Guinness actually paid to have my Guinness animals decorate the hall at Olympia for the circus season. Bertram Mills were so pleased with the effect that they let Guinness do the same thing for years - entirely free!' Gilroy 1981.

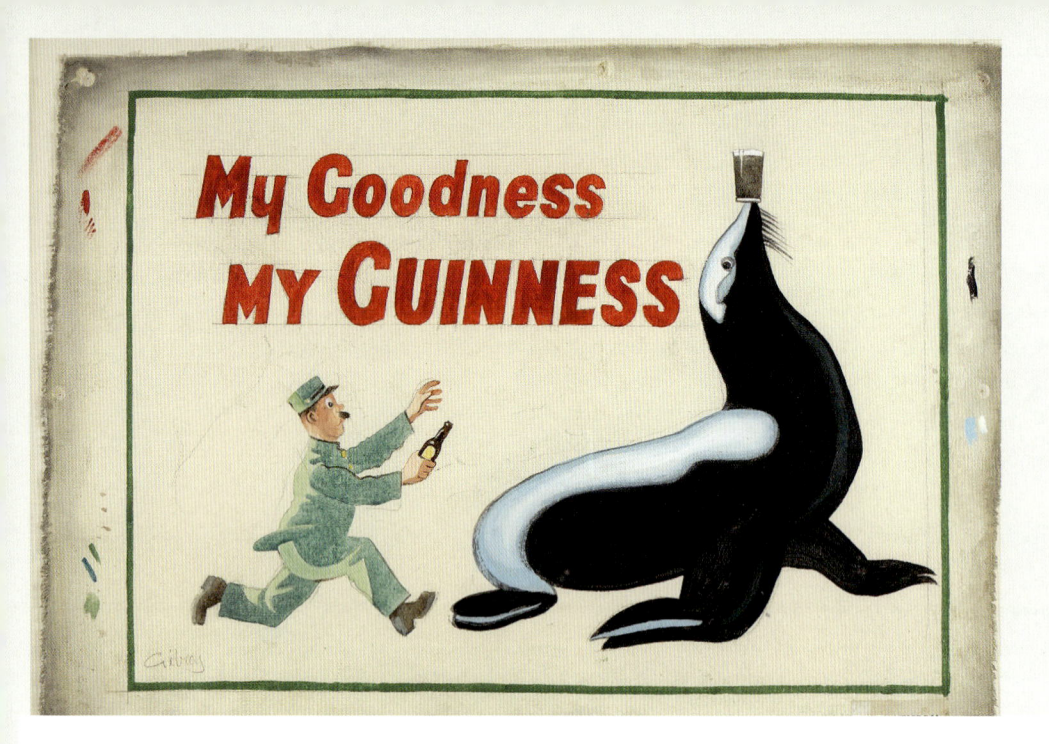

In 1950, the sea lion canvas was also done in Russian, running right to left.

Two sea lion studies in pencil and charcoal. These images were never used.

The Ostrich
1936

'The appearance of this poster evoked floods of letters pointing out that the glass inside the ostrich should have been the other way up. l was working for the famous advertising agency S. H. Benson at the time and couldn't admit to a fault. So l replied that the ostrich had been balancing the glass on his nose flicked it up into the air; opened his mouth and it went down the easiest way to be properly enjoyed in his stomach! At about the same time, on another poster l accidentally drew an axe head back to front. Again, lots of people wrote in. My secretary replied that the artist was now resting in a hospital and all the complainers were either given vouchers for a couple of Guinness pints in their local or invited to visit the brewery. This gave great publicity at the time.' Gilroy 1981.

1935 B&W newspaper advert.

Benson oil on canvas proofs.

The Kangaroo

First used as small size posters in general and on the Underground during the war in 1943 with a dark background so that due to paper shortages, old posters could be overprinted on the back. The Kangaroo was the next in the zoo animal series. Note the Guinness bottle in the kangaroo's pouch and the joey in the zookeeper's apron pocket.

Above is a 1947 watercolour rough sketch of the ad on a white background, whilst to the left is a reversed oil on canvas painting from 1952.

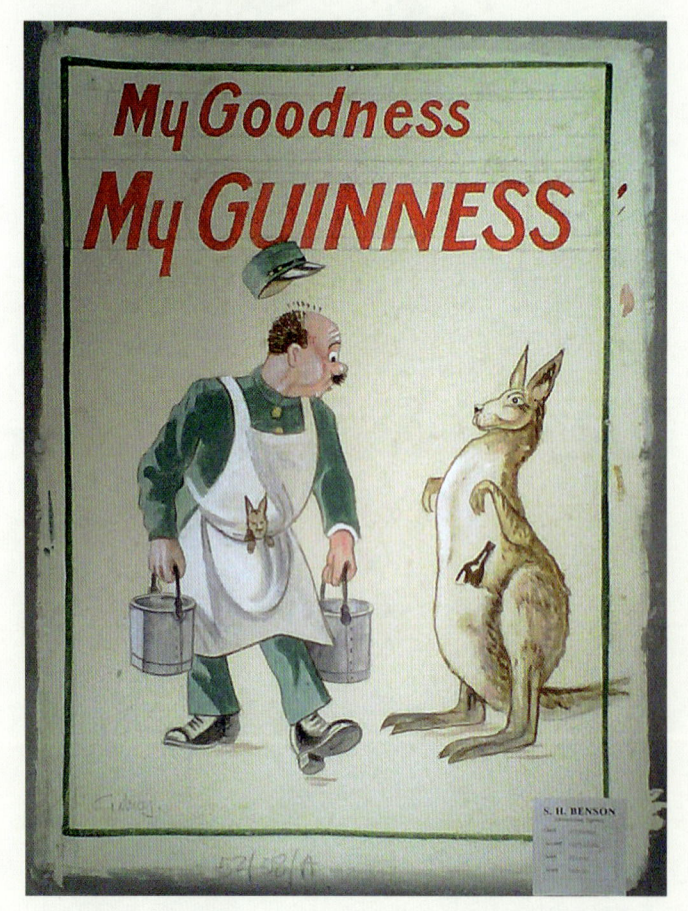

Full size posters with white backgrounds were used in 1947 to 1949.

In 1950, a version like this but in both Hebrew and Russian, was painted for the export market, but never used.

Studies at the zoo, kangaroo, crocodile and tortoise.

Bear Up a Pole
'My Goodness My Guinness'

The poster of the bear up a pole was first used in 1944 and again in 1956. In 1950, an export version in Russian was painted by Gilroy, but in mirror image.

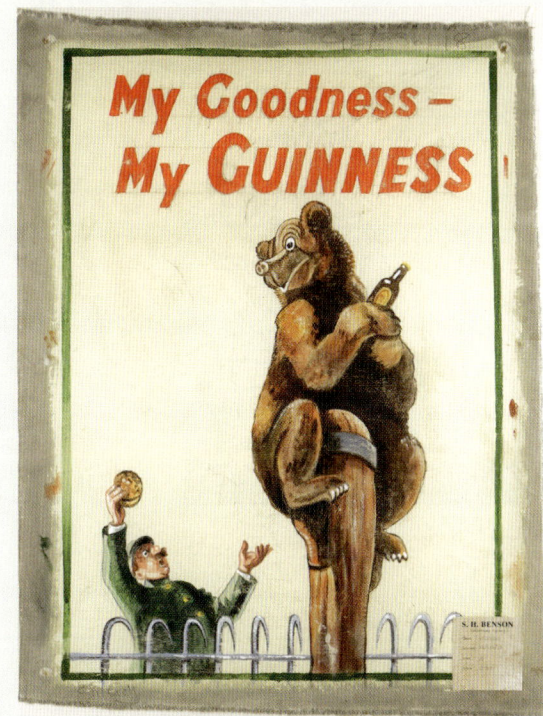

Benson canvas of the bear up a pole, 1953.

Watercolour rough drawing of the bear pose, 1956.

Pencil rough study of a bear holding a bottle, 1956.

Display artwork by Johnson, 1953.

The Menagerie.

Animals in tug of war with the zookeeper in pencil. This frieze was used on pottery and biscuit tins.

The animals outside St James's Gate, pencil drawing.

Animals at the seaside, watercolour in sections from a 1961 poster 'Guinness-The ideal summer resort'.

It was also used in limited numbers at holiday resorts with the slogan, 'Guinness by the sea-the ideal summer resort'.

Below, animals in tug of war with the zookeeper in watercolour.

This frieze was used as a *Guinness for Strength* bus side streamer some 17.5 feet long in 1958 and on pottery and biscuit tins.

My Goodness My GUINNESS

Elephant watercolour, not commercially used.

Camel and seal pencil rough, never used.

Zoo animal Coronation poster without the word Guinness, 1953. Watercolour mounted on board.

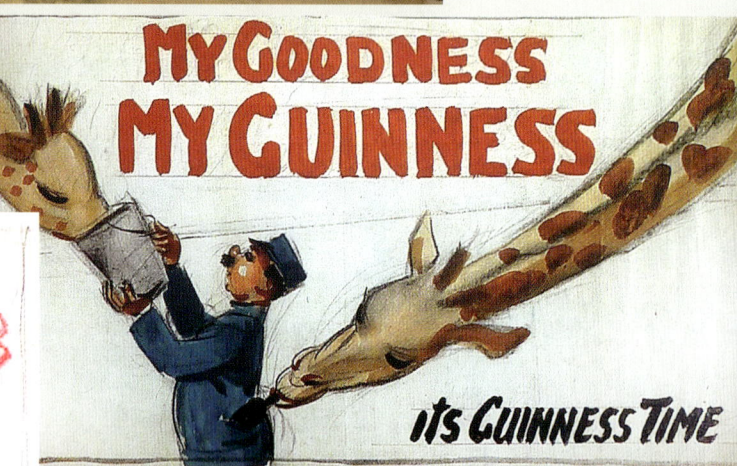

Watercolour of giraffes, 'My Goodness My Guinness – it's Guinness Time'.

Crayon rough drawing of hippos, 'My Goodness My Guinness', neither images were used.

Crayon drawing for Chessington Zoo poster of the Guinness menagerie.

Note that this drawing has the polar bear replacing the Gnu on the Christie's Auction cover.
The penguin was adopted for a one year run only as the image for Draught Guinness.

THE ZOO AND OTHER EXOTIC ANIMALS

The Pelican

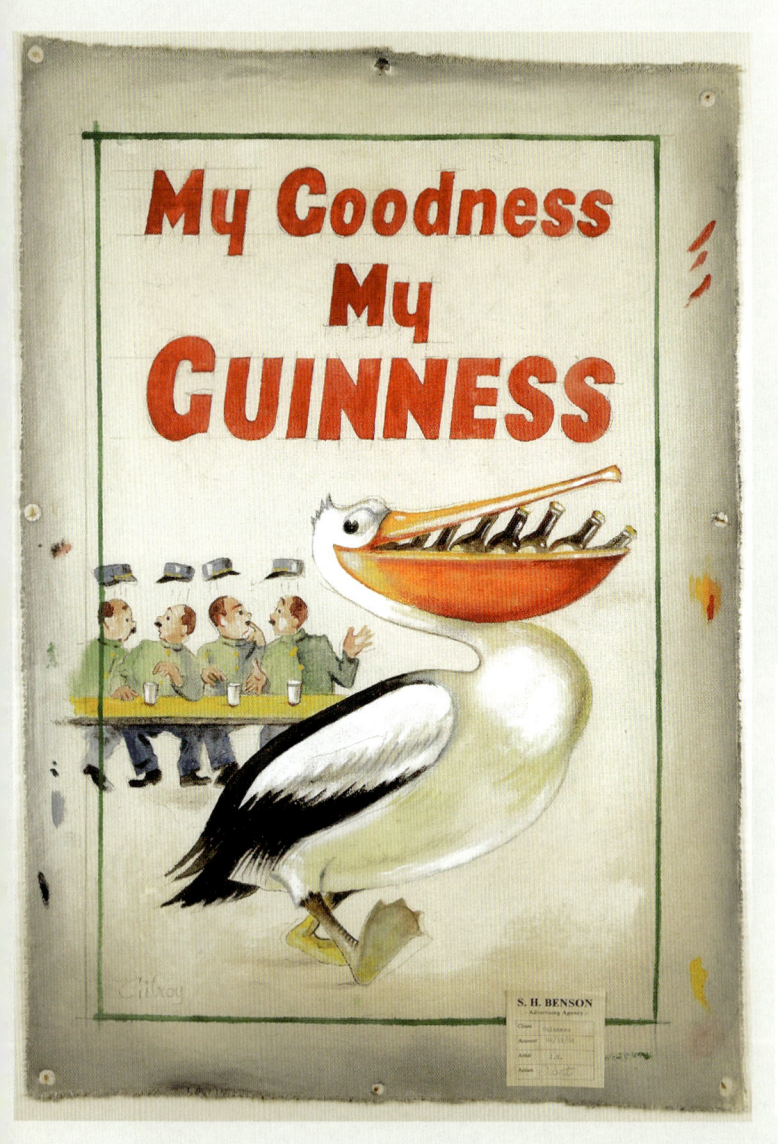

The Pelican with seven bottles in his beak canvas, 1939.

Simple study of the pelican made by Gilroy at London Zoo.

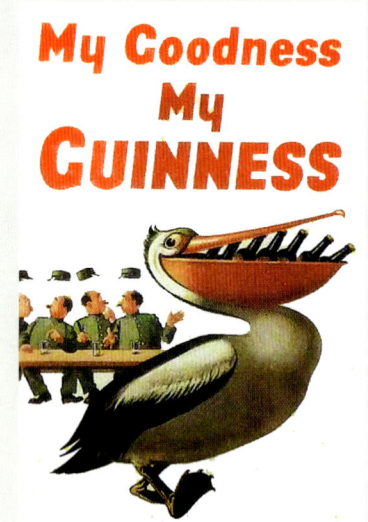

Poster, 1939.

Rough pelican with a full beak.

Watercolour of the Menagerie for the Take Home poster 'Guinness is welcome in the home', also used as an advert, biscuit tin and show card design.

Oil painting by Gilroy of the Menagerie, Storehouse, Dublin Brewery.

THE ZOO AND OTHER EXOTIC ANIMALS

The Rhinoceros

Right Rhino canvas, 1947.
Pencil writing at base - 'make Rhino more threatening'.

Rhino Watercolour.
'2nd idea' in pencil - bottom left corner.

Second Rhino canvas, 1947.
Two horns and facing the other way.

106

The Kinkajou

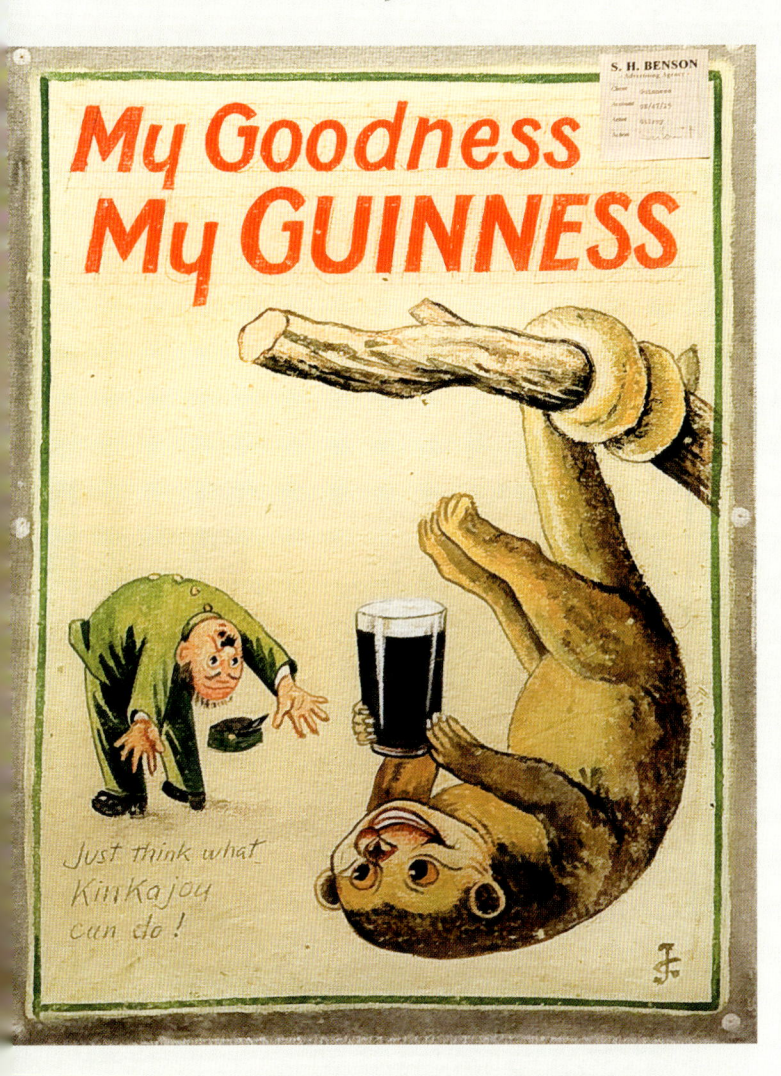

1947 canvas with the 'My Guinness' wording up the correct way and the bottom wording in pencil - 'Just think what Kinkajou can do'.

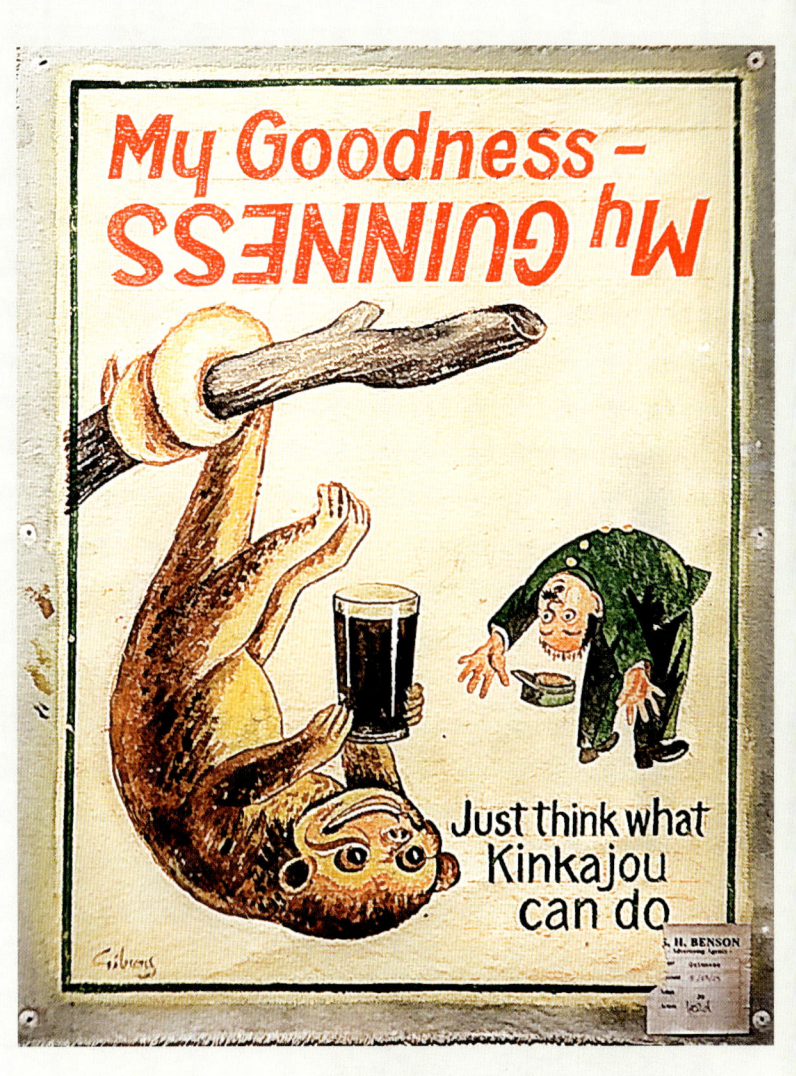

1948 canvas as a mirror image and with the 'My Guinness' wording up the wrong way and the bottom wording in green oil - 'Just think what Kinkajou can do'.

An alternative version of the ostrich from 1936, with some of the lettering in green as well as red.

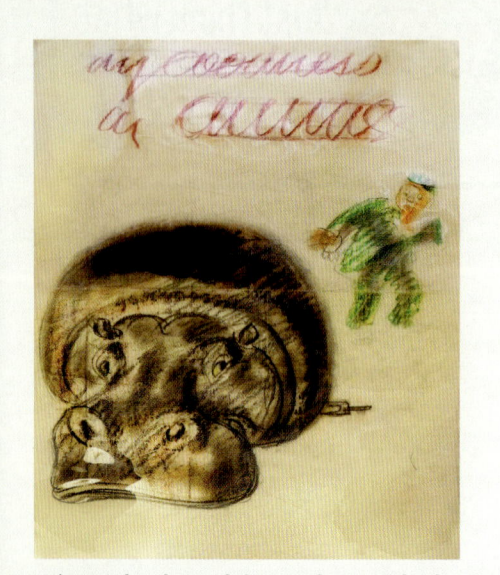

Hippo and zookeeper, below rough crayon sketch.

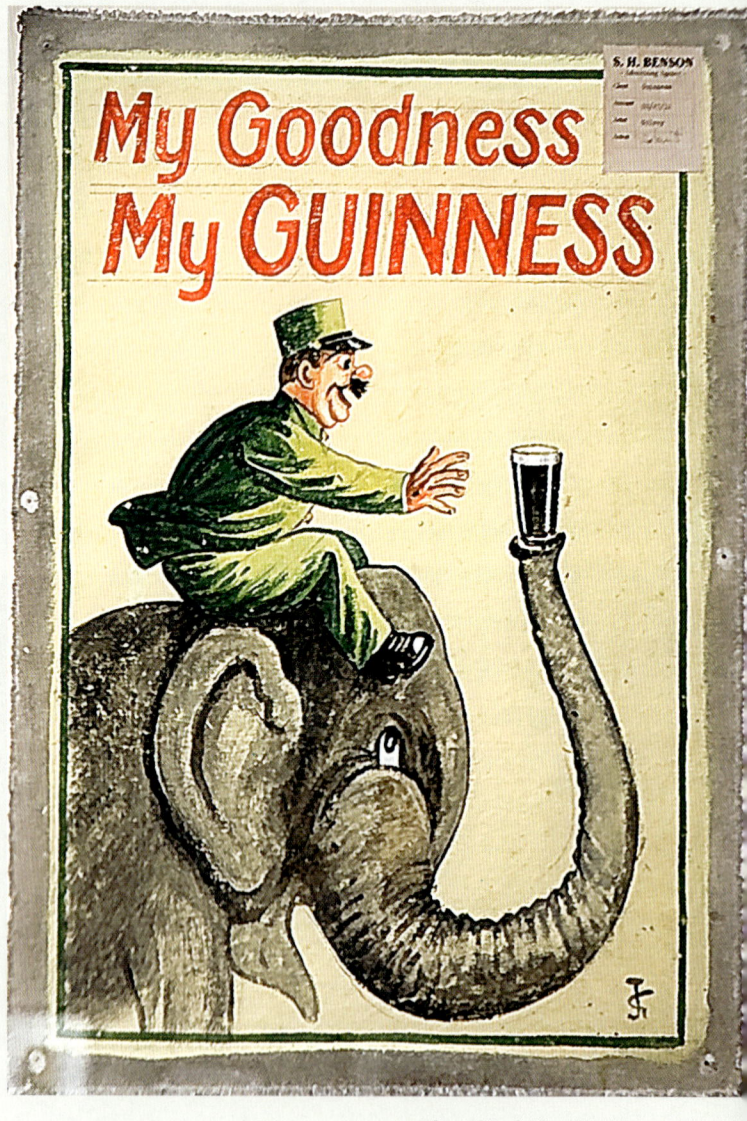

The 1939 elephant poster.

This also exists as two landscape canvases looking left and right, with a small crowd of startled on-lookers in front. These were never adopted commercially.

108

THE ZOO AND OTHER EXOTIC ANIMALS

The Tortoise- Have a glass of Guinness when you're tired

Two canvases from 1936 of the smiling tortoise, balancing a pint on its shell.

109

Golden eagle with a bottle, never used.

I apologise for the poor quality images of these canvases but I thought it important to include them.

A mandrill on a rock, never used.

110

THE ZOO AND OTHER EXOTIC ANIMALS

The Polar Bear and zookeeper

Above, 1949 Landscape Canvas.
Marked in pencil on the top margin, 'Bill Board -GE/49/9'.

Right, 1953 Portrait Canvas.
Pencilled in the top margin –'GE/53b/16'. The advert and poster were first used in 1949. This is a later study for a reissue.
In 1950 an export version in Russian was painted but never used commercially.

The Lion and zookeeper

1939 canvas, marked in pencil on right margin - 'define coat'.
This would normally be a very serious situation, to be chased by a lion, but the zookeeper is only concerned for his Guinness, not his life. In 1950 a Russian version running the other way was painted.

THE ZOO AND OTHER EXOTIC ANIMALS

The Giraffe and the Zebra

Here are two new zoo animals that Gilroy introduced that were never featured either in the UK, Ireland or in overseas markets. These two canvases are in Russian cyrillic script and date from 1950, made for the new export markets.

Gilroy has not taken his usual care with this canvas. The Giraffe is not quite right facially but Gilroy has got him swallowing the Guinness glass, only to get it stuck in his throat like the ostrich.

Here, the zebra is much more life-like and Gilroy has adopted the same pose with the zookeeper as with the Gnu.

113

6
Show cards, lobsters, whales and fish

SHOW CARDS, LOBSTERS, WHALES AND FISH

Show cards

These small plastic laminated stand-up printed cards were a favourite form of pub and off-licence promotion. They very often featured the poster advertisement of the day but many more image types were made than there were poster designs. Gilroy's art appeared on many dozens and often this was the only form of use of this imagery, as is the case with those below. None of these appear as national posters.

Original artwork, watercolour on board, 32 x 22 inches, late 1950s.

Original artwork, watercolour on board, 28 x 14 inches, 1950s.

115

SHOW CARDS, LOBSTERS, WHALES AND FISH

In this artwork, we see the use of pasted on paper sections. The subject of sport was a favourite theme for both Gilroy and Guinness. Guinness was a sport mad company and the association with the beer was inevitable. Many Oxbridge Blues and Rugby Internationals worked for Guinness like Des O'Brien, Chris Chataway, John Ranson, Jim Shanklin and Peter Matthews. Having a prowess in a sport was considered very important. Gilroy was also a very keen golfer, as was his first wife and son.

A finished 'Guinness for Strength' show card on the rugby theme.

A rough sketch of runners for a show card, never commercially used.

A rough sketch of a rugby scrum for a show card, that was commercially used.

116

Two farm scenes under the 'Guinness for Strength' banner.

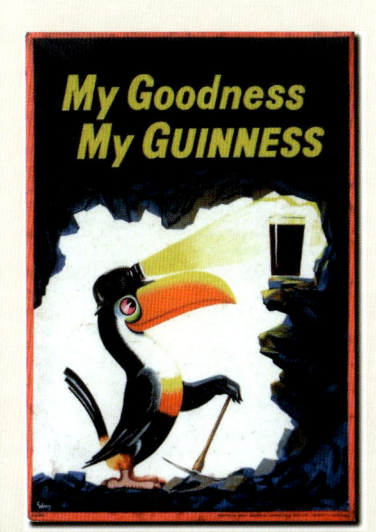

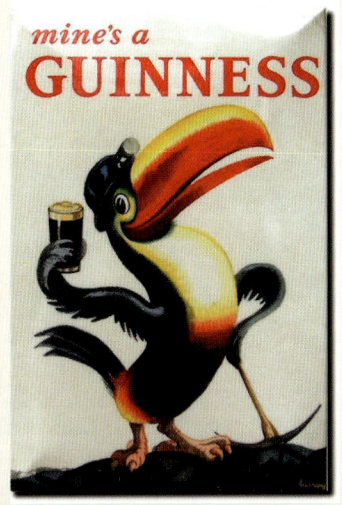

The mining toucan image used in two different formats of show card.

The one on the right is by Gilroy, the left by another Benson commercial artist. Notice how much more animated, three dimensional and likeable the Gilroy bird is. Gilroy's animals and birds had a relationship with the observer that other artists did not achieve.

The rough and finished show cards of a man lifting a boat with one hand to paint the hull.

Artwork for productivity poster, 1947.

Finished show card, farmer carrying a flock of sheep.

'Guinness for Strength' - Fisherman catching a giant fish. Four different attempts at the same theme, a show-card and three sketches.

Gilroy Canvas on the same GFS theme with the giant fish.

Pencil writing bottom right corner - 'John, it's lacking something, 3 ducks or a dog perhaps? Try it portrait'.

Benson's canvases on the fishing theme, the latter being in Hebrew for Israel.

Pencil writing on canvas - 'please check lettering - try Mr Meyer in accounts'.

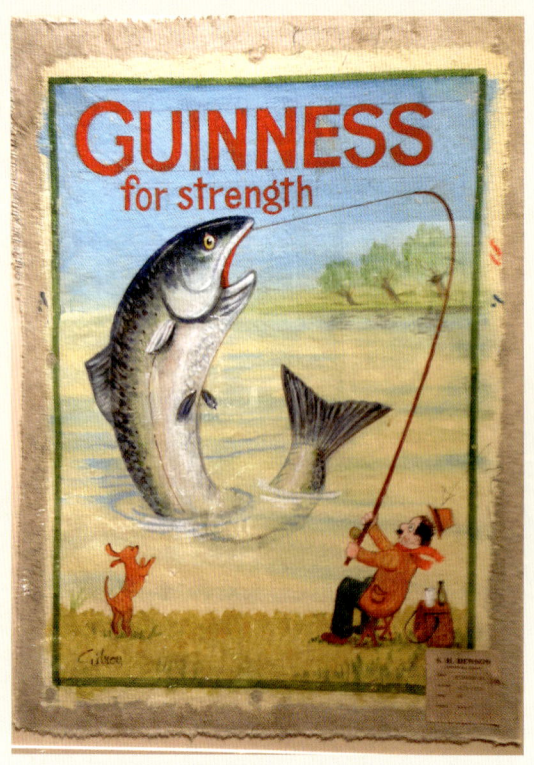

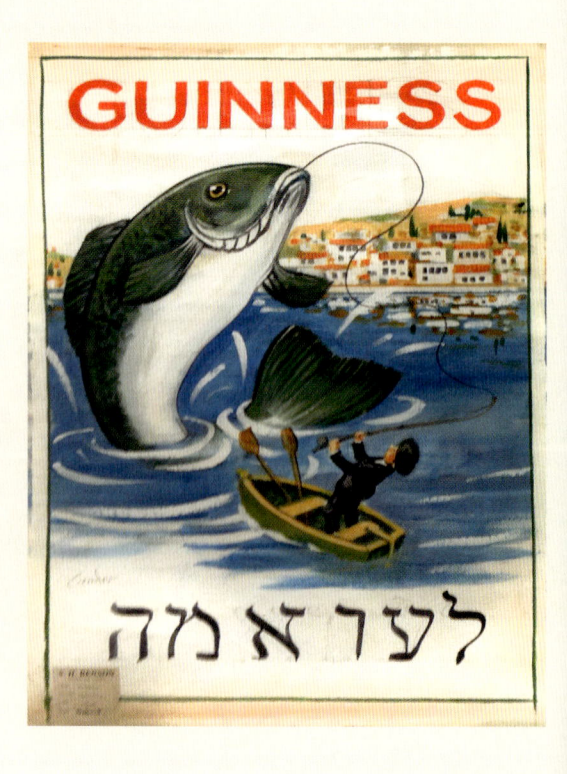

SHOW CARDS, LOBSTERS, WHALES AND FISH

Lobsters and Other Sea Creatures

Different takes on the lobster. Lobsters love… Benson's 1952 Gilroy canvas and the 1939 GE860 printed paper advert. Unknown artist.

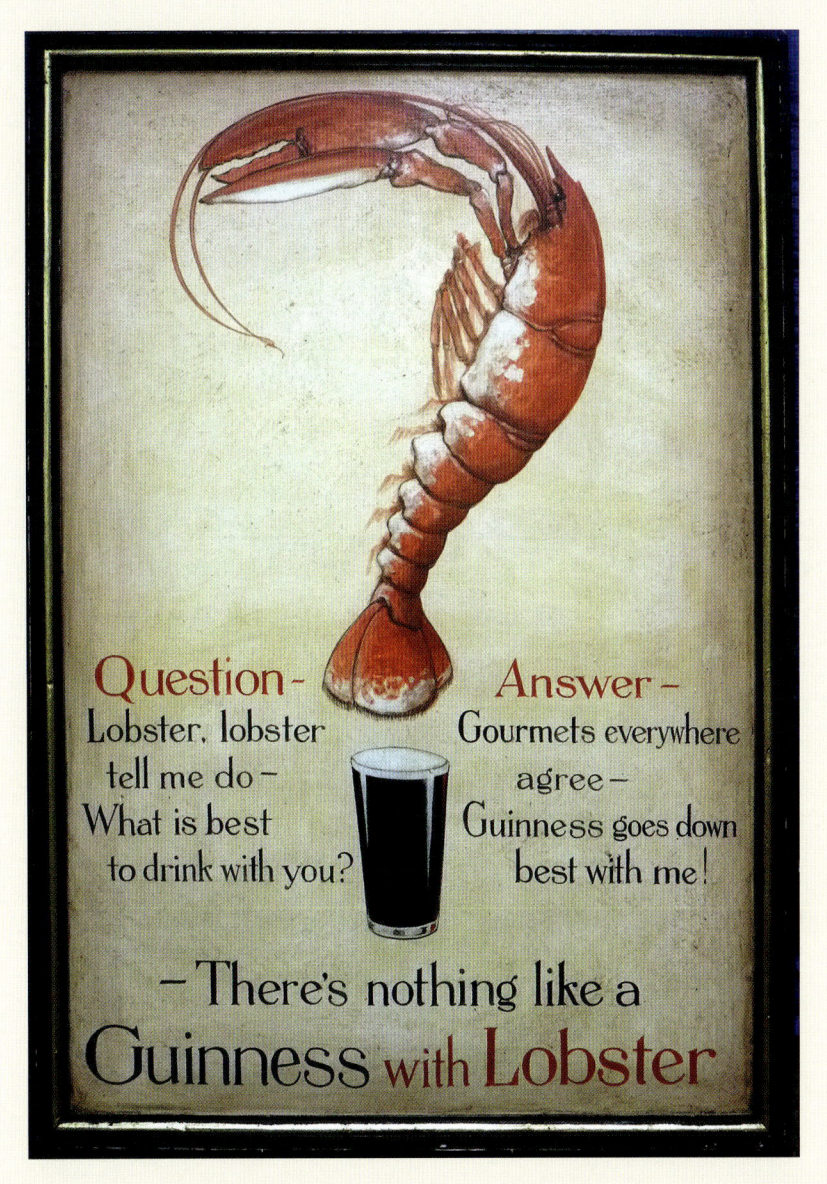

Lobsters love…
GUINNESS

Question –
Lobster, lobster
tell me do –
What is best
to drink with you?

Answer –
Gourmets everywhere
agree –
Guinness goes down
best with me!

– There's nothing like a
Guinness with Lobster

121

'The Jolly Lobster' for the pub in Polpero Cornwall by Lander, oil on canvas.

Pencil writing top left corner - 'presentation board Jolly Roger Polpero'. Bottom right corner - 'make large' and an arrow pointing to the Guinness word.

Lastly a watercolour artwork by Gilroy, lobster and oyster at the piano.

122

The octopus with a glass of Guinness in its tentacles, 'My Goodness My Guinness', 1948, never commercially used.

Probably considered too frightening to ever be used. Even the zookeeper has a worried startled look on his face. Certainly one of Gilroy's more outrageous ideas.

The cheeky squid holding glass of Guinness with the caption, 'creatures in the deep agree - Guinness goes down swimmingly!' 1947-50, never used commercially.

A super image, but not one that fits a particular campaign. The association between Guinness and a squid is also very tenuous and probably caused the rejection of this image.

The Big Blue Whale

A fabulous image of a friendly whale (note the kind eye), stealing the Guinness from the fisherman in the boat and squirting it up from its air hole on a water jet. This canvas exists both in Russian as here, and in Hebrew. The Israeli version is the mirror image and has the fisherman dressed in local middle-eastern costume.

The scene is both amusing and impossible, which makes it classic Gilroy imagery. How on earth could the whale get hold of the Guinness glass from the boat and without spilling a drop, swallow it and exhale it. The zookeeper is transposed into a fisherman wearing his Russian fur hat.

SHOW CARDS, LOBSTERS, WHALES AND FISH

The Fisherman in an overloaded boat, 'Now I feel I've earned a Guinness', canvas by Gilroy, 45cm x 57cm high, 1949.

Written in pencil near the top of the canvas is '2 or 3 seagulls'. These birds were added on the commercially used image and a different text font was employed. This image was first used as a magazine advert GE1308 in 1947 which is confusing if the canvas was from 1949.

7
Toucans

Toucans

The toucan has become synonymous with Guinness and was used in advertising from 1935 up until the *Guinness is Coming Home* series in 2005, when all brewing returned to Dublin with the closure of the Park Royal London brewery. All these canvases exist as their mirror images.

Original oil on canvas artwork, 1953.

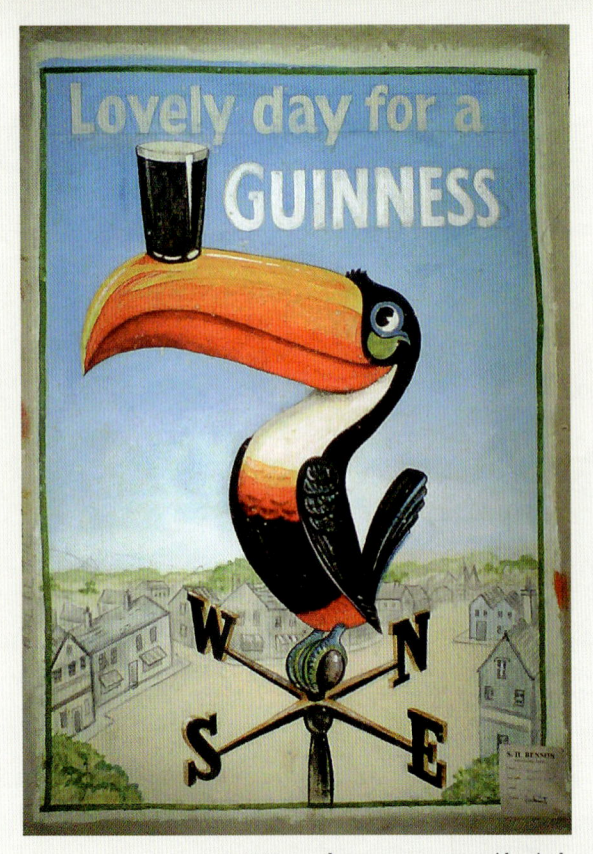

A 1955 weathervane canvas, an identical canvas was recently on sale for $15,000.

1935 Canvas, with extra word Guinness at the top.

Gilroy canvas of a toucan opening bottles with his beak, 1953, blue background.

Reversed Gilroy canvas of a toucan opening bottles with his beak, 1953, white background.

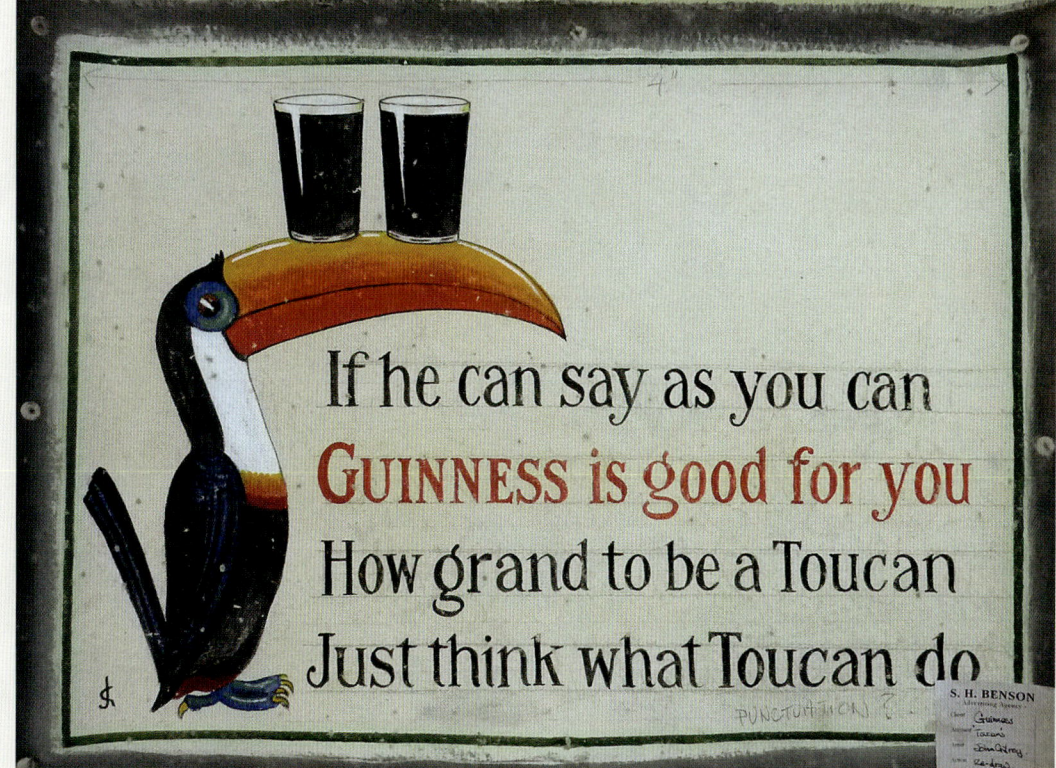

An unusual toucan with two pints on his beak, 1931.

If he can say as you can
GUINNESS is good for you
How grand to be a Toucan
Just think what Toucan do

My Goodness

"Production", said the Toucan.
"Is simply up to you.
So work as hard as you can
And do what Toucan do."

Watercolour artwork for a post-war poster.

Toucans in their nests agree
GUINNESS is good for you
Open some today and see
What one or Toucan do

Toucans in the nest version by Gilroy, 1950. Note the TV aerial.

Final copy for the poster was made in 1957 by the artist Ray Tooby and is almost identical.

A slimmed down and squarking version of the running toucan by Gilroy from the 1980s.

The classic flying toucan with two pints of beer balancing on his beak.

Pencil sketches.

Pencil sketches of a running toucan, never commercially used. Very comical birds with stubby wings and prancing feet.

Weathervane canvases, 1955 with toucans facing the reverse way, two different colour backgrounds.

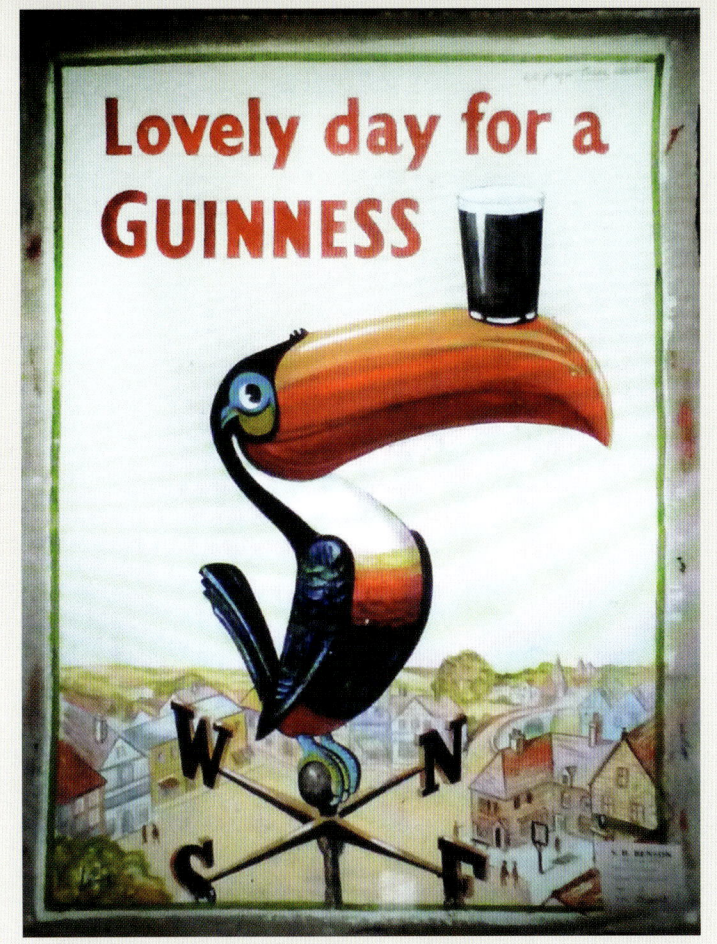

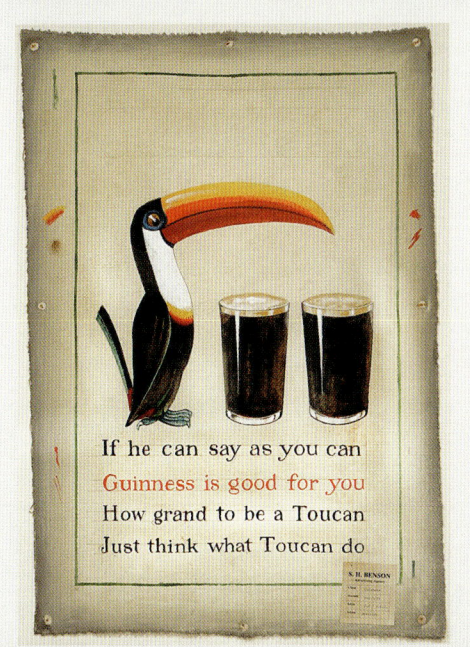

The correct canvas, 1935 without the word Guinness at the top. Famous copy written by Dorothy Sayers.

8
Classic Cars

Classic Cars
New York 1939 World Fair

This is an unusual subject for Guinness, but Benson asked Gilroy on several occasions to produce classic car images. In 1939, Benson wrote to Gilroy in the letter - right, to paint car images for a calendar to be used at the World's Trade Fair in New York, just at the outset of WWII. This he did and the results are striking. Each of the twelve months are illustrated, although December is listed twice instead of November (corrected in pencil). Car pictures for the 1948 Earls Court Motor Show in London were also produced for Guinness and mainly painted by R. Clifford. Note that none of these adverts are for the cars themselves.

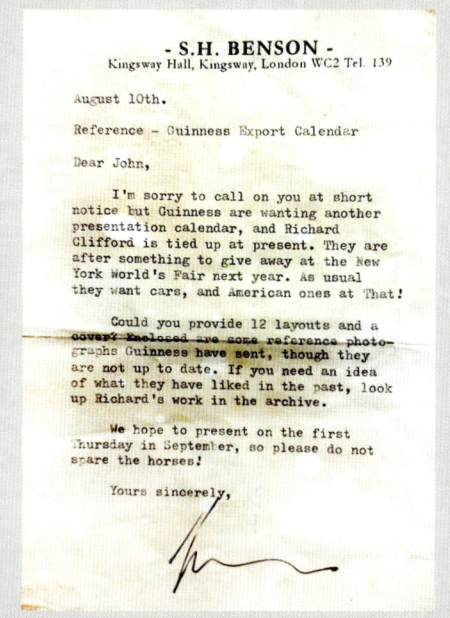

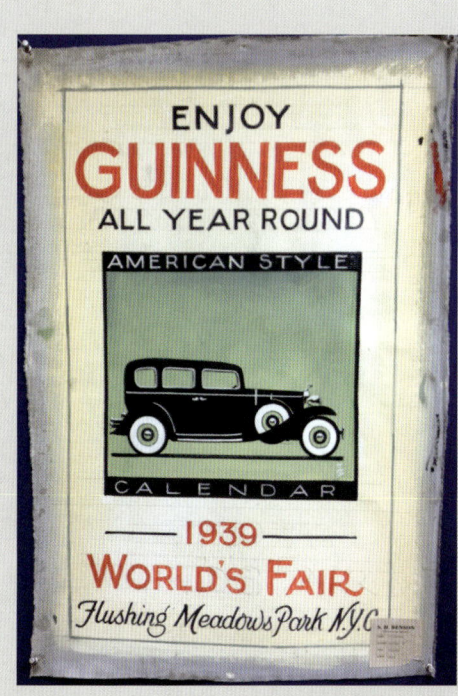

- S.H. BENSON -
Kingsway Hall, Kingsway, London WC2 Tel. 139

August 10th.

Reference - Guinness Export Calendar

Dear John,

I'm sorry to call on you at short notice but Guinness are wanting another presentation calendar, and Richard Clifford is tied up at present. They are after something to give away at the New York World's Fair next year. As usual they want cars, and American ones at That!

Could you provide 12 layouts and a cover? Enclosed are some reference photographs Guinness have sent, though they are not up to date. If you need an idea of what they have liked in the past, look up Richard's work in the archive.

We hope to present on the first Thursday in September, so please do not spare the horses!

Yours sincerely,

January 1939, Chrysler CL Phaeton 1933.

New York 1939 World Fair.

February 1939, Cadillac 452 Imperial V-16 1931.

March 1939, Auburn 851 Cabriolet 1935.

April 1939, Cadillac V-12 Coupe 1933.

May 1939, Packard 443 Roadster 1928.

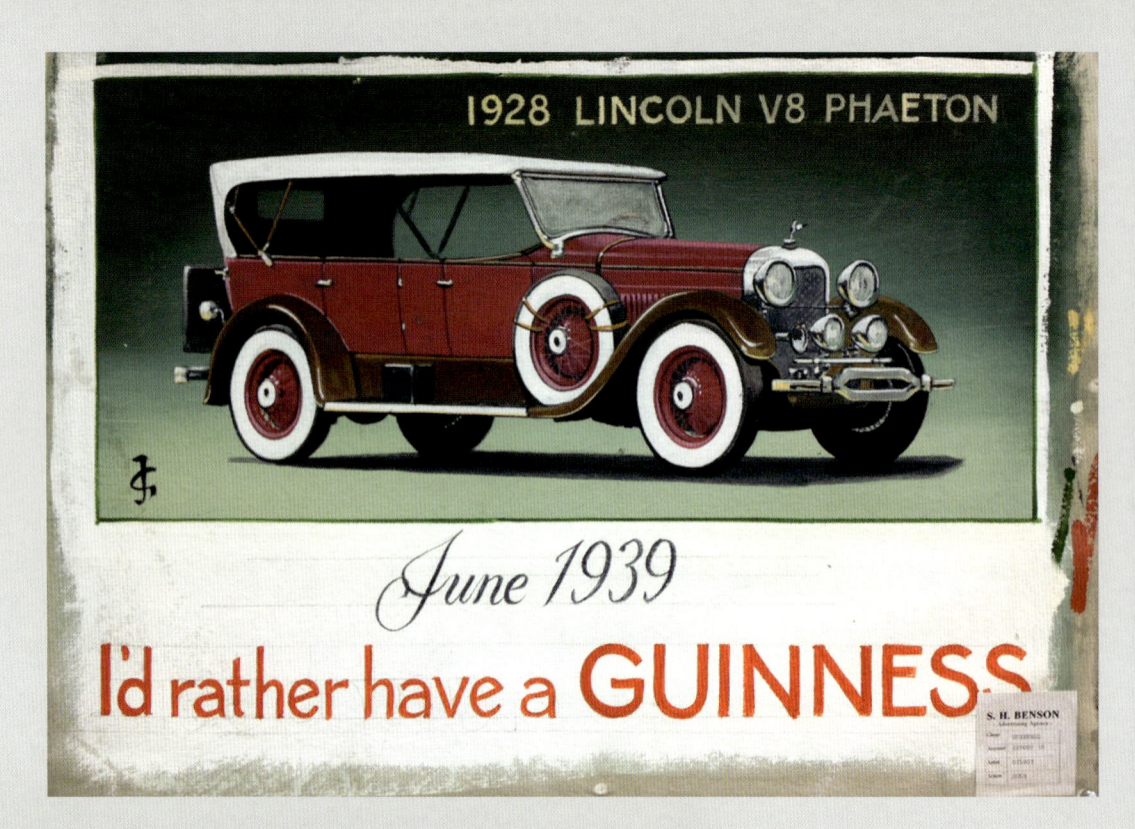

June 1939, Lincoln V-8 Pharton 1928.

July 1939, Packard 640 Roadster 1929.

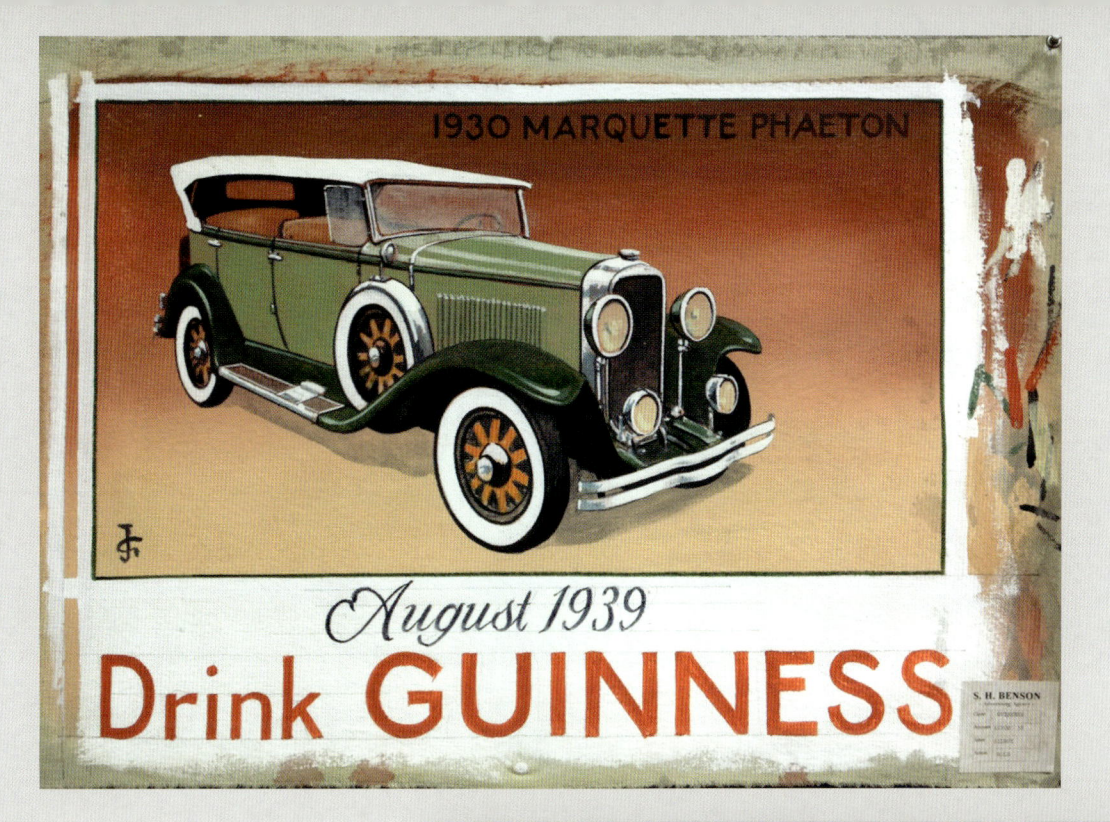

August 1939, Marquette Phaeton 1930.

September 1939, Auburn V-12 Boat tail Speedster 1935.

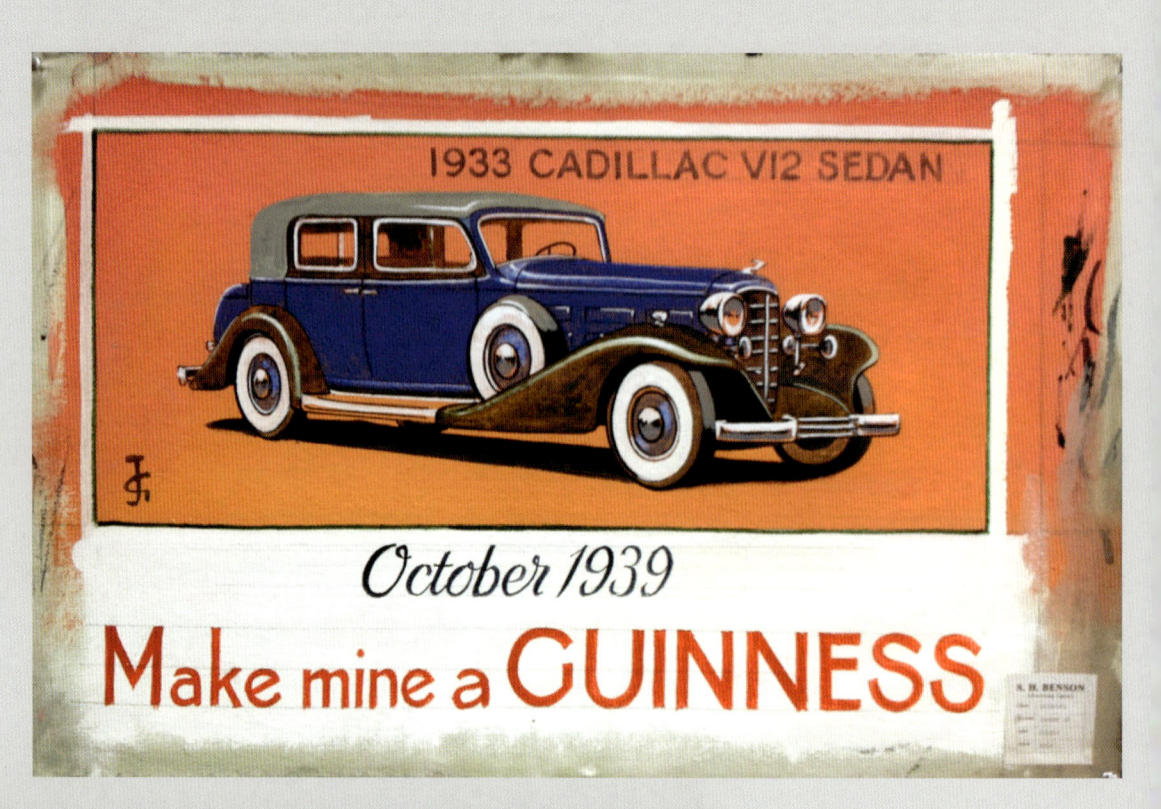

October 1939, Cadillac V-12 Sedan 1933.

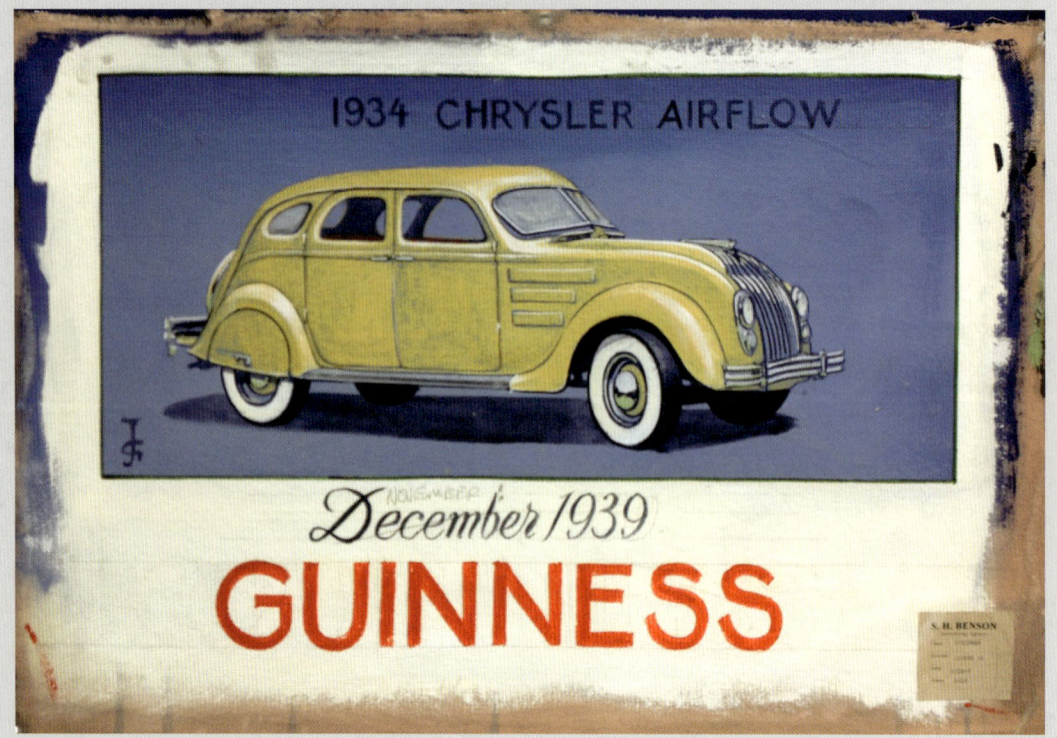

November 1939, Chrysler Airflow 1934 (wrong month).

A number of different advertising slogans were used in this set of twelve, some familiar such as 'Guinness for Strength', and some new, like 'Drink Guinness'.

December 1939, Cord 812 SC Coupe, 1937.

Earls Court Motor Show 1948

The new Morris Minor and MG Morris.

These images were also commissioned by Benson for Guinness for the 1948 London Motor show, but were painted by R. Clifford. Notice the state of post-war British car manufacture compared to the US.

Earls Court Motor Show, 1948, The Land Rover.

Earls Court Motor Show, 1948, Rover P3.

In pencil - top right margin, 'BE/13'.

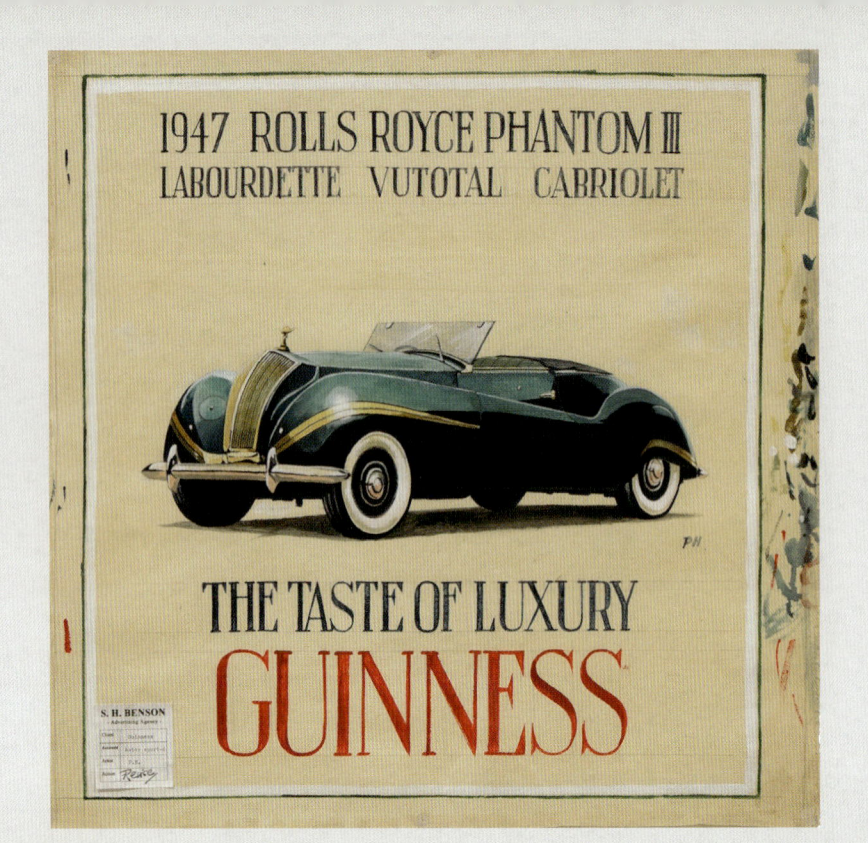

Rolls Royce Phantom III Labourdette Vututal Cabriolet, 1947.

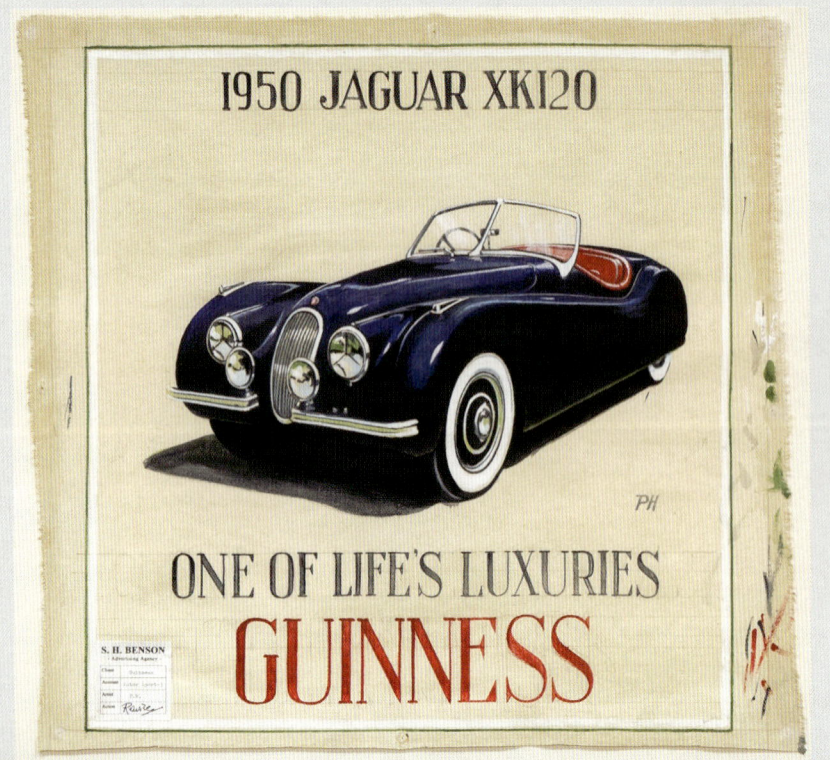

Jaguar XK150, 1950.

Another commercial artist simply known as 'P. H.' also produced some wonderful UK classic car canvases for Guinness.

Rolls Royce Silver Dawn, 1953.

All these various car theme calendars are true representations of actual models and employ no humour or wit in design or text. In this way they are unusual, especially as Guinness advertising. They do show great draughtsmanship and in this respect Clifford's images are probably superior to Gilroy's.

Bentley MKVI Drophead Coupé.

Bentley 8 Short Chasis.

Jaguar XK120 Coupé.

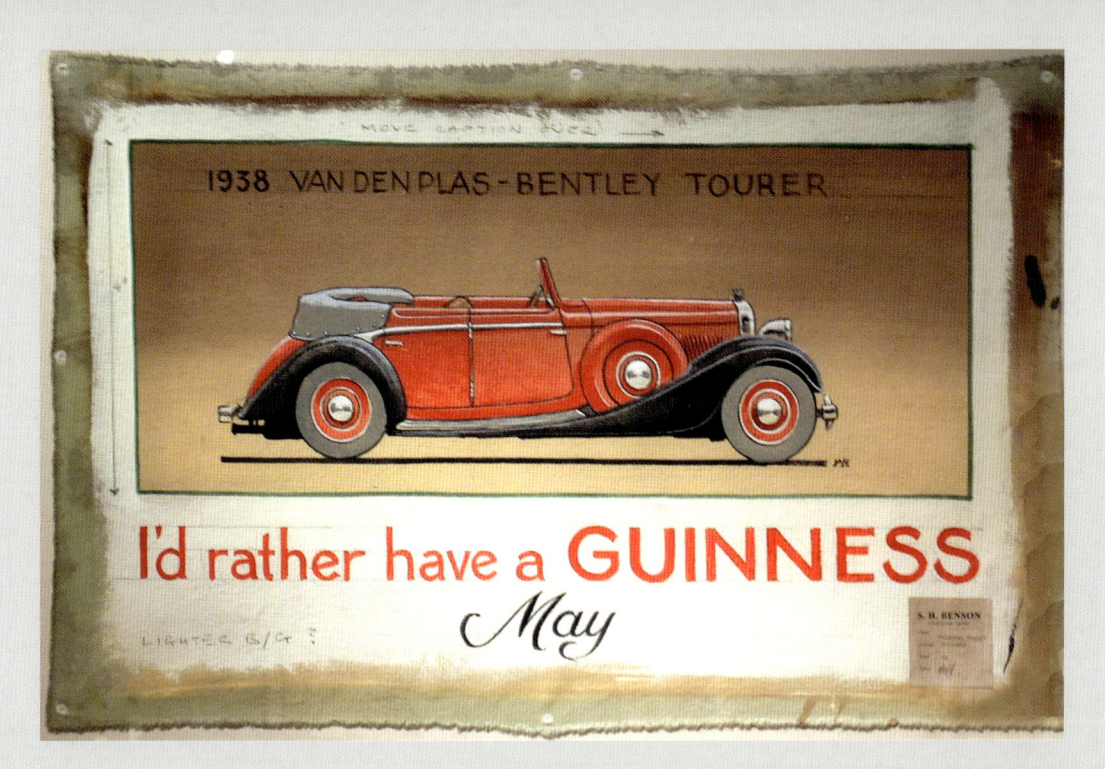

May 1938 Van Den Plas - Bentley Tourer.

In pencil on the canvas - top margin, 'move caption over' and bottom left corner, 'Lighter B/G?'

Bentley Tourer, 1936, 4.25 Litre.

Bentley Tourer, 1929, 4.5 Litre.

Bentley Convertible, 1937.

Bentley Saloon, 1953.

Derby Bentley, 1935, 3.5L Saloon.

CLASSIC CARS

Earls Court Motor Show, 1948, Ford V8 Pilot.

'Any colour – so long as it's black!'

CLASSIC CARS

Earls Court Motor Show calendar 1950 project

Gilroy was commissioned by Benson to produce a classic car calendar for Guinness at the 1950 Earls Court Motor Show in London. Again whilst he was not the regular Benson artist to paint cars, he did this job very well. Note the months are added in pencil. It is likely these were never used.

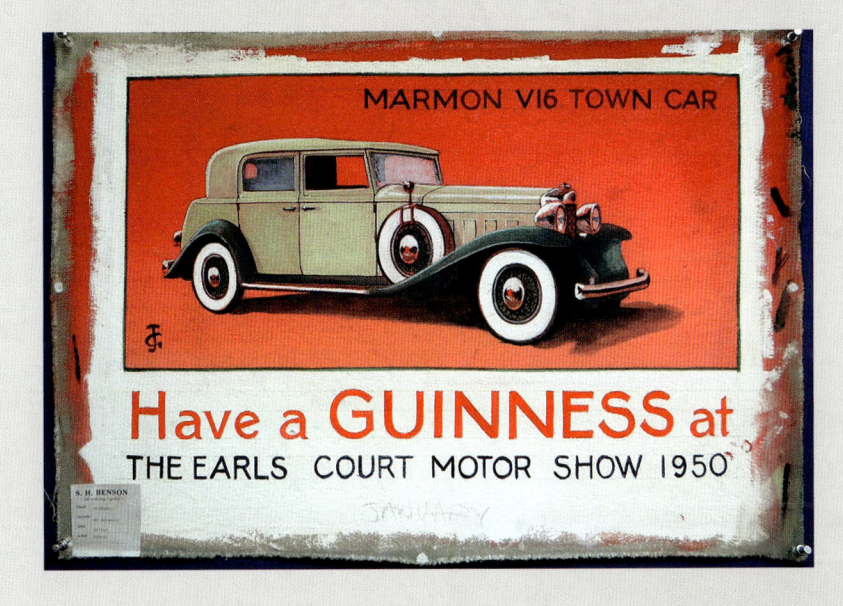

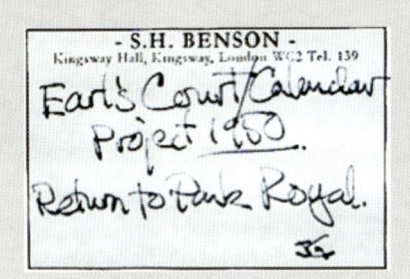

January, Marmon V16 Town Car.

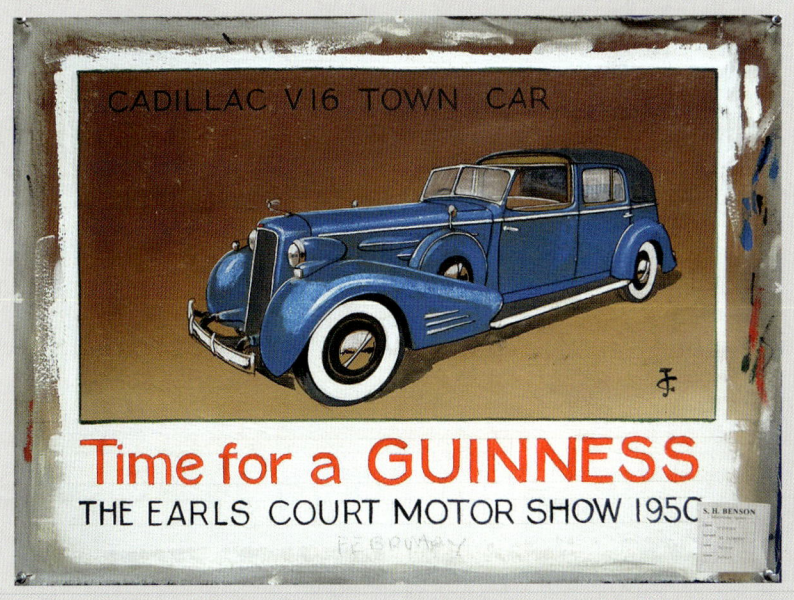

February, Cadillac V16 Town car.

March, Rolls Royce Silver Ghost.

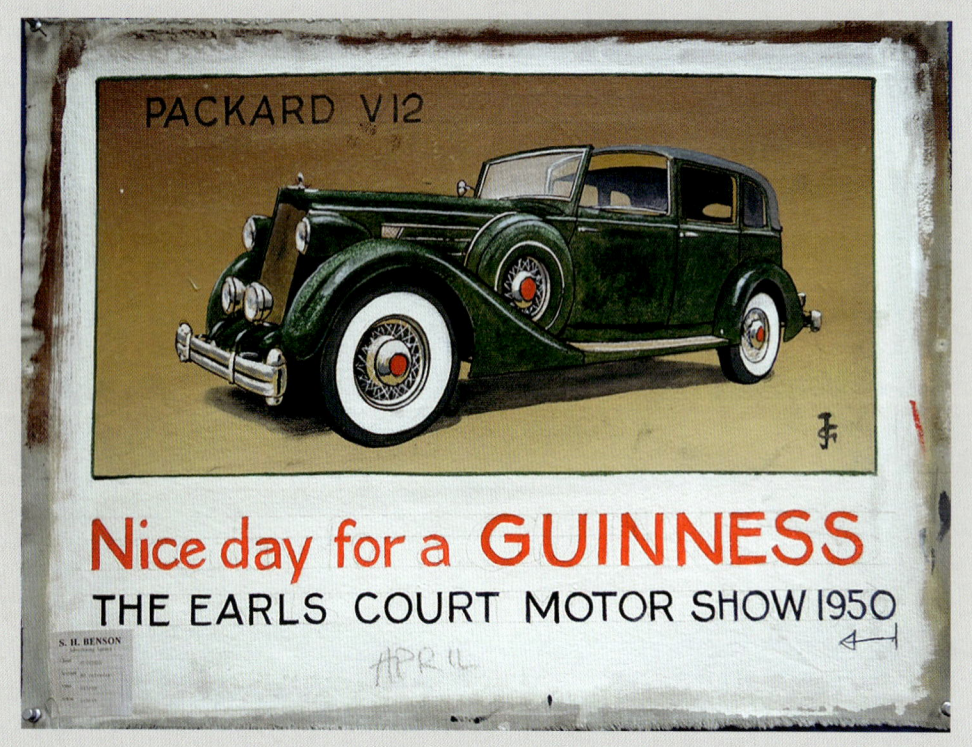

April, Packard V12.

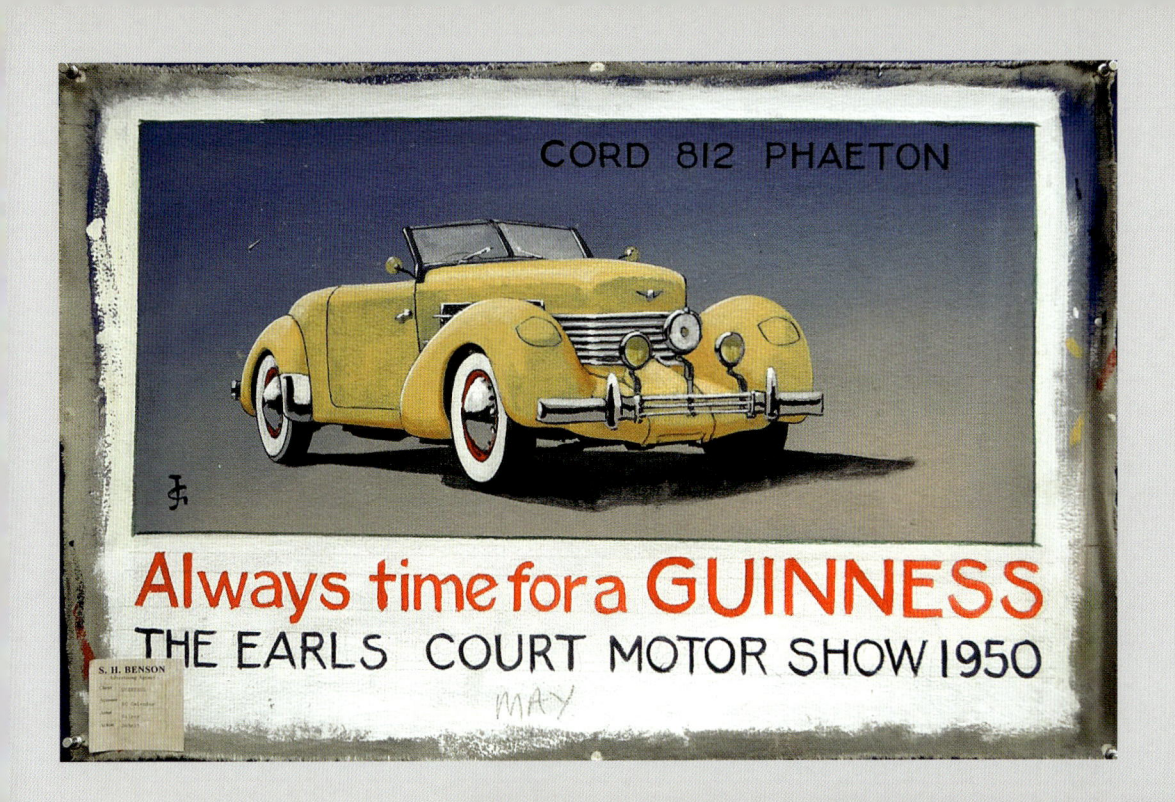

May, Cord 812 Phaeton.

June, Isotta - Fraschini Tipo 8A.

153

July, Duesenberg Torpedo.

August, Bugatti 57C Aravis.

154

September, Stutz 'BB' Tourer.

October, Speed Six Bentley.

November, Isotta Fraschini Type 8.

December, Chrysler Imperial CG Limousine.

Note the misspelling of 'Guinness' annotated in pencil at the bottom margin. Also the top margin is annotated with an arrow instructing, 'Point car the other way'.

9
London, the Olympics and Coronation

London, the Olympics and Coronation

Gilroy produced a set of at least twelve canvases to celebrate the post-war London 1948 Games held in Wembley Stadium. We have examples here of five of the canvases that look finished. They are each marked 'submit' on the Benson sticker so one assumes they 'passed muster', and where to be used. However there is no record of their commercial use as posters, calendars or press adverts. One wonders where the seven missing canvases are and which sports were illustrated?

Toucans flying past the Olympic rings, 1948. Canvas, 54cm wide x 71cm high.

Marked in pencil as no 7.

LONDON, THE OLYMPICS AND CORONATION

The weightlifter is a tribute to the Guinness for strength girder man, 73cm wide x 54cm high.

Marked in pencil as no 9.

LONDON, THE OLYMPICS AND CORONATION

The runner harkens back to the zoo animals running away with the zookeepers. Guinness canvas, 59cm wide x 44 high.

Marked in pencil as no 11.

LONDON, THE OLYMPICS AND CORONATION

The pole-vaulter. Here the athlete takes his Guinness with him over the bar whilst the bemused official who looks remarkably like the zookeeper, stands beneath gesturing.

Canvas, 44cm wide x 59cm high.

Marked in pencil as no 8.

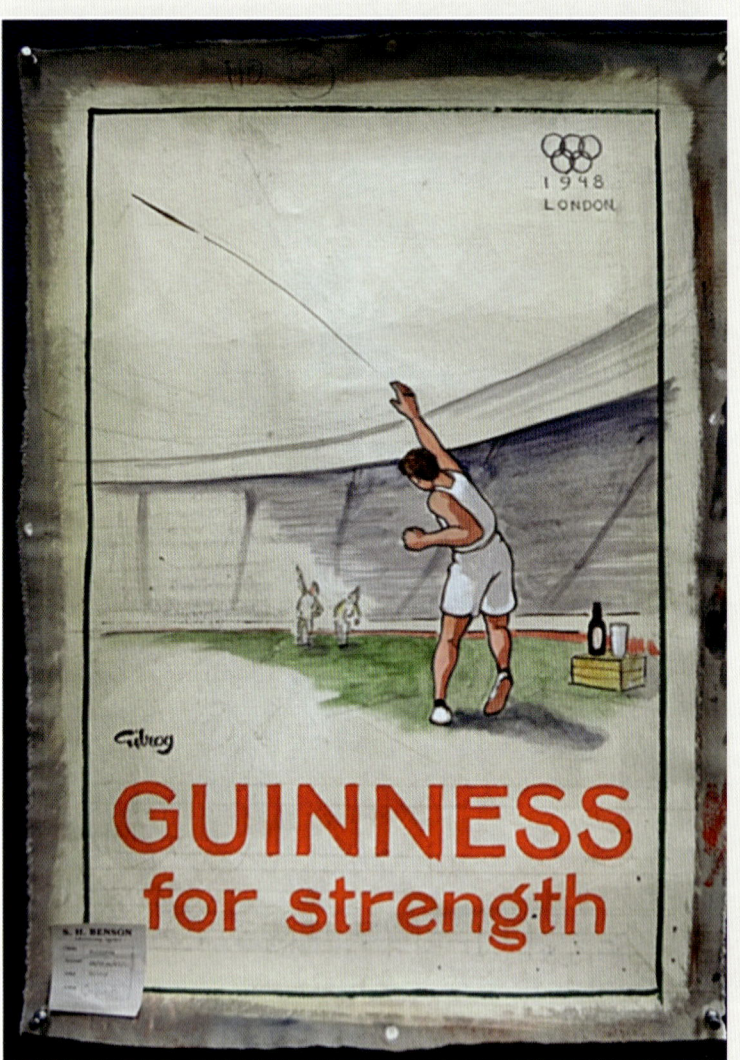

The javelin thrower throws high into the air, way beyond the measuring officials, all because he drank his Guinness. Even in 1948, I doubt athletes could take beer into the arena.

Canvas, 51cm wide x 71cm high.

Marked in pencil as no 12.

162

Coronation

Commemoration of the Coronation of Queen Elizabeth II in 1953. Canvas, 60cm wide x 87cm high.

Gilroy painted this version facing the opposite direction for the commercially used poster. Also the pelican is missing from the final line-up. This canvas was painted in early 1953 after the death of Princess Elizabeth's father, King George IV. In this version the crowd is not fully painted in and the caption MGMG was employed. On the printed poster, no caption was used, not even the word Guinness, so well-known was the product imagery. A huge banner poster of this image was placed on the procession route near St Paul's Cathedral, which said 'Loyal Greetings'.

LONDON, THE OLYMPICS AND CORONATION

London

Tower Bridge, 1950.
Intended for the House of Commons, Terrace Pavilion.

A set of three unique London scenes with flying Toucans, offered by Guinness Park Royal Brewery to the Houses of Parliament to aid their post-war renovation. Each picture was inscribed with a dedicated room in which to be hung.

St Paul's Cathedral and a bishop, 1950.

LONDON, THE OLYMPICS AND CORONATION

Nelson's Column, England Expects, 1950 – Guinness.

Letter reads - House of Commons, 14th July, 1950.
Dear Sir,
It is with regret that I inform you that we will not be proceeding our refurbishment plans. Whilst your samples were well received, the committee felt that given the prevailing 'climate', neither of our masters would welcome too close an association with the other!

Yours sincerely,
Major S. E. Sidwell, Chairman of the Services Committee.

Covent Garden porter carrying boxes – 'Guinness for Strength', 1938. Never used commercially.

165

10
Foreign Countries and War Time

Germany

S. H. Benson was asked by St James's Gate Brewery in 1936 to produce a set of images for use with a German distributor. Gilroy submitted these oil on canvas pictures, none of which were ever used. Viewed post-WWII - they now appear rather naive and inappropriate, especially those depicting the military.

Brandenburg Gate, Berlin. This comes in two versions.

Bismarck statue in Hamburg.

Wehrmacht soldier holding a glass. *Berlin Olympic stadium with swastikas.*

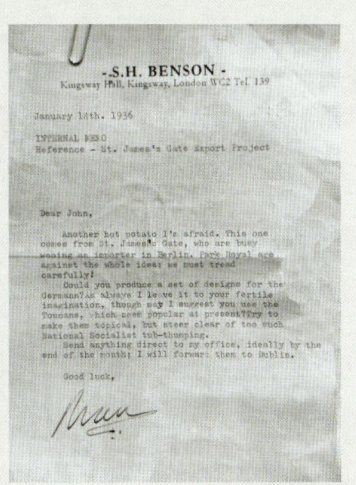

Jan 14th 1936. Internal Memo.

Dear John, Another hot potato I'm afraid. This one comes from St James's Gate who are busy wooing an importer in Berlin. Park Royal are against the whole idea; we must tread carefully. Could you produce a set of drawings for the Germans? As always I leave it to your fertile imagination, though may I suggest you use the toucans which seem popular at present? Try to make them topical, but steer clear of too much Nationalist Socialist tub-thumping. Send anything direct to my office, ideally by the end of the month; I will forward them to Dublin.

Good luck,

Bevan

Letter from Bensons to Gilroy, 1936, asking for German advertising poster ideas.

Graf Zeppelin Airship in Nazi regalia.

'Question.. Answer… There's nothing like Guinness with lobster'. Inset advert and c 1936 watercolour on board, German version with the lobster wearing an SS helmet, probably not by Gilroy.

A strangely politically incorrect image for Guinness, but in 1936, people were naive about 3rd Reich Germany.

Sie Angekommen! (It's Coming!)
In pencil at top margin – 'Check translation!' and bottom margin – 'Schloss Neuschwanstein'.
Toucans over Schloss Neuschwanstein in Bavaria, 1936.

FOREIGN COUNTRIES AND WAR TIME

Celebrating 50 years of German car invention in 1936

Mercedes G4. In pencil at the base- 'congratulations from Guinness'. The G4 was a German three-axle off-road vehicle first produced by Mercedes-Benz as a staff/command car for the Wehrmacht in 1934. The cars were designed as a seven-seat touring car or closed saloon, and were mainly used by upper echelons of the Nazi regime in parades and inspections as they were deemed too expensive for general Army use. This staff car is the one Hitler used. The six wheeled Mercedes were ordered by the German Army and fifty-seven were built. There are only three left, one of them belongs to the Spanish royal family.

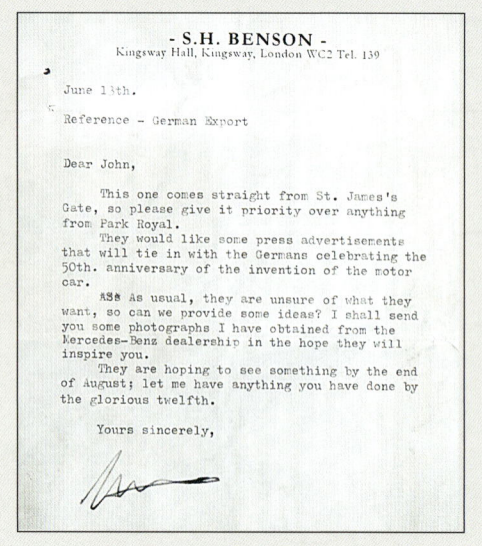

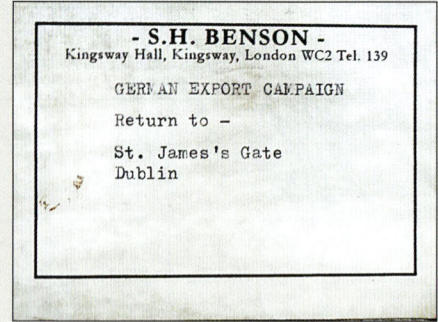

Letter to Gilroy from Bevan at Benson, dated 13th June 1935, asking him to provide German motor car adverts for St James's Gate Brewery Guinness.

FOREIGN COUNTRIES AND WAR TIME

This compact Mercedes came out in 1936 and was rear engined like the Volkswagen, hence no front grill.

In the 1930s there were attempts to move car engines from the forward compartment to the rear of the car. Such a move allows a reduction in the volume of the front compartment. At the same time, the voluminous rear provides a lot of space above and behind the rear axle. When engines are rear mounted, the drive shaft is eliminated. The first attempt was the Mercedes 130, followed by the 150 and then the 170. Few were built due to its poor road handling and production ceased in 1939. Today they are rare.

Mercedes Benz 170H with the German caption 'Small car-Great beer! Guinness'.

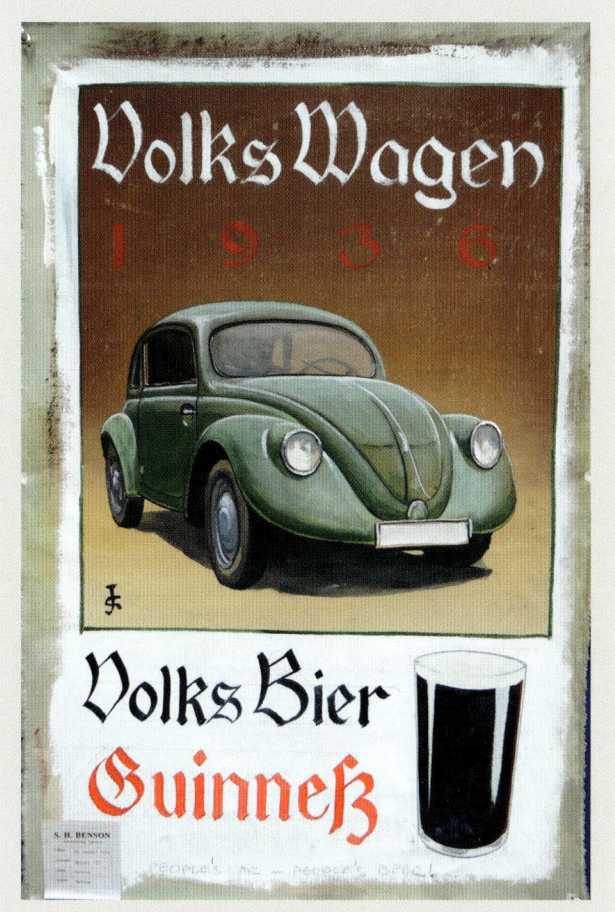

Volkswagen 1936 with the caption 'Peoples beer Guinness', also marked in pencil at the base.

The famous Volkswagen people's car was designed in 1931, just before the war, by Dr Ferdinand Porsche with the patronage of Hitler, who instructed Ferdinand Porsche to go and steal the Tatra T97 design from the Czechs, turning the design into the Volkswagen Beetle. It was a small low cost family car that the Third Reich had great hopes for. However production initially was low and its future in doubt before the war.

FOREIGN COUNTRIES AND WAR TIME

Mercedes Benz 540K.

With an eight cylinder five litre engine, four speed gear box with twin carburettors, this was a fast roadster. Both Hitler and Göring owned one of these cars, known as the 'blue goose'.

Mercedes Benz 150.

This is the mid-engine roadster version designed in 1934 as a two seater sports car. Only thirty-two built.

FOREIGN COUNTRIES AND WAR TIME

Mecedes Benz 770K, Congratulations from Guinness.

The 770k was used during the war as an armoured staff car. Also known as the Großer Mercedes (large Mercedes) this was a luxury car built by Mercedes-Benz from 1930 up to 1943. It is probably best known from archival footage of being used by high-ranking Nazi officials before and during World War II, including Adolf Hitler and Hermann Göring. Hitler's car was black. In 1938 the Mercedes 770 is thought to have been the most expensive German passenger car for sale up to that time, though it appeared on no price list: the price was published merely as 'auf Anfrage' ([available] by request). Less than two hundred were built before production ceased in 1944.

The 770 was powered by an inline eight-cylinder engine of 7,655 cc (467.1 cu in) capacity with overhead valves and aluminium pistons. This engine produced 150 brake horsepower (110 kW) at 2800 rpm without supercharging.

FOREIGN COUNTRIES AND WAR TIME

World War II Themes

Sailor loading a torpedo on a submarine, 1944. These are spin-offs from the girder man idea.

Airman loading a Lancaster bomber with ordinance, 1944.

Benson's Gilroy canvases with wartime themes. None of them were commercially used.

   In pencil on canvas- top middle,
   'Make figures smaller,
   Longer torpedo,
   Longer gang plank,
   Find reference for conning tower'
   Bottom right corner- 'Add man in hatch'.

Another variation of the girder man theme, with a man lifting a very heavy weight. Pencil note made in top right margin - 'add bird for humorous effect' with an arrow to a faint bird in top right corner. Top middle margin, 'Add slogan' with arrow. Pencil drawing of an oil drum and Guinness in bottom right corner. 'Berlin or bust!' is written on the bomb. Submit to censor on the sticker. Pencil annotated at bottom right corner with an oil drum and glass of Guinness.

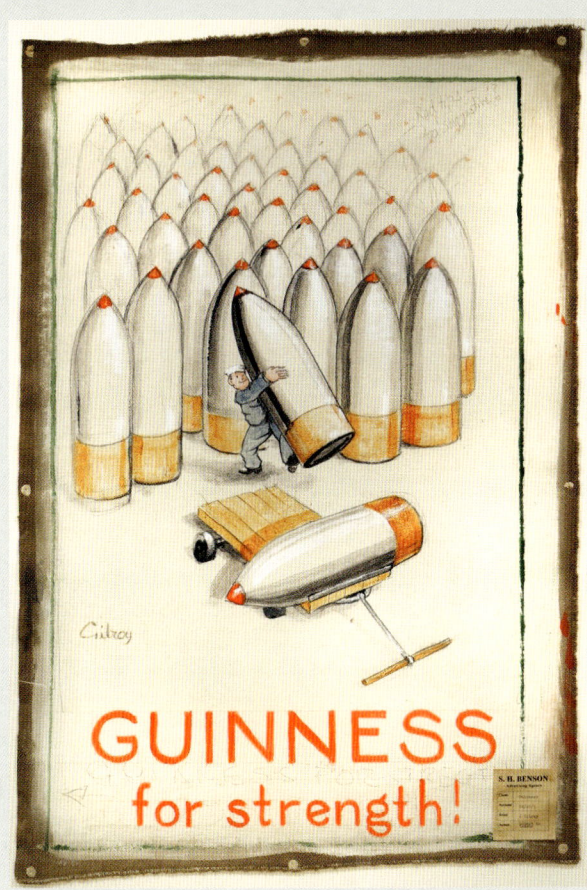

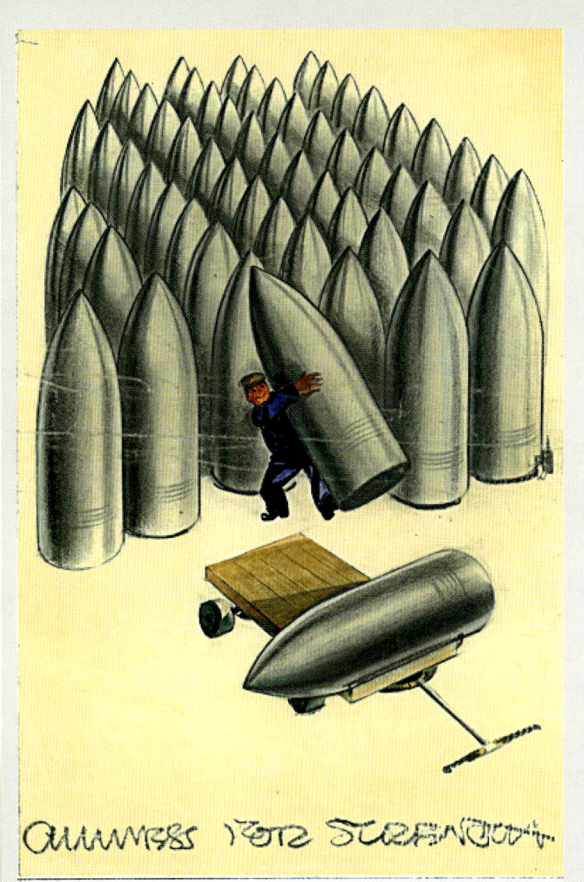

Canvas and rough sketch of a sailor loading ordnance onto a trolley 1940, never commercially used. The canvas is marked in pencil in the top right hand corner- Red tips, too suggestive? The sticker says –submit to censor.

Airman loading a Lancaster bomber with ordinance 1944.

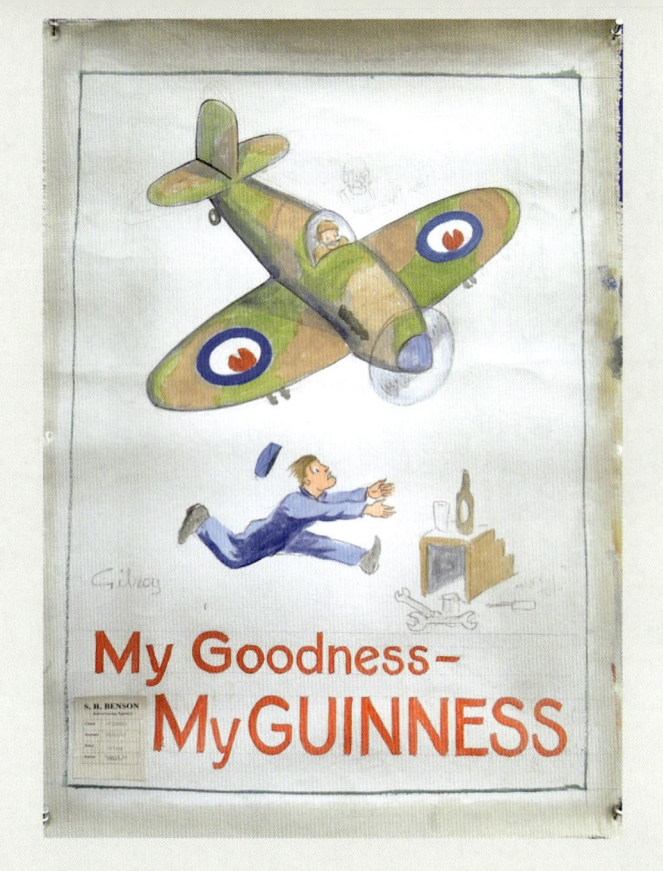

This proof canvas of the spitfire poster from 1942, has the aircraft diving from the other side.

Tools drawn in pencil beneath the box and pilots head just above the cockpit. The poster was used in small format mainly for window displays from 1941-42. The larger 30" x 40" landscape version has the man running from the other direction.

Wartime GFS man lifting a tank one handed, canvas, unfinished.

Guinness For Strength man carrying an enormous gun barrel is a different take on the girder man, two versions, top on canvas, beneath is a watercolour from 1943.

The workman carrying the enormous gun barrel jogs along the wooden plank with the same swagger as in the girder man poster, providing the visual joke. Note the startled bird in all.

GUINNESS for strength!

GUINNESS FOR STRENGTH

GUINNESS FOR STRENGTH

Above, finished commercially used advert, 1943.

FOREIGN COUNTRIES AND WAR TIME

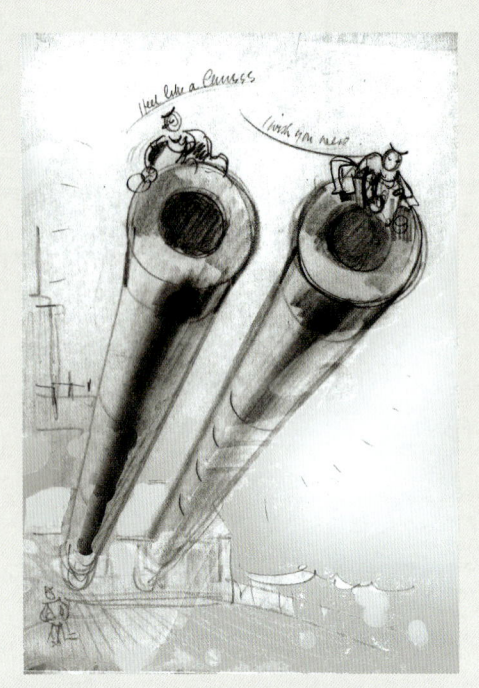

Rough sketch of naval guns being cleaned under the slogan, 'I Feel Like a Guinness! I wish you were!'

This was one in the series of ads under the slogan, 'I Feel Like a Guinness! I wish you were!' Again strong visual image and humour in the task.

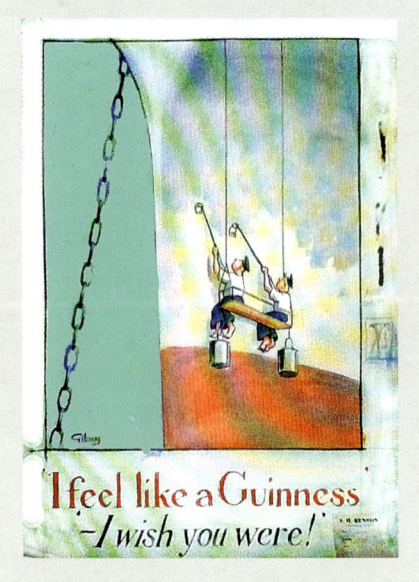

Canvas of a smaller section of the same picture, with just the two sailors painting, 1944. Not used commercially.

Full size poster of two sailors painting the side of the aircraft carrier, 1944.

The above canvas is marked in pencil in several places.
Top left corner- 'more detail on superstructure'.
Top right- 'make (deck) wider'.
Mid right- 'move planes up'.

180

Lovely day for a GUINNESS

This poster in 48 sheet format, won the National Outdoor Advertising Award in 1955, sponsored by the Worlds Press News and Advertisers Review. Gilroy won this award many times with Guinness posters.

Five toucans in formation flying over an RAF base, 1955 canvas.

Two rarely seen wartime Gilroy adverts

Now I feel I need a GUINNESS

Sailor returning from overseas with fruit. Spring 1944 poster.

My Goodness — where's My GUINNESS?

Lost Guinness at a camouflaged gun emplacement. 1941 magazine advert.

Man sitting on a torpedo canvas, 1942.

Above,- actual advert, 1943.
Note the side of the ship and the shorter take off distance.

The optically reversed version in canvas, 1942.

Subtle differences especially with the bird. In pencil base margin – 'Horizon' with an arrow pointing up.

FOREIGN COUNTRIES AND WAR TIME

United States of America

Three 1947 American market canvas views with toucans flying over New York and San Francisco: The Empire State Building, The Chrysler Building and a New York cop and The Golden Gate Bridge with a cop. All completed in 1947 for a campaign that did not run.

Bensons had asked Gilroy to prepare a series of poster designs for the US market post the Second World War, as they tried to re-establish the brand and break Guinness sales right across the USA. Mistakes had been made in relaunching Guinness in 1934 at the end of Prohibition, because they were still trying to sell bottled Foreign Extra Stout which contained 7% alcohol. It was too strong for the post-war American market and remained as a niche East Coast product. The new campaigns were about bottled Extra Stout at 4% alcohol and Draught Guinness. These Bensons ideas were not used. Guinness began working with Ogilvy Mather in New York, who favoured a more realistic advertising style, but sales and distribution growth was slow.

Toucans over Brooklyn Bridge, New York.

Toucans over Golden Gate Bridge, San Francisco.

A different version in landscape with a man in a boat fishing and no cop. This slogan mentions 'Draught Guinness'.

Two fabulous poster designs, never used.

Toucans flying over Monument Valley, Arizona with a cowboy, 1952.

185

Toucans over Mount Rushmore, South Dakota, 1952. Two versions, never used.

Golden Gate Bridge, San Francisco.

Some canvas soiling top and bottom. Pencil drawing of a policeman in bottom left corner and –'add figure' in margin.

New York Statue of Liberty, 1949.

In pencil at top margin –'Change angle of Toucans' and at base- 'More Liberty!!!'

FOREIGN COUNTRIES AND WAR TIME

It is clear that in 1950, Guinness were planning to conduct a major American campaign under the slogan 'It's arrived', suggesting that this was the launch of a new type of Guinness, across many States, not just the usual target of the East Coast. Benson asked Gilroy to provide a set of suitable canvases and he chose the toucans in formation flying past major US tourist attractions. None of these posters were later used.

Empire State Building and toucans, 1950.
Pencil writing top margin- 'Give the tower more room'.

The Statue of Liberty in New York, 1950.

FOREIGN COUNTRIES AND WAR TIME

Never used commercially, these American canvases are some of Gilroy's best non-British market designs.

USA campaign poster artwork from 1950.

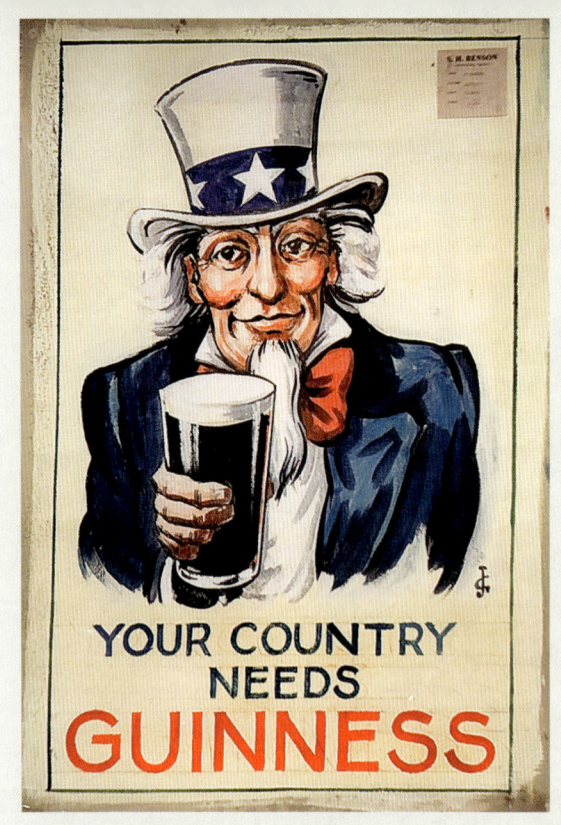

Above, a spoof on the US recruiting poster of Uncle Sam, 1950 canvas (insert by J.M. Flagg).

Notated in pencil in the top margin - 'Apologies to James Montgomery Flagg'. Never used.

An original illustration by Flagg.

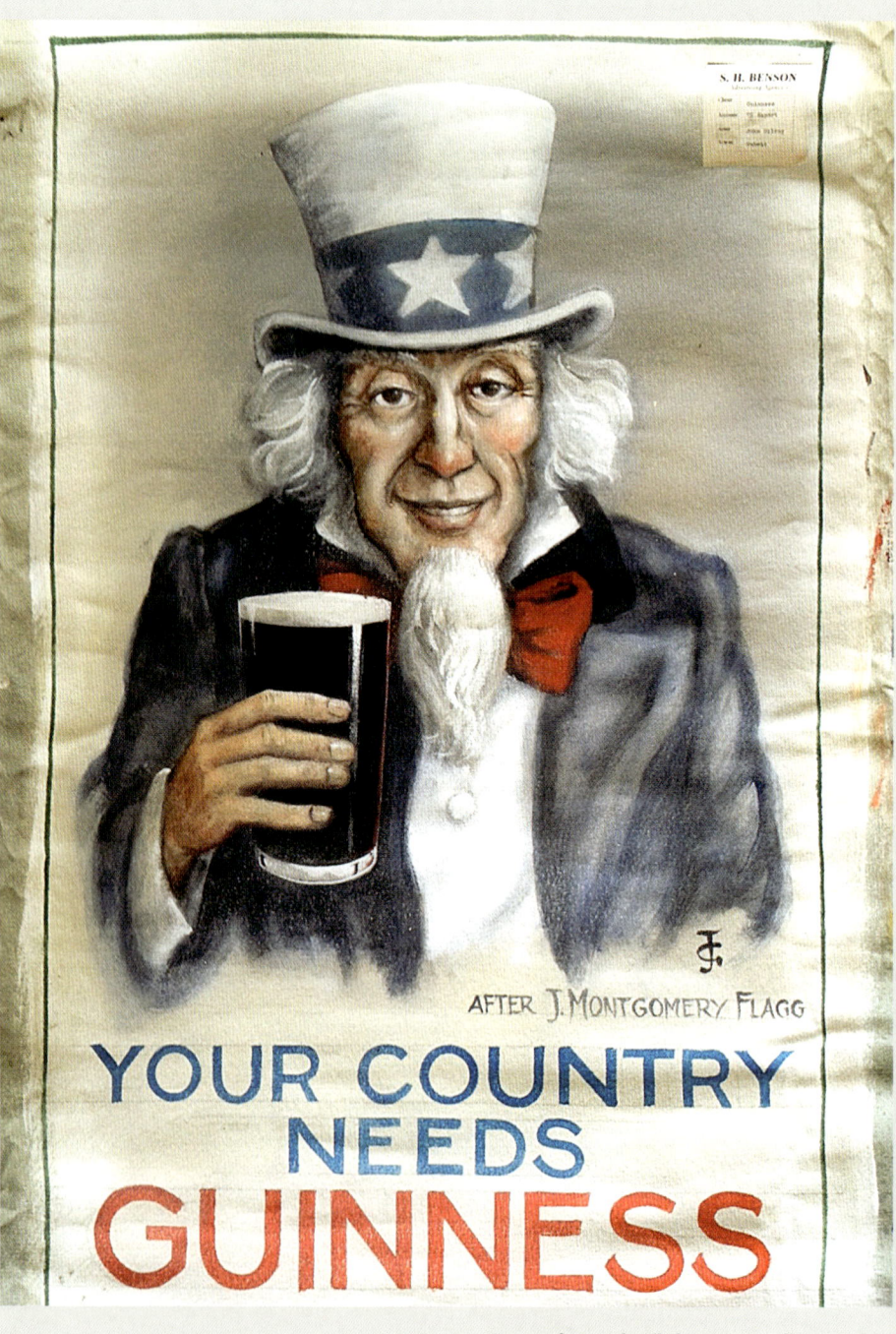

A second more detailed canvas, no date.

France

Eiffel Tower, Paris, two canvases.

Pencil writing in top left margin
- 'set tower at an angle'.
Top right margin – 'check spelling'.

Pencil drawing of de Gaulle.

Italy

Leaning Tower of Pisa, Italy, 1947 canvas.

FOREIGN COUNTRIES AND WAR TIME

Venice

Benson canvas, 1949. Unfinished scene of gondoliers in Venice.

Benson canvas, 1949. A more completed scene of gondoliers in Venice.

Written in pencil, right side - 'Smaller toucans'.

FOREIGN COUNTRIES AND WAR TIME

Russia

The Kremlin wall, Red Square, Moscow.

In pencil left margin - 'Not Stalin!!!!'
A look-a-like is standing by the wall. Bottom margin - 'For Strength', 'GE/30c'.

Two canvases of Russian Orthodox Churches in Moscow, 1952.

FOREIGN COUNTRIES AND WAR TIME

Israel

Toucans flying past the old city walls of Jerusalem.

The Jewish man in Orthodox clothing is saying in Hebrew 'Lachiam!' - 'to life!'

FOREIGN COUNTRIES AND WAR TIME

Nigeria

Guinness has had a presence in Nigeria since the late 19th and early 20th century. They traded with the support of the United Africa Company UAC, a part of Unilever. The first Stout brewery was built in Ikeja, Lagos in 1963 (not as below in 1949), followed by Benin in 1978 and later Ogba in Lagos. It is a huge Guinness market, the largest in Africa and very important to the company.

1962 Gilroy poster painting along the 'Guinness for Strength' woodcutter lines, but with the caption 'Guinness gives you Power'.

195

11
Watercolours and Roughs

WATERCOLOURS AND ROUGHS

Watercolours and roughs

Watercolours were done on paper or card. None of these images progressed to become accepted for advertising, more's the shame.

'I feel I've earned a Guinness', a rower, watercolour. A simple and well-constructed image.

'I feel I need a Guinness', GFS, rough of a barber and an exceedingly hairy man, watercolour.

'Guinness for strength', rough of a single skuller, watercolour.

197

'Guinness is so refreshing' and 'Have a Guinness when you're tired' roughs, watercolour on paper.

Gardener asleep in a hammock, having just had his Guinness. The grass can wait!

'Guinness Time' caption, man leading a huge bull with an apple, watercolour.

Sculptor making an abstract reclining man out of stone, 'Guinness for strength'.

My Goodness My Guinness - Seagull

The strapline, 'Take some with you in cans' dates from the late 1950s when Guinness in cans first became available.

Two versions on this theme of the seagull stealing a man's Guinness, watercolour on paper roughs.

Scarecrow stealing Guinness, watercolour.

Two crayon roughs - man with dog and a juggler.

Donkey, footballers and photographer roughs.

A new caption is tried out here in the image of the photographer, 'Take Guinness and develop strength'.

Milkman with churns, soldier overloaded with kit and a giant tree going through a buzz saw.

Great exaggeration of strength as seen in these pictures was the hallmark of Gilroy's art.

Man lifting a piano, man ploughing a field without a horse and man lifting a car.

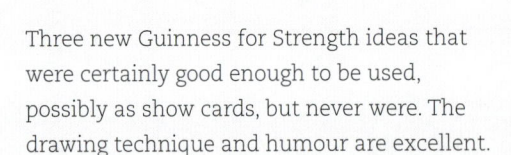

Three new Guinness for Strength ideas that were certainly good enough to be used, possibly as show cards, but never were. The drawing technique and humour are excellent.

A watercolour and two pencil drawings of wonderful poster ideas.

What a shame that more of these impossible advert concepts were not used.

Two pencil sketches on paper. Gilroy as the feisty boxer, signed and dated 1948.

The toucan on the shoulder of the strong man was a clever take on the Dorothy Sayers toucan advert.

A park keeper carrying two huge stacks of chairs, a rough 'Guinness for strength', watercolour.

Greetings from Gilroy

Gilroy and the zookeeper carol singing, personal Christmas card, pencil and crayon, 1937.

The sea lion balancing a barrel of Guinness, entering the stage door, watercolour.

A personal Christmas Greetings card from Gilroy.

Gilroy's script for a card.

12
The Smiling Glass, Guinness Time and Christmas

THE SMILING GLASS, GUINNESS TIME AND CHRISTMAS

The Smiling Glass

1947 and 1938 canvases.

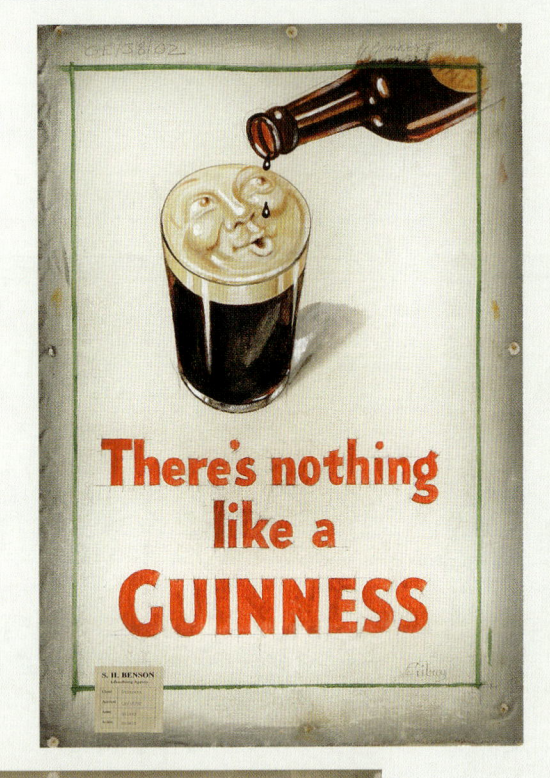

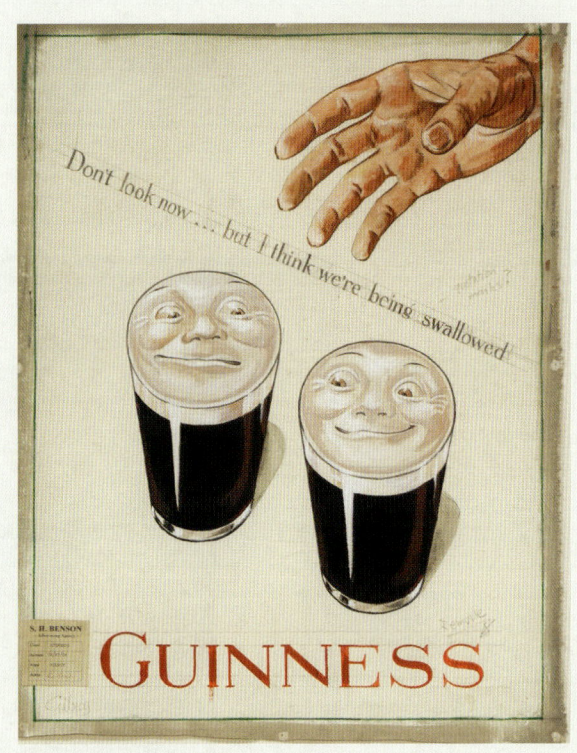

'Reach for a Guinness' canvas painted by W Brearley, 1939.

Written on the canvas top right hand corner in pencil is, 'Billy, the whole thing is too Soviet, please revise, S'. The image without the lines did appear as an advert, below GE134.

209

Smiling Guinness glasses

It was Gilroy who gave the head on the pint of Guinness a face and personality for the first time in 1933. This theme was to be reused many times and over many years. The very early black and white ads were not signed so it is difficult to assign them to an artist, however all these six canvases in this set are by Gilroy.

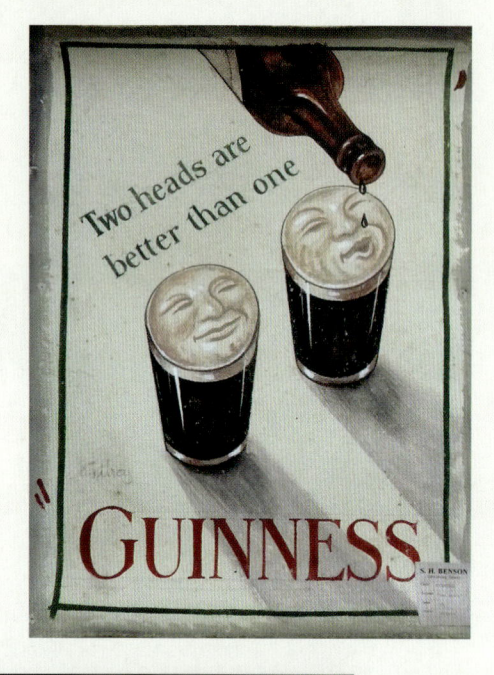

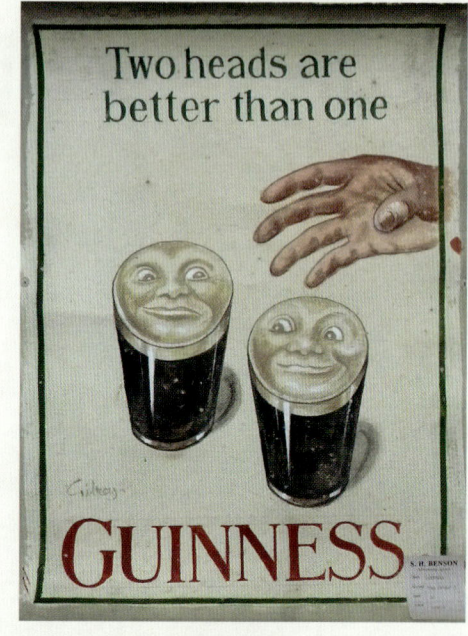

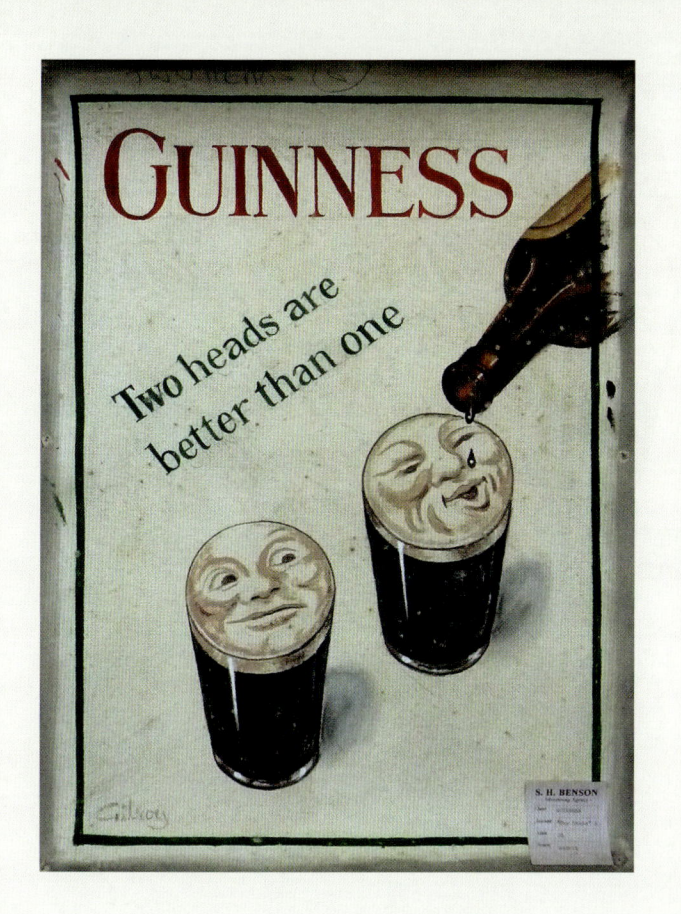

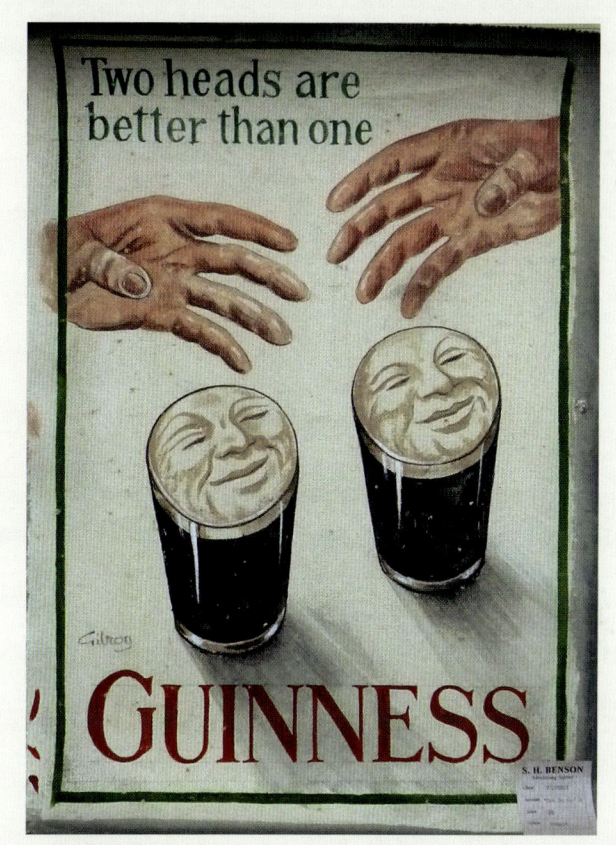

Christmas 1930 Advert GE227, using the same smiling glass imagery as the posters (unsigned by Gilroy).

The Benson archive contained two complete sets of six variations on the theme of 'Two Heads are better than one', the smiling glass and the hand or pouring bottle, painted by Gilroy.

A signed Gilroy canvas, 'Unmistakable' from 1937.

'A Guinness a day' poster seven glass 1932 Gilroy canvas signed and clearly ascribed to him on the Benson sticker.

This is important as many early 1929 -31 adverts used this glass theme and many would have been drawn by Gilroy, albeit unsigned.

Gilroy canvas in Russian.

1950s Russian show card.

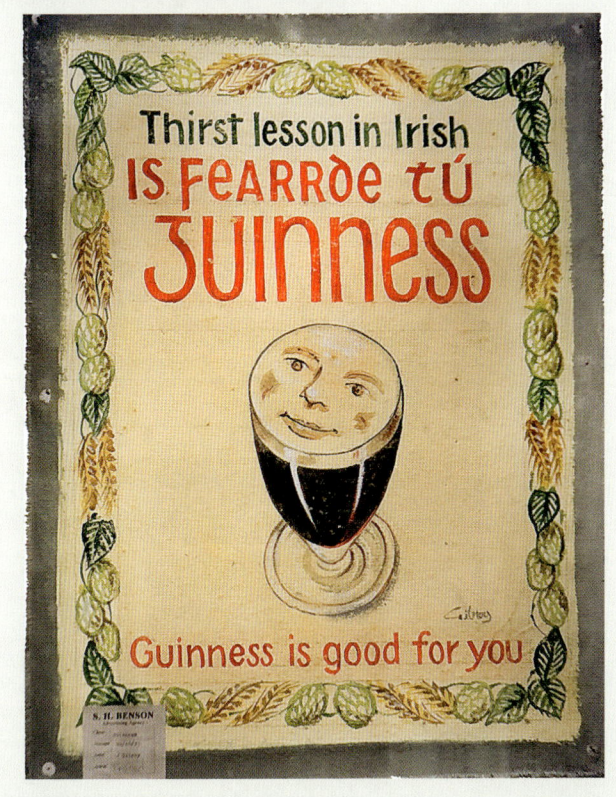

Thirst lesson in Irish, Gilroy canvas and advert, 1964.

Guinness Time

Guinness Time was a great theme for Guinness that started with the simple clock face, then the face and hands went wobbly with eyes added, and the clock became embodied in the London Piccadilly neon clock. The concept ended with the fabulous mechanical Festival Clocks of 1951.

'Guinness Time' and crying oysters canvas, 1936. Same advert GA145, issued in 1933.

'Guinness Time' with hops and barley, 1931.

'Ten to one it's Guinness time' canvas variant, 1931.

'Guinness Time' and smiling glass Underground poster, 1936.

214

Christmas Posters

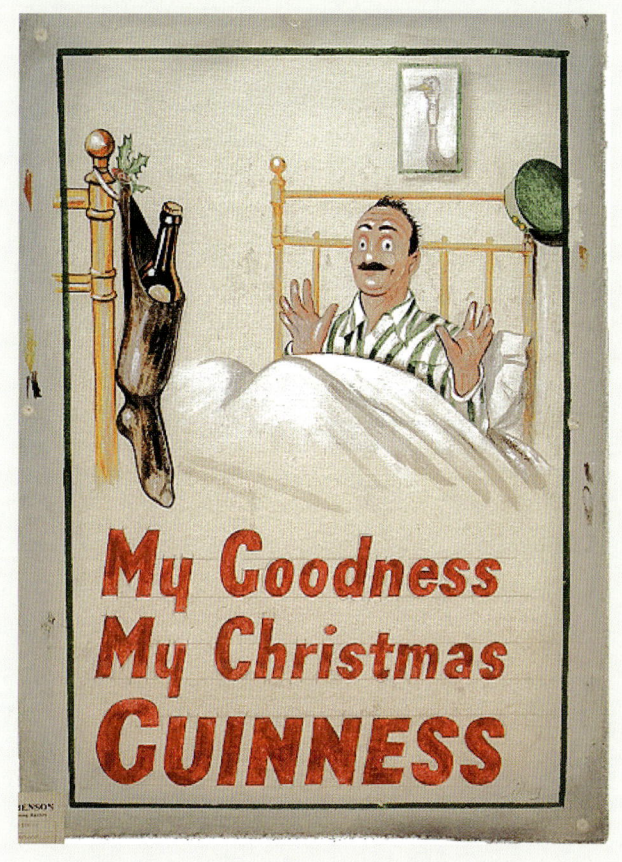

'My Goodness My Christmas Guinness' canvas, 1952.

'Guinness Time' small poster, 1958.

'Guinness is Good for You' advert GE62, 1930.

13
Golf courses, knights in armour, Hastings 1066

Golf Courses

In 1950, Guinness Exports asked Benson to provide some golf course images for advertisements or calendars overseas. Gilroy, a keen golfer and an accomplished landscape artist set about the project and produced the following set of famous holes on Championship Courses. These serious studies carry no visual jokes. They were never commercially used.

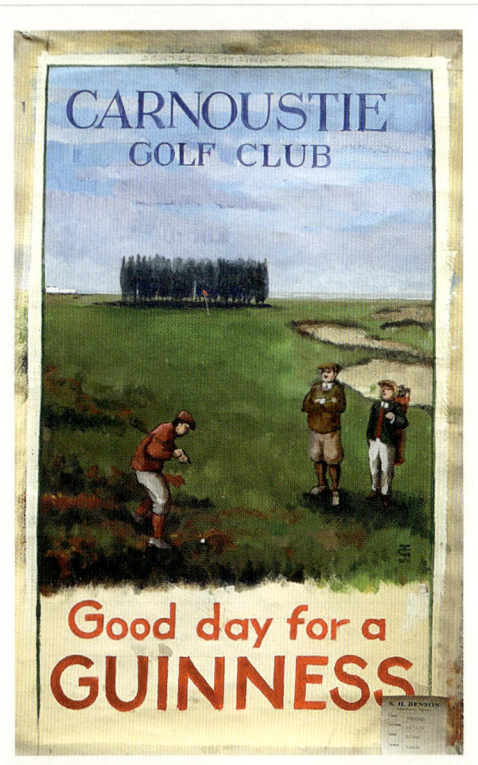

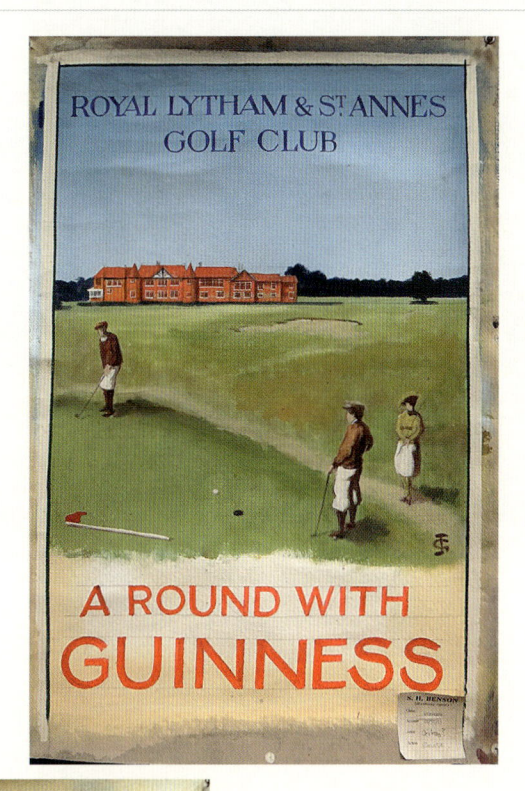

Were these the only pictures done of golf courses or were there more in these sets? Why just paint Caesarea course on its own? These were done by W. Brearley, another of the Benson Commercial artists.

Caesarea Golf Club in Israel.

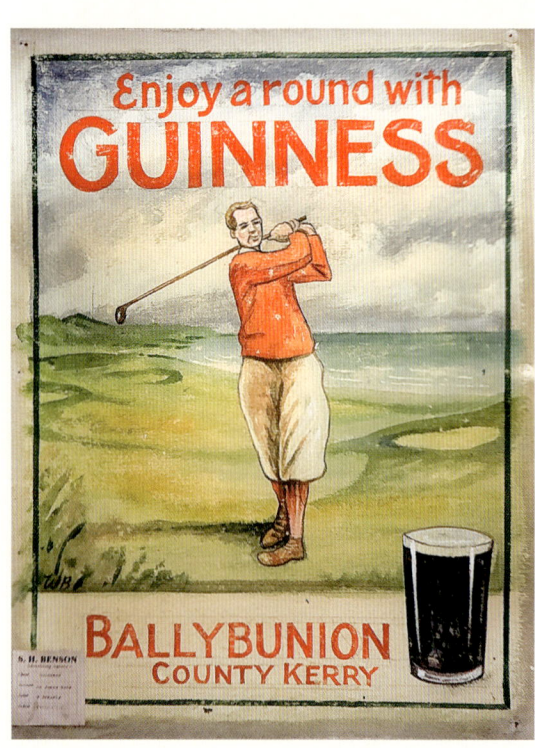

Irish golf courses produced by Benson for St James's Gate, painted by artist W. Brearley.

218

My Goodness My Guinness, the Mechanical Grab

The crane driver is borrowed from the rough sketch of the girder man on an early page. This famous poster from 1937 was rarely used. It was displayed in Éire during December 1938, making it one of the earliest poster adverts used there and certainly the first Gilroy. It appeared in UK magazines but again on a restricted basis.

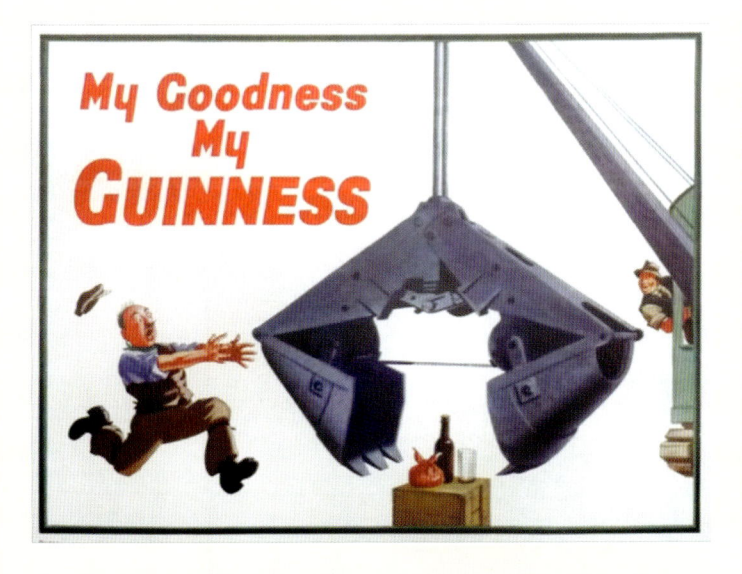

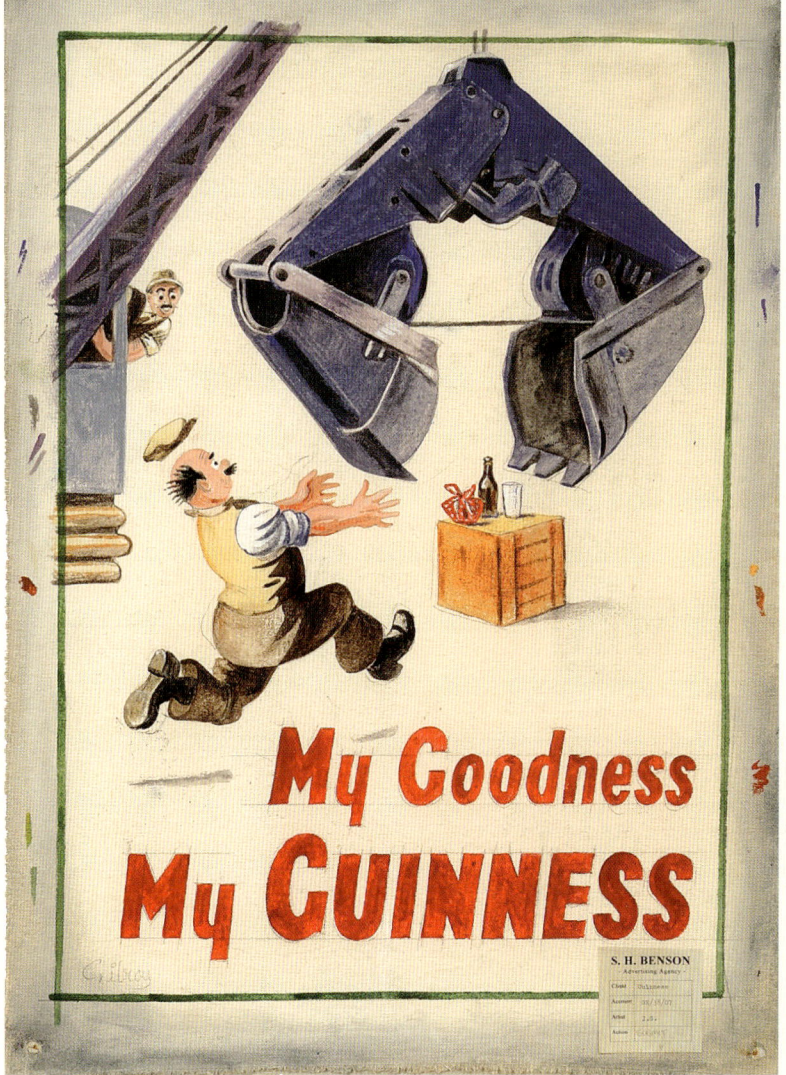

This landscape version of the finished advert is very different to the above portrait view. The man is running into the scene rather than running away as above. It is not signed and could well be by another artist.

Opening time is Guinness Time

The Knight in armour with a glass.

This poster offers a neat visual and verbal joke as to how the knight will drink the beer and how the helmet opens so he can reach his mouth. The double meaning refers of course to pub opening times. On this occasion the artist is Lander who painted it in 1957.

A rough sketch of an armoured glove, the gauntlet.

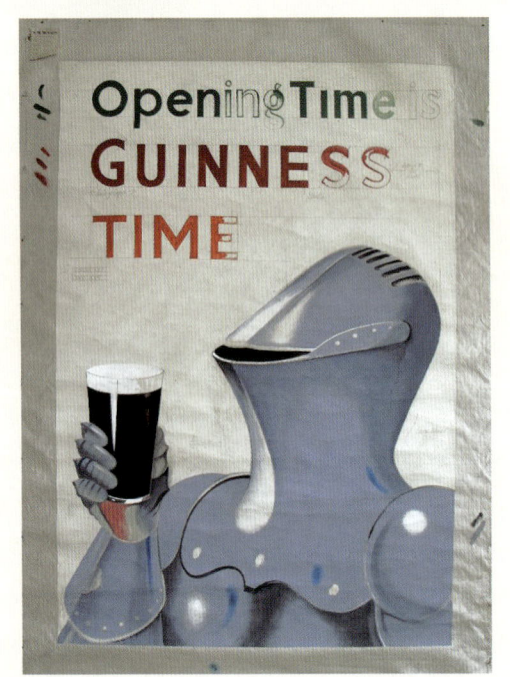

The knight's armoured helmet, a very large but less complete canvas, 1957.

The knight's armoured helmet in French.

GOLF COURSES, KNIGHTS IN ARMOUR, HASTINGS 1066

The French and Italian versions of the armoured Knight drinking Guinness, 1957.

The helmet in the poster is a Stech-helm, a heavy German jousting helmet of the 15th and 16th centuries. It has a bluntly pointed front with a V-shaped slit for viewing.

GOLF COURSES, KNIGHTS IN ARMOUR, HASTINGS 1066

Battle of Hastings 1066

Two different canvases partially finished, of the Battle of Hastings, 1066 poster, 1966.

GOLF COURSES, KNIGHTS IN ARMOUR, HASTINGS 1066

Ascribed on the Benson label to an 'in-house artist'.

This canvas also exists as the English and Italian version, La Battaglia di Hastings 1066, again unfinished.

14
Early Black and White Adverts

EARLY BLACK AND WHITE ADVERTS

The first Gilroy black & white Guinness advertisements

We are all familiar with the classic colour posters from Gilroy's brush, but his early black and white pen drawn newspaper ads are not so often seen. They are no less miniature masterpieces of draughtsmanship and humour. His characters are well observed and benign; and the situations they find themselves in are often surprising.

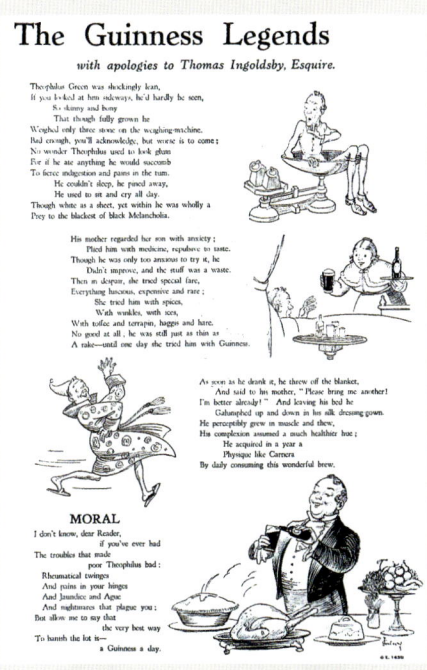

225

EARLY BLACK AND WHITE ADVERTS

I Feel I've earned a Guinness, Guinness for Strength

The Guinness for Strength campaign started with the strong man lifting or pulling huge weights. There was humour involved in these early ads, but much more was to come. Gradually the concept matured into exaggerated situations where the impossible task was accomplished by a person after drinking Guinness. The girder man was probably the most famous.

Of Henry Hercules I sing
The Man who can Lift Anything;
See him supporting with one hand
(The right) a full size Concert Grand,
While poised upon the other are
Four adults in a baby car.
Three times a night the hall is packed
To see his Record-breaking Act.

He does his stuff, he makes his bow—
Behind the scenes observe him now
And let us learn how he acquires
The muscles which the world admires.
Upon a silver tray are brought
A glass and bottle; as I thought,
His secret stands revealed at length—
Guinness—the sovereign source of strength.

Guinness for Strength

'I feel I've earned a GUINNESS'

CHRISTMAS TIME IS GUINNESS TIME

I feel I've earned a GUINNESS

GUINNESS for STRENGTH

226

EARLY BLACK AND WHITE ADVERTS

Guinness and Oysters

An association between drinking Guinness and eating oysters was firmly cemented following the early 1930s run of press and magazine adverts.

The Oyster Bed

or "Call me at
GUINNESS TIME"

Guinness and Oysters are Good for you

Always popular with the Natives

GUINNESS
is good for
OYSTERS

"The Oyster is a gentle thing,
And will not come unless you sing"
OLD PROVERB

Remember this. Remember, too,
Not every kind of song will do.
So profit by this little rhyme
And always sing in "Guinness Time"

GUINNESS is good for Oysters
—good for you

GUINNESS TIME
Cried the OYSTERS

EARLY BLACK AND WHITE ADVERTS

Humpty Dumpty and Alice

The 'Alice' and 'Humpty Dumpty' theme was much used by Gilroy, combined with clever words from the copywriters that were borrowed from Lewis Carroll.

Humpty Dumpty 'Unmistakability', GE434, 1934.

Humpty dumpty re-cited GE775, 1938.

Guinness glass logic GE442, Tweedle Dum and Tweedle Dee, 1935.

Humpty Dumpty 'Guinness is Good for You', GE393, 1934.

Maddening GE320, 1933 and *The Hunting of the Stout* GE144, 1931.

'Off with its head' GE72, 1929.

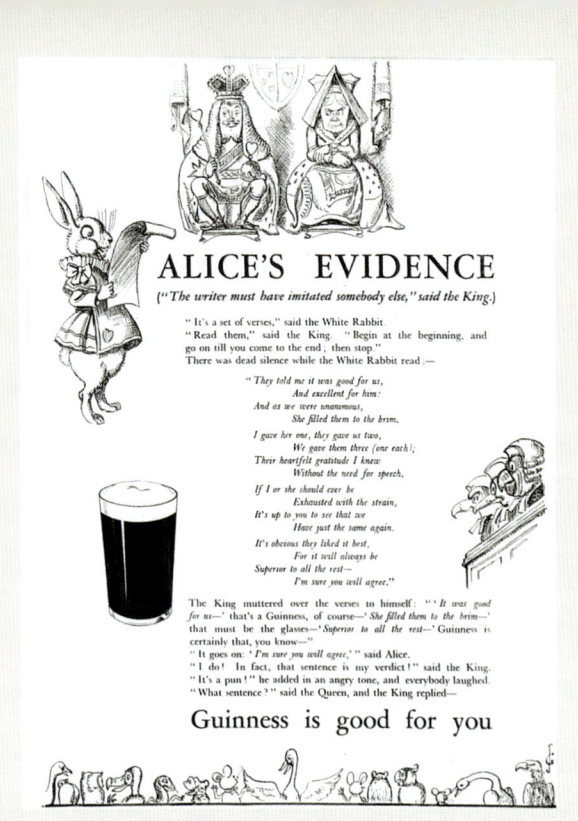

'Alice's Evidence' GE193, 1931 and 'Alice through the Guinness Glass' GE768, 1937.

'Oh my ears and whiskers!' GE252, 1932.
'Questions by Queens and Answers by Alice' GE576, 1936.

'As the birdie said to the eagle', GE842, 1939.

'Father William', GE250, 1932.

'Where's that Tiger?', GE769, 1932.

'Second Sight', 1930.

231

'Guinness Time', Cleaning Big Ben GE180, 1931.

GFS boat race crew carried by the cox GE493, 1935.

EARLY BLACK AND WHITE ADVERTS

A Guinness a Day is Good For You

'Be careful with that Guinness', GE315, 1933.

'It's someone he knows', GE314, 1933.

'Someone is waiting for that Guinness', GE316, 1933.

'Underground escalator – when you're tired', 1936.

EARLY BLACK AND WHITE ADVERTS

Guinness Time

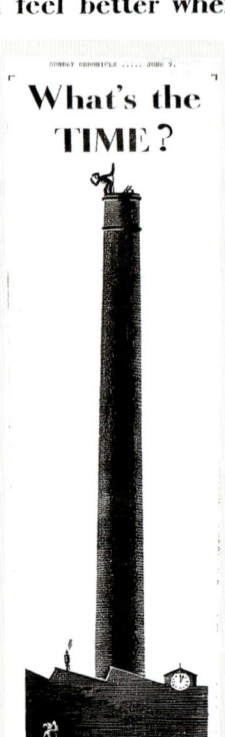

Even when an ostrich buries its head in the sand you still know it is an ostrich and nothing else.

Even if someone were to give you a glass of Guinness, having first removed the distinctive creamy head, you would know it was Guinness. If you hold it up to the light you can tell it by its deep rich colour, but the best, most unmistakable test of all is to taste it.

The invigorating strength of Guinness is as distinctive as its flavour: that is why people feel they've had something worth drinking when they've had a Guinness.

A golfing ostrich, 1934 and a depressed stork in two press adverts, 1935.

Have a glass of Guinness when you're Tired

GUINNESS FOR STRENGTH

Ostrich and zookeeper, GE547, 1935.

EARLY BLACK AND WHITE ADVERTS

Christmas

The sea lions used in a Christmas card by Gilroy.

'Spreading Christmas Tree', GE839, 1939.

Under the spreading Christmas tree
    A glass of Guinness stood.
Its strength and goodness, as you see,
    Does Father Christmas good.
And would it do the same for me?
    My Guinness — yes it would!

236

'Christmas is coming said the tortoise', Gilroy
GE665, 1936.

'My Goodness My Christmas Guinness'
GE747 Gilroy, 1937.

Two smiling glasses and a bottle, 1932.

Guinness and mistletoe – 'Who can resist … at Christmas?' GE133, 1930.

Father Christmas, 1934.

'Guinness is coming - Christmas is good for you' GE135, 1930.

Guinness Glasses

Guinness gets home

Doctors are recommending Guinness as a great tonic beverage with meals, as an aid to natural sleep. The widespread advertising campaigns are emphasizing this health value of Guinness.

The "home trade" in Guinness is thus soundly based—on the firm conviction of the public that—"Guinness is good for you."

GUINNESS IS GOOD FOR YOU

'Guinness gets home',
GE251, 1932.

GUINNESS IS GOOD FOR YOU

'Three glasses filling',
GE536, 1935.

EARLY BLACK AND WHITE ADVERTS

GIGFY and the glass theme

Finished 1930s ads probably not by Gilroy.

'How to find the ruby....', GE91, 1930.

'Three perfect things for Christmastime', GE63, 1929.

'Put your heads together', Two glasses and mistletoe, GE228, 1931.

240

Hand and Glass. 'Guinness is GOOD for you', GE533, 1935.

Man in the moon GE456, 1946.

FULL MOON

Chuckle, chuckle, through the night,
You are such a cheerful sight,
Up above the world so high,
Like a Guinness in the sky.

GUINNESS IS GOOD FOR YOU

But there's nothing like a Guinness Ark.

but there's nothing like a Guinness

241

15 Conclusion

CONCLUSION

So how does the discovery of this artwork change our perception of the artist? Gilroy came as close as any commercial artist has done, to achieving a form of proprietary rights to his Guinness art. Whilst he did not own the copyright, he did have some control as the preferential artist for the huge Guinness account. Apart from the very first black and white Guinness adverts using images of clock faces or glasses of Guinness, which Gilroy drew in abundance but were unsigned, from 1930 onwards he was the first artist to sign his work in the finished form. Benson and Guinness allowed him that recognition.

We now know more about how Guinness and Benson were interacting as client and agent, and how this clever artist interposed himself between them. We can see how Benson viewed his art from the comments made at the first point of review, notated in pencil on the canvases, which show us what was trying to be achieved visually. The great variety of shapes and layouts on the same theme shows the flexibility of imagery they were seeking. This was to fit the advertising site that the image was destined to fill, albeit a poster hoarding viewed either from left or right or magazine page with the centre fold either side.

It was always a mystery as to exactly how Guinness posters were taken through from concept to printed copy. Neither the Guinness archives in Scotland, which houses the Park Royal Brewery records and collection, nor the archives in Dublin; contain examples of final proof Gilroy adverts on canvas. They do contain the post 1950 Gilroy sketches and drawings on paper, but little older, pre-war material. Some of these drawings were then worked up into commercially accepted images and others died a natural death. So, where was the finished article of say the 'Sea lion at the Zoo' as artwork? The answer, we now know is that Benson retained them as a source of reference, since Guinness tended to keep reverting to tried and tested campaigns and imagery.

The Benson art room contained bundled up canvases by year and by campaign. Every canvas had a sticker attached, giving data on the artist, the year it was produced and what action to take post-presentation to Guinness. Canvases were often rolled into cardboard tubes and labelled accordingly. By 1971 when Benson was sold, the room contained forty-two years of Guinness advertising history. Guinness tended to have four different poster campaigns each year, making about 150 campaigns in total across that period. Very often, different configurations of an image were produced (portrait or landscape, left or right facing). Add in the images never used which number as many as those used, and it is possible that the archive contained about 1,000 Guinness items.

Where is all the original artwork for the plethora of magazine and newspaper adverts? By 1955, Guinness had used and code numbered about 2,500 different adverts. Again it must have been produced by Benson for supply to the Press. Was it then stored or simply discarded after use? There would have been large amounts of it, given the diversity of print advertising. None of it remains, unless there are future surprises to come from this source? The only advertising record that remains, is the advertising guard books held in the Guinness archives. Whilst not original artwork, there is a copy of each printed advert, together with date and print source detail typed across the base or top.

Historically, Guinness in Dublin and Park Royal had been rather casual when it came to retaining and conserving their advertising legacy. In 1969, when they withdrew the contract with Benson and went to J. Walter Thompson, they did not require Benson to transfer their archive to the new advertiser, or back to Guinness. Indeed over the years this treasure was forgotten by Guinness. Advertising managers came and went, all focused on the here and now. Pre-1986 there was no archive and no archivist employed to list and protect their legacy. Over the years, some advertising material either drifted out of the Brewery or was flood damaged in storage. Material had been stored randomly in cardboard boxes, without being listed or catalogued. It was kept in disused parts of the Brewery such as old hop stores or trade stores and basements. Luckily, a large quantity of marketing material has survived and been retained and is now available for the public to view in Dublin but not in Scotland. Guinness would never usually buy and certainly never sell off any of their advertising heritage. It is only because Benson held the Gilroy artwork in their store room, which has led to it being available to the public now. Before the discovery of these canvases, Gilroy artwork for Guinness was rarely on the market, and never oil on canvas.

These oil paintings were the costliest part of the whole poster production procedure. They consumed considerable studio time and materials. They appear not to have been framed ever, rather pinned to a wooden stretcher. The pin marks clearly show through the application of base paint. For storage they were simply cut out or unpinned from the stretcher and laid flat. We know they were not always completely oil dry when stored, as many canvases ended up stuck together. Bobby Bevan's father was an artist and he appreciated art. Is that why all these were done on canvas rather than cheaper card or board?

One of the fascinating features of the discovered pictures is the large amount of new images that were never commercially used. Not only have they not been used, but they have lain unknown by even Guinness for the last forty to sixty years. Who knew that Gilroy painted twelve classic American cars in 1939, for a World Trade Fair calendar in New York? Who has seen toucans flying past Mount Rushmore in South Dakota, USA or flying past Red Square in

CONCLUSION

Moscow? Did anyone know about lobsters in German helmets or Guinness and golf courses? To the famous zoo menagerie was added the rhino, gorilla, elephant, golden eagle, octopus, hippo, giraffe, zebra, orangutan, mandrill, and koala bear.

The flying formation of three toucans in front of a famous landmark tends to dominate many of these newly found canvases, with the earliest being assigned in 1936 to the German set. Given the flying toucans prolific usage by Gilroy in this collection of canvases, it is strange that the first commercially used flying toucan poster came much later in 1955, with the toucan flying past the Royal Air Force base. The evolution of the toucan image over twenty years is fascinating, as it has matured from a tall skinny serious standing bird with an over long beak, into a chubby smiling bird with a shorter fatter beak. The toucan was used first in 1935 as a standing bird in front of two glasses of Guinness together with the immortal Dorothy Sayers words. It was employed twice as a standing bird in 1953, as the toucan on the weathervane and the toucan opening the bottle with its beak. Later, in 1957 we get the two toucans standing in the nest, painted by Ray Tooby. The toucan was always present when Gilroy drew all the zoo animals together, but these menageries tend to be painted after 1955. So why did Gilroy use the three flying toucans so prolifically on the foreign canvases from 1936 if they were not used in the UK until 1955? It's quite a mystery? It also suggests that the single toucan canvas done as an illustration, which has no sticker and therefore has no year attached to it, probably dates from around 1956 – '58, towards the end of his time on the Guinness account when he was a freelance for Benson. If his involvement was not finishing, why would he offer up the secret of how to paint the toucan.

It is clear that around 1950, Guinness was looking at the export markets of Russia, Turkey, Greece and Israel, having seen sales growth stagnate in Europe. Gilroy was asked to re-work successful British posters for these markets, but they were never used. An abundance of American imagery was also commissioned from 1948 into the 1950s, but these American campaigns did not proceed. Instead, the growth came from in-country brewing of Foreign Guinness in Asia, the Caribbean and Africa. To support sales of the Foreign Stout, Guinness used many of the current posters from the UK market. Benson never seem to have been involved in Asian marketing.

Will we ever know how the Benson archive got sold off and to whom? I suspect we will, maybe as a result of this book. The original buyer wishes to remain very secretive, which is his right. Who this was, we can speculate about, based on there being three owners of Benson around 1971.

Benson, was a public listed company in some financial difficulty, whose major client, Guinness, had left them in 1969. They would have always harboured a hope that they could win the Guinness account back in the future so would they have sold their art history and store of creativity? Given the long and successful relationship between the two organisations, would Benson cash in on it by selling off their art heritage?

Ogilvy, was a prosperous and growing US agency, whose very birth had been financed partly by Bobby Bevan, the ex-MD of Benson. Ogilvy were by 1971 already working for Guinness in the US. If they had discovered and sold off the archive, one imagines Guinness would not have been at all appreciative.

Lord Rothschild's Investment company, RIT bought out Benson, sold off their valuable office leases and property, and then sold on the agency business as a going concern to Ogilvy. Could this have been how the art got sold, as just another asset? Rothschild had no reason to fear any consequences from Guinness from such a sale.

And why did the new owner of the archive wait forty years to get a return on his considerable investment? Why was the art stored in the UK after the sale and up until the present day? It possibly suggests a UK resident? Maybe like some collectors, he was just happy to own it stored away, or maybe over time he forgot he had it. Maybe he is rich enough not to worry about selling the archive. He has certainly been very cautious and only released the canvases at the rate at which they were selling, so as not to flood the market. There are still more canvases to come, which will be beyond the reach of this book, maybe another sixty to eighty, who knows? There are bound to be more surprises.

For as much Guinness poster advertising has been discovered, there is still a lot missing from this Benson collection, especially the earlier period, from 1929 to 1939. Was this the artwork that was damaged in storage and discarded? Or does this early artwork exist in someone's very private collection?

As for Gilroy's life, considering his talent, his prolific and brilliant output and its huge popularity, it is surprising that he lived quite modestly in the later part of his life. He was salaried for the period when he worked for Benson in the 1930s when he was at his most commercially creative. He would have earned nothing from repeat fees or merchandising. The copyright to the material was assigned to Benson, who in 1933 assigned it by letter to Guinness.

The life of an artist can be turbulent but he must have enjoyed periods of considerable prosperity. He rented one of the best houses in Queens Park, London, raised a family and sent his son to private school and then Cambridge University, He paid for his two children by marriage to go to good private schools, and Robin to Harrow School. This has laid the foundation for the grandchildren to enjoy the same private educational benefits and they are all prosperous. It is no coincidence that Jim Gilroy, his grandson, runs his own advertising agency. There is great affection for John's memory amongst the entire family.

CONCLUSION

He spent at least one day a week at the very select Garrick Club; membership of the Garrick is by invitation and would not come cheap, and I suspect his monthly bar bill would be healthy. Membership was free to him from the age of eighty.

Maybe he did not plan for reduced income and old age and spent the money as it became available. Overall I think he had a rich and varied life, full of friends, travel and good humour. He knew and painted the rich and famous, some of whom took him away on their travels or to their villas, so they could enjoy his wit, his storytelling and his company.

I certainly think he is underrated as a portrait painter, hence I have included a number of his works in the book. Did he charge his sitters enough for this work? For some he charged nothing. What would he have made of the selling off in America of his Guinness canvases for very good money? When one looks at other British contemporary artists, such as Hirst and Emin, Hockney, Vettriano and Rolf Harris, they are making an excellent living. This newly discovered Gilroy art is classic for its period and valuable, except to the deceased artist. At least we can now more fully appreciate his painted work, and some can now own an original and iconic piece of advertising history.

This is the first time the complete biography of Gilroy's life has been written, and we witness a man who used his wit, his skill and his considerable personality to create a lasting body of work that is widely acknowledged as being at the pinnacle of commercial art. For the first time in these pages we see the breadth of his imagination. I hope the book has raised people's awareness of Gilroy's considerable talent and will allow for a reappraisal of his art, both commercial and portraiture. Those who knew Gilroy found him entertaining and interesting. He had a good life, rich in experience and achievement. Yes, one can truly say that 'Gilroy was good for Guinness', and vice versa.

David Hughes

Bensons archive original oil on canvas artwork - Catalogue

Note that not all canvases are illustrated in the book

Picture description	Marketing Strapline	Year	S H Benson sticker code/artist/comment	Landscape or portrait	Page
Zoo Animals					
Polar Bear in pool and Zookeeper	My Goodness my Guinness	1938	GE/38/Gilroy/Print	Portrait	
Polar Bear in pool and Zookeeper	My Goodness my Guinness	1953	GE/53b/16/Gilroy/Submit	Portrait	
Polar Bear in pool on LHS and Zookeeper	My Goodness my Guinness	1949	GE/ JG/49/9/Submit	Landscape	111
Polar Bear in pool on LHS and Zookeeper	My Goodness my Guinness in Russian	1950	GER/50/10/JG/Hold	Portrait	
Polar Bear in pool on RHS and Zookeeper	My Goodness my Guinness	1949	GE/ JG/49/11g/Submit	Landscape	111
Lion chasing Zookeeper right to left	My Goodness my Guinness	1953	GE/53b/15/Gilroy/Submit	Portrait	
Lion chasing Zookeeper right to left	My Goodness my Guinness in Russian	1950	GER/50/11/JG/Hold	Landscape	
Lion chasing Zookeeper left to right	My Goodness my Guinness	1939	GE/39/05/Gilroy/Submit	Portrait	112
Bear up a pole and zookeeper right			Gilroy	Portrait	
Bear up a pole and zookeeper left	My Goodness my Guinness	1953	GE/53b/18/Gilroy/Submit	Portrait	99
Bear up a pole and zookeeper	My Goodness my Guinness in Russian	1950	GER/50/14/Gilroy/Hold	Portrait	
Crocodile and Zookeeper	My Goodness my Guinness	1953	GE/53b/17/Gilroy/Submit	Portrait	92
Crocodile and Zookeeper	My Goodness my Guinness	1948	GE/48/05/Gilroy	Portrait	
Crocodile and Zookeeper	My Goodness my Guinness in Russian	1950	GEX/50/09/JG/Hold	Landscape	
Crocodile and Zookeeper	My Goodness my Guinness in Hebrew	1950	GE/50/42d/JG/Hold	Landscape	
Zookeeper chasing sea lion right to left	My Goodness my Guinness	1953	GE/53b/20/Gilroy/Submit	Landscape	
Zookeeper chasing sea lion right to left	My Goodness my Guinness in Russian	1950	GER/50/06/JG/Hold	Landscape	
Zookeeper chasing seal lion left to right	My Goodness my Guinness	1946	GE/46/22/Gilroy/Submit	Landscape	95
Zookeeper chasing seal lion left to right	My Goodness my Guinness	1935	GE/35/22/Gilroy/Submit	Landscape	96
Ostrich and Zookeeper lhs	My Goodness my Guinness	1936	GE/36/23/Gilroy	Portrait	
Ostrich and Zookeeper lhs	My Goodness my Guinness (my Goodness in green)	1953	GE/53/14/JG/Submit	Portrait	108
Ostrich and Zookeeper rhs	My Goodness my Guinness	1953	GE/53b/13/Gilroy/Submit	Landscape	97
Ostrich and Zookeeper rhs	My Goodness my Guinness	1946	G/46/24/Gilroy/Submit	Landscape	97
Ostrich and Zookeeper dancing	Keeping Guinness Time		Gilroy /Faded sticker	Square	92
Kangaroo right and Zookeeper	My Goodness my Guinness	1952	GE/52/18/Gilroy/	Portrait	98
Kangaroo right and Zookeeper	My Goodness my Guinness in Russian	1950	GER/50/11/Gilroy/Hold	Portrait	
Kangaroo right and Zookeeper	My Goodness my Guinness in Hebrew	1950	GE/50/42e/Gilroy/Hold	Portrait	
Kangaroo left and Zookeeper	My Goodness my Guinness	1943	GE/43/11/Gilroy/Submit	Portrait	
Gnu to left and Zookeeper	"The new Gnu knew, Guinness is good for you"	1946	GE/46/13/Gilroy/Submit	Portrait	49
Gnu to left and Zookeeper	"The new Gnu knew, Guinness is good for you"	1952	GE/52/09b	Portrait	49
Gnu to left and Zookeeper	"As the new Gnu knew, very soon at the zoo, Guinness is good for you"		GE//Gilroy/Submit	Landscape	49
Gnu and Zookeeper in blue outline	"The new Gnu knew, very soon at the zoo, Guinness is good for you"	1946	GE/46 sketch/Gilroy/Draw up	Landscape	48
Gnu to right and Zookeeper on left	"As the new Gnu knew, very soon at the zoo, Guinness is good for you"		No sticker	Portrait	
Tortoise with Guinness glass on its back	Have a Guinness when you're tired	1936	GE/36/12/Gilroy/Submit	Portrait	109
Tortoise with Guinness glass on its back	Have a Guinness when you're tired	1946	G/46/25/Gilroy/Submit	Portrait	109
Pelican with seven pints in beak	My Goodness my Guinness	1939	GE/39/04/Gilroy/Submit	Portrait	104
Pelican with seven pints in beak	My Goodness my Guinness in Russian	1950	GER/50/12/Gilroy/Hold	Landscape	104
"Kinkajou right on a branch with glass, zookeeper"	"Just think what Kinkajou can do in pencil, MGMG"	1947	GE/47/15/Gilroy/Submit	Portrait	107
"Kinkajou left on a branch with glass, zookeeper"	"Just think what Kinkajou can do, MG reversed MG"	1948	GE/48/25/Gilroy/Hold	Portrait	107
Giraffe and Zookeeper	My Goodness my Guinness in Russian	1950	GER/50/13/Gilroy/Hold	Portrait	113
Zebra and Zookeeper	My Goodness my Guinness in Russian	1950	GER/50/07/Gilroy/Hold	Portrait	113
Elephant left and fat Zookeeper	My Goodness my Guinness in Hebrew	1950	GE/50/42c/Gilroy/Hold	Portrait	
Gorilla right and Zookeeper	My Goodness my Guinness	1939	GE/39/15/Gilroy/Hold	Portrait	94
Gorilla left and Zookeeper	My Goodness my Guinness	1948	GE/48/8/Gilroy/Submit	Portrait	
Orangutan right and Zookeeper	My Goodness my Guinness	1939	GE/39/18/Gilroy/Hold	Portrait	94
Orangutan left and Zookeeper	My Goodness my Guinness	1948	GE/48/7/Gilroy/Submit	Portrait	
Rhino looking left and zookeeper	My Goodness my Guinness	1948	GE/48/25b/Hold	Landscape	106
Rhino looking right and zookeeper	My Goodness my Guinness	1947	GE/47/13/Submit	Landscape	106

Elephant facing left and zookeeper with a bun	My Goodness my Guinness	1939	GE/39/17/Gilroy/Hold	Portrait	93
Elephant facing right and zookeeper riding	My Goodness my Guinness	1947	GE/47/12/Gilroy/Submit	Portrait	109
Elephant facing right and zookeeper small crowd	My Goodness my Guinness	1947	GE/47	Landscape	
Elephant facing left and zookeeper small crowd	My Goodness my Guinness	1947	GE/47/4/Gilroy/Submit	Landscape	
Mandrill on a rock and glass of Guinness	My Goodness my Guinness		Gilroy	Portrait	110
Golden Eagle on a stump and glass of Guinness	My Goodness my Guinness		Gilroy	Portrait	110

Fish, Shell fish

"Salmon, crab and lobster"	Bonte Devine. C'est le Guinness!		Export-France/Gilroy/Submit	Portrait	55
"Salmon, crab and lobster (in pencil-Old Neptune Free House)"	My Goodness Where's the Guinness		Presentation board/Gilroy/Submit	Portrait	55
Lobster and glass of Guinness	Lobsters love….. Guinness	1952	GE/52/16/Gilroy/Redraw	Portrait	121
Lobster and glass of Guinness	Lobsters love Guinness			Portrait	
Lobster in apron on beach and glass of Guinness	The Jolly Lobster - Guinness	ND	Presentation board/Lander/Submit	Portrait	122
Squid and Guinness glass	"Creatures of the deep agree, G goes down swimmingly"			Portrait	123
Octopus and Guinness glass	My Goodness my Guinness	1948	GE/48/28/Gilroy/Submit	Landscape	123
Whale and man in boat	My Goodness my Guinness in Hebrew	1950	GER/50/42b/Gilroy/Hold	Portrait	
Whale and man in boat	My Goodness my Guinness in Russian	1950	GER/50/05/Gilroy/Hold	Portrait	124
Galway Oyster Festival. Neptune at table	Pub menu board design		Kerry board/in-house artist/Proceed	Portrait	
"Tipperary Bar, EC4 Salmon crab and cucumber"	Pub menu board design unfinished		in-house artist	Portrait	
"Oliver St John Gogarty, Temple Bar. Salmon lobster"	Pub menu board design unfinished Guinness Irish stout		in-house artist	Portrait	

Guinness for Strength

Covent Garden porter carrying boxes of veg	Guinness for Strength	1938	GE/38/15/Gilroy/Redraw	Landscape	165
Rome- Roman breaking a column at the forum	Guinness per forza!		GE/export-sp/Gilroy/Archive	Portrait	70
Porter leaning on breaking column	Guinness for Strength	1952	GE/52/15/Gilroy/Redraw	Portrait	
Man carrying US Yale boat rowing crew R to L	Guinness for Strength	1939	GE/39/08/Gilroy/Submit	Portrait	
Man carrying US Yale boat rowing crew L to R	Guinness for Strength	1939		Portrait	
Man carrying boat rowing crew L to R	Guinness for Strength	1939		Portrait	
Man lifting old car to service	Guinness for Strength	1944	GE/44/17/Gilroy/Submit to censor	Portrait	74
Fisherman catching giant dark blue fish	Guinness for Strength	1953	GE/53/11/Gilroy/Redraw	Landscape	120
Fisherman and brown dog catching giant fish	Guinness for Strength			Landscape	
Fisherman and brown dog catching giant salmon	Guinness for Strength				120
Med Fisherman in boat catching giant green fish	Hebrew	1953	GE/53/32b/Gilroy/Submit	Landscape	120
5 Million sold every day man with bent girder	Guinness for Strength	1960	GA/60/14/Gilroy/Redraw	Portrait	81
Man carrying steel girder	Guinness for Strength	1934	GE/34/14/Gilroy/Submit	Landscape	82
Man carrying steel girder	Guinness for Strength		Gilroy no sticker	Portrait	48
Man carrying steel girder	Guinness for Strength		Gilroy	Landscape	82
Man pulling horse in cart going right	Guinness for Strength	1939	GE/39/19/Gilroy/Redraw	Portrait	79
Man pulling horse in cart going right	Guinness for Strength	1952	GE/523/12/Gilroy/Redraw	Portrait	79
Man pulling horse in cart going left	Guinness for Strength	1952	GE/52/22E/Submit	Portrait	66
Man pulling horse in cart going right	Guinness for Strength	1952	GE/52/22	Portrait	66
Man pulling horse in cart going right	Guinness for Strength in Hebrew	1952	GE/52/22	Portrait	79
Man pulling horse in cart going right	Guinness for Strength in Greek	1952	GE/52/22	Portrait	79
Man pulling horse in cart going left	Guinness for Strength in Russian	1952	GE/52/22	Portrait	79
Man carrying tree trunk	Guinness for Strength	1948	GE/48/05/Gilroy/Submit	Portrait	69
Man lifting steamroller	Guinness for Strength	1951	GE/51/09/Wilkinson/Submit	Portrait	68
Man lifting steamroller	Guinness for Strength	1952	Gilroy/Revise	Portrait	
Man lifting steamroller	Guinness for Strength in Greek	1952	Gilroy	Portrait	78

Man lifting steamroller	Guinness for Strength in Hebrew	1952	Gilroy	Portrait	78
Man lifting steamroller	Guinness for Strength in Russian	1952	GE/52/24/Gilroy	Portrait	78
Man carrying huge globe	I'd give the world for a Guinness Guinness for Strength	1934	GE/369A/Submit	Portrait	70
Man with wheelbarrow full of vegetables	Guinness for Strength	1944	GE/44/07/Gilroy/Submit	Portrait	
Man with wheelbarrow full of vegetables	Guinness for Strength	1938	GE/38/14	Portrait	77
Man with wheelbarrow full of vegetables	Hebrew writing	1952	GE/52/25/2i/Gilroy	Portrait	77
Man with wheelbarrow full of vegetables	Russian cyrillic writing	1952	GE/52/25/Gilroy	Portrait	78
Man with wheelbarrow full of vegetables	Greek writing	1952	GE/52/25/Gilroy	Portrait	78
Musician cutting cello in half	Guinness for Strength	1948	GE/48/11/Gilroy/Submit	Portrait	80
Man carrying huge scythe to left from cornfield	Guinness for Strength	1952	GE/52/16/Gilroy/Redraw	Portrait	75
Man carrying huge scythe to left sunset cornfield	Guinness for Strength	1952		Portrait	75
Man carrying huge scythe to left from field	Guinness for Strength Russian	1952	GE/52/23/Gilroy	Portrait	76
Man carrying huge scythe to right from cornfield	Guinness for Strength Greek	1952	GE/52/23/Gilroy	Portrait	76
Man carrying huge scythe to right from cornfield	Guinness for Strength Hebrew	1952	GE/52/23/Gilroy	Portrait	76
Toucans					
Toucan opening bottle with beak blue ground	Opening Time is Guinness Time		GE///Submit	Landscape	128
Toucan opening bottle with beak white ground	Opening Time is Guinness Time	1953	GE/53/30	Landscape	129
Toucan on weathervane looking left over town	Lovely day for a Guinness		GE/Toucan/5/Submit	Portrait	133
Toucan on weathervane looking right over town	Lovely day for a Guinness	1955	GE/55/17e/Gilroy/Submit	Portrait	128
Toucan on weathervane looking right over town	Lovely day for a Guinness	1955	GE/55/17c/Gilroy/Submit	Landscape	127
Toucan on weathervane looking left over countryside	Lovely day for a Guinness	1955	GE/55/17d/Gilroy/Submit	Landscape	127
Toucan standing with two pints on its beak	If he can say as you can	ND	Toucan/Gilroy/Redraw	Landscape	129
Toucan standing in front of two pints Guinness word at top	If he can say as you can	1935	GE/35/1/Gilroy DS/Print	Portrait	
Toucan standing in front of two pints	If he can say as you can	1935	GE/Pos.35/Gilroy DLS/Develop	Portrait	133
Toucans flying over RAF base	Lovely Day for a Guinness	1955	GE/55/10/Gilroy/Print	Landscape	181
Two toucans in nest with two Guinness	Toucans in their nests agree GIGFY	1950	G/HP/50/06/Gilroy/Present	Portrait	130
Single flying toucan	Instruction piece to Benson drawing room artists	c1955	None	Landscape	57

Cars

World Trade Fair Flushing Meadows NY calendar cover	Enjoy Guinness all year round	1939	Export/Gilroy/Hold	Portrait	135
January 1939 Chrysler CL Phaeton 1933	Nice day for a Guinness	1939	Export/Gilroy/Hold	Landscape	135
February 1939 Cadillac 452 Imperial V-16 1931	Always time for a Guinness	1939	Export/Gilroy/Hold	Landscape	136
March 1939 Auburn 851 Cabriolet 1935	Make mine a Guinness	1939	Export/Gilroy/Hold	Landscape	136
April 1939 Cadillac V-12 Coupe 1933	Time for a Guinness	1939	Export/Gilroy/Hold	Landscape	139
May 1939 Packard 443 Roadster 1928	Drink Guinness	1939	Export/Gilroy/Hold	Landscape	139
June 1939 Lincoln V-8 Pharton 1928	I'd rather have a Guinness	1939	Export/Gilroy/Hold	Landscape	138
July 1939 Packard 640 Roadster 1929	Always time for a Guinness	1939	Export/Gilroy/Hold	Landscape	138
August 1939 Marquette Phaeton 1930	Drink Guinness	1939	Export/Gilroy/Hold	Landscape	139
September 1939 Auburn V-12 Boat tail Speedster 1935	Guinness for Strength	1939	Export/Gilroy/Hold	Landscape	139
October 1939 Cadillac V-12 Sedan 1933	Make mine a Guinness	1939	Export/Gilroy/Hold	Landscape	140
November 1939 Chrysler Airflow 1934	Guinness	1939	Export/Gilroy/Hold	Landscape	140
December 1939 Cord 812 SC Coupe 1937	Time for a Guinness	1939	Export/Gilroy/Hold	Landscape	141
Earls Court Motor Show 1948 The new Morris Minor	Drink Guinness	1948	R. Clifford	Square	142
Earls Court Motor Show 1948 The Land Rover	Guinness for Strength	1948	R. Clifford	Square	143
Earls Court Motor Show 1948 Rover P3	Time for a Guinness	1948	GE/13/48/R Clifford/Submit	Landscape	143
Earls Court Motor Show 1948 Bentley 8 short chasis	Time for a Guinness	1948	R. Clifford	Landscape	146
Earls Court Motor Show 1948 Jaguar XK120	Guinness time	1948	R. Clifford	Landscape	146

Earls Court Motor Show 1948 Ford V8 Pilot	Any colour so long as it's black! Guinness	1948	R. Clifford	Landscape	150
Rolls Royce Phantom III Labourdette Vutotal Cabriolet 1947	The taste of Luxury. Guinness		Motor sport 4/PH/Revise	Square	144
Jaguar XK150 1950	One of life's luxuries Guinness		Motor sport 3/PH/Revise	Square	144
Bentley MKVI drophead Coupe	Always time for a Guinness	1952	GE/52/03/R Clifford/Submit	Landscape	145
Rolls Royce Silver Dawn 1953	Guinness- The best!	1953	GE/53/16/R Clifford/Submit	Landscape	145
February 1936 4.25L Bentley Tourer	Drink Guinness		RC	Landscape	147
April 1935 Derby Bentley 3.5L Saloon	Time for a Guinness		RC	Landscape	149
May 1938 Van Den Plas- Bentley Tourer	I'd rather have a Guinness		PH	Landscape	147
August 1928 4.5L Bentley Tourer	Time for a Guinness		PH	Landscape	148
October 1937 Bentley Convertible	Guinness for Strength		RC	Landscape	148
November 1953 Bentley saloon	Make mine a Guinness		RC	Landscape	149
January Marmon V16 Town Car	Have a guinness at ….	1950	50 Calendar/Gilroy/Submit	Landscape	151
February Cadillac V16 Town car	Time for a Guinness	1950	50 Calendar/Gilroy/Submit	Landscape	151
March Rolls Royce Silver Ghost	Time for a Guinness	1950	50 Calendar/Gilroy/Submit	Landscape	152
April Packard V12	Nice day for a Guinness	1950	50 Calendar/Gilroy/Submit	Landscape	152
May Cord 812 Phaeton	Always time for a Guinness	1950	50 Calendar/Gilroy/Submit	Landscape	153
June Isotta- Fraschini Tipo 8A	Enjoy a Guinness	1950	50 Calendar/Gilroy/Submit	Landscape	153
July Duesenberg Torpedo	Time for a Guinness	1950	50 Calendar/Gilroy/Submit	Landscape	154
August Bugatti 57C Aravis	Time for a Guinness	1950	50 Calendar/Gilroy/Submit	Landscape	154
September Stutz 'BB' Tourer	Enjoy a Guinness	1950	50 Calendar/Gilroy/Submit	Landscape	155
October Speed Six Bentley	Nice day for a Guinness	1950	50 Calendar/Gilroy/Submit	Landscape	155
November Isotta Fraschini type 8	Drink Guinness	1950	50 Calendar/Gilroy/Submit	Landscape	156
December Chrysler Imperial CG Limousine	Time for a Guinness	1950	50 Calendar/Gilroy/Submit	Landscape	157
Mercedes Benz 150 Deutsches Kraftwagen 50 Jahre	Gluckwantsche von Guinness	1935	St James gate/export/35/Gilroy/Review	Landscape	174
Mercedes Benz G4 Deutsches Kraftwagen 50 Jahre	Gluckwantsche von Guinness	1935	St James gate/export/35/Gilroy/Review	Landscape	172
Kleines Auto- Mercedes Benz 170H	Grosses bier! Guinness	1935	St James gate/export/35/Gilroy/Review	Portrait	173
VolksWagen 1936	Volks bier! Guinness	1935	St James gate/export/35/Gilroy/Review	Portrait	173
Mercedes Benz 540K Deutsches Kraftwagen 50 Jahre	Gluckwantsche von Guinness	1935	St James gate/export/35/Gilroy/Review	Landscape	174
Mercedes Benz 770K Deutsches Kraftwagen 50 Jahre	Gluckwantsche von Guinness	1935	St James gate/export/35/Gilroy/Review	Landscape	175

Countries

Italy-Toucans fly over Leaning Tower of Pisa	It's Arrived Guinness	1947	GE/47/04/Gilroy/Redraw	Portrait	191
Venice- gondalier and toucans on Grand Canal	Guinness has arrived! E Arrivato!	1949	GE/49/11/Gilroy/Submit	Landscape	192
"Venice- gondalier and toucans on Grand Canal, incomplete "	Guinness has arrived! Essere Arrivato!	1949	Gilroy	Landscape	192
"USA- Toucans over Golden Gate Bridge, fisherman in boat"	It's Arrived! Draught Guinness	1948	GE/48/17/Gilroy/Submit	Landscape	184
"USA- Toucans over Golden Gate Bridge, Policeman"	It's Arrived! Guinness	1948	GE/48/17/Gilroy/Submit	Portrait	184
"USA- Toucans over Golden Gate Bridge, no Policeman"	It's Arrived! Guinness	1949	GE/49/06/Gilroy/Revise	Landscape	187
USA- Toucans over American Flag	It's Arrived! Guinness	1950	GE/50/18/Gilroy/Submit	Portrait	189
USA- Uncle Sam holding Guinness glass	Your country needs Guinness	1950	Gilroy/50/17/Submit	Portrait	190
USA- Older Uncle Sam holding Guinness glass	Your country needs Guinness		ES Export/Gilroy/Submit	Portrait	190
USA- Toucans over Statue of Liberty	It's arrived! Guinness	1949	GE/49/08/Gilroy/Revise	Square	187
USA- Toucans flying past the Statue of Liberty	It's arrived! Guinness	1950	GE/50/15/Gilroy/Submit	Portrait	188
USA- Toucans over Chrysler Building and cop	Guinness	1947	GE3/47/7/Submit	Portrait	183
USA- Toucans over Empire State Building	Lovely day for a Guinness	1947	GE3/47/4/Submit	Portrait	183
USA- Toucans past erect Empire State Building	It's arrived! Guinness	1950	GE/50/19	Portrait	188
USA- Toucans flying left over Monument					

Description	Caption	Year	Code	Orientation	Page
Valley with a cowboy USA- Toucans flying right over Monument Valley with a cowboy	Guinness across the nation! (lower case)	1952	GE/52/04/Gilroy/US Submit	Landscape	185
	Guinness across the nation! (upper case)	1949	GE/49/04/Revise	Landscape	185
USA- Toucans fly over Mt Rushmore	Across the nation. Draught Guinness	1952	GE/52/03/Gilroy/US Submit	Landscape	186
USA- Toucans fly over Mt Rushmore (blueish)	It's Arrived! Guinness	1949	Gilroy/Revise	Landscape	186
USA-Toucans Brooklyn Bridge & policeman	Coming soon… Draught Guinness	1947	GE3/47/3/Gilroy/Submit	Square	184
Moscow- Toucans Fly Over Red Square Church with Cossack right	(written in Cyrillic) Guinness It's arrived	1952	GE/52/13/Gilroy/Redraw	Portrait	193
Moscow- Toucans Fly past Russian Church with Cossack left	(written in Cyrillic) Guinness It's arrived		Gilroy	Portrait	193
Moscow- Toucans Fly Over Kremlin Wall Red Square two men left	(written in Cyrillic) Guinness for Strength		Gilroy	Landscape	193
London- Toucans over Tower Bridge with running man	Lovely day for a Guinness	1950	G/HP/50/1/Present	Landscape	164
London- Toucans over St Pauls with Bishop	My Goodness my Guinness	1950	G/HP/50/3/Present	Landscape	164
London- Toucans over Nelsons Column	England expects- Guinness	1950	G/HP/50/2/Present	Portrait	165
Germany- Toucans and Bismark Statue	Es ist Angekommen! Guinness	1936	St JG/ export/Gilroy/Submit	Portrait	167
Germany- Toucans and Olympic stadium	Es ist Angekommen! Guinness	1936	St JG/ export/Gilroy/Submit	Portrait	168
Germany- Toucans going R-L Brandenburg Gate and officer	Meine Gute! Guinness	1936	St JG/ export/Gilroy/Submit	Portrait	167
Germany- Toucans going L-R Brandenburg Gate and soldier	Es ist Angekommen! Guinness	1936	St JG/ export/Gilroy/Submit	Portrait	
Germany- German soldier holding glass	Es ist Zeit fur ein Guinness	1936	St JG/ export/Gilroy/Submit	Portrait	168
Germany- mechanic lifting half track	Fur Starke- Guinness	1936	St JG/ export/Gilroy/Submit	Landscape	169
Germany- Toucans flying by Zepplin airship	Meine Gute! Guinness	1936	St JG/ export/Gilroy/Submit	Landscape	169
Germany- Toucans Schloss Neuschwanstein	Sie Angekommen! Guinness	1936	St JG/ export/Gilroy/Consult	Portrait	171
Israel-Toucans over Jerusalem City Wall with Jew	Hebrew writing- Lachaim Guinness		Gilroy	Landscape	194
Paris- Toucans flying over leaning Eiffel Tower flag with Gendarme	C'est arrivee! (in red) Guinness (De Gaulle sketch)		Gilroy	Portrait	191
"Paris- Toucans flying over Eiffel Tower streamer, with Gendarme"	C'est arrivee! (in black) Guinness	1953	GE/F/53/6/Submit	Portrait	191
Nigeria- red train and Mt Kilimanjaro	For a refreshing change - Drink Guinness!	1949	GE/49/17/Clifford	Landscape	195

Wartime

Description	Caption	Year	Code	Orientation	Page
Man carrying bomb to bomber. Berlin or bust!	Guinness for Strength	1944	GE/44/Gilroy/Submit to censor	Portrait	176
Man carrying torpedo to submarine over plank	Guinness for Strength	1944	GE/44/Gilroy/Submit to censor	Landscape	176
Spitfire diving right towards a mechanic	My Goodness my Guinness	1942	GE/42/17/Gilroy/Submit to censor	Portrait	178
Spitfire diving left towards a mechanic	My Goodness my Guinness	1942	Gilroy	Portrait	178
Sailor sitting on a torpedo moving left to right	My Goodness my Guinness	1942	GE/42/13/Submit to censor	Landscape	182
Sailor sitting on a torpedo moving right to left	My Goodness my Guinness	1944	GE/44/19/Gilroy/Submit to censor	Landscape	182
Man carrying huge gun barrel across plank	Guinness for Strength	1943	GE/43/26/Gilroy/Submit to censor	Landscape	179
Man bombing up a Lancaster Bomber	Guinness for Strength	1944	GE/44/Gilroy/Submit to censor	Landscape	177
Aircraft Carrier with painters	I feel like a Guinness …I wish you were	1944	GE/44/15/Gilroy/Submit to Censor	Portrait	180
Detail of painters on Aircraft Carrier	I feel like a Guinness …I wish you were		Gilroy	Portrait	180
Man loading large ordinance onto a trolley	Guinness for Strength (comment about 'red tips too suggestive')	1940	GE/40/5/Gilroy/Submit to Censor	Portrait	177
Man lifting a tank with one hand (unfinished)	Guinness for Strength		Gilroy	Landscape	178
Sailor with fruit	Now I feel I need a Guinness	1949	GE/49/14/Gilroy/Submit	Portrait	181

Guinness Time

Description	Caption	Year	Code	Orientation	Page
Smiley clock face	10 to 1 its Guinness time	1931	GE/31/11/Gilroy/Submit	Portrait	214
Smiley clock face and hops at base	"Ten to one, it's Guinness time "	1931	GE/31/11/Gilroy/Redraw	Portrait	214
Clock and oysters crying	Guinness time cried the oysters	1936	GE/36/145/Gilroy/Submit	Portrait	214

Golf courses

Description	Caption	Year	Code	Orientation	Page
Gleneagles The Kings Course 16th hole	A round with Guinness	1950	Golf Club/GE/50/12/Gilroy/Submit	Portrait	217

Royal Lytham and St Anne's Golf Club	A round with Guinness	1950	Golf Club/GE/50/15/Gilroy/Submit	Portrait	217
Wentworth Golf Club	Time for a Guinness	1950	Golf Club/GE/50/11/Gilroy/Submit	Portrait	217
Carnoustie Golf Club	Good day for a Guinness	1950	Golf Club/GE/50/14/Gilroy/Submit	Portrait	217
Putting at Caesaria Golf Club	Guinness available everywhere! Hebrew	ND		Landscape	218
Golfer Royal Portrush Co Antrim Golf course	Relax with Guinness	ND	St James Gate/W Brearley/Proceed	Portrait	218
Golfer Ballybunion Co Kerry Golf Course	Enjoy a round with Guinness	ND	St James Gate/W Brearley/Proceed	Portrait	218

Smiling Glasses

Two smiling glasses and a pouring bottle	Two heads are better than one		Gilroy/Submit	Portrait	210
"Two glasses glum and smiling, pouring bottle from right"	Two heads are better than one		Two heads/6/Gilroy/Submit	Portrait	211
"Two glasses glum and smiling, pouring bottle from right"	Two heads are better than one		GE/TH/Gilroy	Portrait	210
Two smiling glasses and a pouring bottle from top	Two heads are better than one		Two heads/8/Gilroy/Submit	Portrait	210
Two smiling glasses and a pouring bottle from top	Two heads are better than one		GE/TH/Gilroy	Portrait	
Two smiling glasses and a hand	Two heads are better than one		Two heads/7/Gilroy/Submit	Portrait	210
Two glasses one only smiling and a pouring bottle	Two heads are better than one. Green and red writing		Gilroy/Submit	Portrait	
Two smiling glasses and a pouring bottle and hand	Two heads are better than one		Two heads/5/Gilroy/Submit	Portrait	210
Two smiling glasses and a pouring bottle and hand	Two heads are better than one		GE/TH/08/Submit		
Two smiling glasses and two hands	Two heads are better than one		Two heads/4/Gilroy/Submit	Portrait	211
Two smiling glasses and two hands	Two heads are better than one		GE/TH/Gilroy	Portrait	
Two smiling glasses	Two heads are better than one		Two heads/3/Gilroy/Submit	Portrait	210
Two smiling glasses	Two heads are better than one		GE/TH/Gilroy	Portrait	
Hand reaching for two smiley Guinness glasses	Don't look now but I think were being swallowed	1947	GE/47/06/Gilroy/Redraw	Square	209
Smiling glass sipping Guinness drops from a bottle	There's nothing like a Guinness	1938	GE/38/02/Gilroy/Submit	Portrait	209

Generic

Man cutting topiary	Lovely day for a Guinness	1956	Tom Eckersley	Portrait	
Guinness bottle with neck label	Think Big! Guinness goes home better in a bigger bottle	1951	GE/51/36/Eckersley/Submit	Portrait	
Single smiley goblet glass -Hop barley border	Thirst lesson in Irish - Gaelic Is Fearrde tú Guinness GIGFY	1946	GE/46/33/Gilroy/Proceed	Portrait	213
Full and MT glass -Hop barley border	Russian	1946	GE/46/32/Gilroy/Proceed	Portrait	213
Single smiley glass	UNMISTAKABLE - Guinness is Good for You	1937	GE/37/10/Gilroy/Redraw	Landscape	212
Knight on RHS in helmet with glass facing left	Opening Time Guinness Time	1956	G/56/07/Lander/Revise	Portrait	220
Knight on RHS in helmet with glass facing left	Opening Time Guinness Time (green words Opening Time)	1936?	GE3/36/a/Lander	Portrait	220
French Knight on LHS in helmet with glass	Le temps d'ouverture est le temps de Guinness (green words)			Portrait	220
French Knight on LHS in helmet with glass	Le temps du debut est temps pour Guinness (green words)	1957	GE/57/17/Lander/Submit	Portrait	220 221
Italian Knight on RHS in helmet with glass	Il tempo di apertura e tempo di Guinness (green words)	1957	GE/57/18/Lander/Submit	Portrait	221
Seven Guinness Pints	A Guinness a day	1932	GE/32/01/Gilroy/Submit	Landscape	212
Hand reaching for a glass	Reach for a Guinness ('too soviet looking')	1939	GE/39/Brearley/Redraw	Square	209
Steam shovel grabbing Guinness	My Goodness my Guinness	1938	GE/38/07/Gilroy/Submit	Portrait	219
Eagle Brand Special Export Quality	Machen & Hudson Liverpool	1923	Export - GE/23/1/38/in-house artist/Submit	Portrait	42
Speakman brand Melbourne Australia	Guinness's Export Stout	1918	G/18/36.83.A4	Landscape	42
Stork brand Extra Guinness Stout	C Stone & Co London	1918	GE/18/36.83.02/	Portrait	43
Guinness Stout Vat brand	"J. S. Woodfield, Liverpool"	1918	GE/18/36.82.13/	Portrait	43
Probyns Guinness Stout Argus Brand	Probyn London	1918	GE/18/36.82.14b	Portrait	43
Guinness & Cos Extra Stout. Hops and barley wreath	In Bottle Guinness bottling plant Park Royal	1936	GE/B/36.70.18	Landscape	

Dogs Head brand Bass & Guinness Man seated on crate					
Burkes Dublin bottled Guinness Stout Lobster salad	The Old'uns advice is right		Read Bros London- unknown artist	Square	42
	An appetising digestive beverage E&J Burke Dublin	1932	GE/32/i4/Brearley/Revise	Landscape	
Burkes bottled Guinness Stout. Ships and airship	Above all be sure it's Burkes E&J Burke Dublin		Unknown artist	Landscape	42
La Battaille de Hastings 1066	French spoof on the Bayeaux Tapestry	1966	GE/66//in-house artist/Consult	Landscape	222
La Battaille de Hastings 1066	French spoof on the Bayeaux Tapestry	1966	GE/66//in-house artist/Consult	Landscape	223
La Battaglia di Hastings 1066	Italian spoof on the Bayeaux Tapestry	1966	GE/66/09/in-house artist/Consult	Landscape	
Battle of Hastings 1066. Bottle of Guinness 1966	Spoof on the Bayeaux Tapestry	1966	Export- France/in-house artist/Submit to client	Landscape	
Fisherman in overloaded boat	Now I feel I've earned a Guinness	1949	GE/49/21/Gilroy/Submit	Portrait	125
Coronation. Zookeeper lifting animals on a bench	My Goodness My Guinness	1952?	GE/ /Gilroy/Submit	Portrait	163
Guardsman with pint in busby	Lovely day for a Guinness	1951	GE/51/12/Lander/Submit	Portrait	

Christmas
Santa & animals trimming tree with bottles	Guinness Time	1937	GE/T377/Gilroy/Redraw	Portrait	
Santa & animals trimming tree with labelled bottles	Guinness Time	1949	GE/49/16/Gilroy/Submit	Portrait	215
Guinness bottle in stocking and man in bed	My Goodness My Christmas Guinness	1952	GE/52/28/Gilroy/Submit	Portrait	215

Olympics 1948 London
Pole-vaulter	My Goodness My Guinness	1947	GE/Olys/47/8/Gilroy	Portrait	162
Toucans flying past rings	Guinness	1947	GE/Olym/47/7/Gilroy	Portrait	159
Runner	My Goodness My Guinness	1947	GE/Olym/47/11/Gilroy	Landscape	161
Weightlifter	Drink Guinness for Strength	1947	GE/Olym/47/9/Gilroy	Landscape	160
Javelin thrower	Guinness for Strength	1947	GE/Olym/47/12/Gilroy	Portrait	162

Index

Canvases in bold print

A

129 Kingsway. Holborn   3, 39, 45
1st Lord Iveagh   31, 33, 39, 55, 62
A E Mason   26
A G Bryant   26
A Guinness a day   212, 233
A K Lawrence   9, 10
A P Herbert,   40
A R (Tommy) Thompson   25, 27, 29
Air Chief Marshal Sir Hugh Constantine   18, 19
Aircraft Carrier   180
Airman loading a Lancaster bomber   176, 177
Alan Wood   3, 55, 60
Alexander de Karlowski   40
Alexander Fleming   25
Alice Doctors Book   85
Alice in Wonderland   43, 61, 228, 230
aluminium plates   50
Ampney St Peter, Gloucestershire   19
Anderson Hewitt   45
Andrews' Liver Salts,   39
Animals at the seaside   101
Animals in tug of war with the zoo keeper   100, 101
animals outside St James's Gate   100
Anna Morgan   20
Annigoni   30
antelope and the hippo   94
Anthony d'Offay,   40
Anthony Powell   40
Armstrong College Art School   9
Arthur Ransome   27
Attorney for Western Electric (Canada)   27
Auburn   136, 139
Augustus John   27, 29, 30
Austin Cars   11
Austin Reed Ltd   16
Avenue Studios, Sydney Close, London SW3   12, 27

B

B. Heckstall-Smith and Wm.McMeek   40
Baker-Baker girls   27
Ballybunion   218
Bandsman   67, 80
Barbara Hepworth   10
Barber   197
Baron (Charley) Janssen, Belgian banker   31
Battersea Park   59
Battle of Hastings   222, 223
BEA   59
bear up a pole   44, 99
Beechams   45
Ben Newbold the Deputy Managing Director   39
Benjamin Britten   40
Bentley   145, 146, 147, 148, 149, 155
Berlin Olympic stadium   168
Bertram Mills Circus   95
Beth Chatto   40
Bicentenary   62, 63, 87
Big Blue Whale   124
Bill Gillie   14
Billposters   52
Bismarck Statue in Hamburg   167
boat race crew carried by the cox   232

Bottle Royal   85
Bovril   11, 39, 40
boxer   26, 206
Boxted House, Boxted, Suffolk   40, 41
Brandenburg Gate, Berlin   167
Brendan Bracken   28
Brendan Nolan   60
Brian Sibley   3, 5, 20
British Institute Scholarship for decorative painting   10
British Naval Intelligence   40, 45
Brooklyn Bridge, New York   184
Buckingham Palace   18
Bugatti   154
Burlington House   29

C

Cadillac   136, 137, 140, 151
Caesarea Golf Club in Israel   218
Café Royal ballads   26
calendar   135, 145, 151, 159, 217, 244
Camberwell School of Art   10
Camel and seal   101
camouflaged gun emplacement   181
Canada Club dinner   30
Canada visit   28
Carnoustie   217
Casterton Boarding school in the Lake District   14
CBS   28
Cedric Morris,   40
Centenary Exhibition 1998   20
Chairman of the Works of Art Committee, Garrick   16, 17
Charles Cundall   25
Charles Dickens   27
Charlie Moore   55, 60
Chelsea Arts Club   25, 29, 30
Chelsea studio   13, 14, 27
Cheltenham   12, 27
Cheltenham College   12
Chessington Zoo   103
Chris Chataway,   116
Christ Church College, Oxford   40
Christie Scholarship   9
Christies Auctions   20, 103
Christmas   4, 9, 25, 50, 54, 61, 63, 69, 207, 208, 211, 215, 236, 237, 238
Chrysler   135, 140, 157
Chrysler Building   183
Churchill   5, 12, 27, 28, 30, 32, 33, 74
Churchill College Cambridge   32
Clarence House   31
classic cars   41, 135, 144, 151, 244
Cleaning Big Ben   232
Clementine Churchill   27
Col. Harvey QC   29
Coleman's mustard   39
Colonel Harry Morritt   10
Commandant Dominé   40
Commanding Officer Colonel Hugh Davies   30
Commercial TV   58
Cord   141, 153
Coronation of Queen Elizabeth II   163
Coronation poster   102
Countess Miranda Iveagh   62
Court Denny   40
Crazy Gang as the zookeeper   58

Cresswell Gardens London   16
crocodile   86, 91, 98

D

Dancing ostrich and zookeeper   92
Dangerfield Printing Co   52
David Jagger   30
David Ogilvy   41, 45
David Tatham   19
Deputy Chief of Naval Information   40
Derby Day June 1967   17
Des O'Brien   116
Devonshire Place, Belgravia   14
Dig for Victory   27, 77
Diploma in Decorative Painting   9
Director of General Production at the Ministry of Information   40
Doctor Roland Bramley   14
Dod Osbourne   27
Donald Sinden   17
Donkey   79, 202
Dorothy Gilroy nee Tilley   29
Dorothy L Sayers   11, 39, 40
Dr. Breen   26
Dr. Cyril James, the Principal of T E McGill University   28
Dr. Thomen Agency of the Ambassador Dominion Republic   29
Duesenberg   154
Duke of Northumberland   22
Dyson Smith   27
Dyson Smith the Sculptor   25

E

E & J Burke of Dublin   39
Earls Court Motor Show in London   135, 142, 143, 151
Edward Guinness   3, 19, 61
Edward Heath   33
Eiffel Tower, Paris   191
Elephant and zookeeper   88, 89, 93
Elizabeth Bramley   14
Elizabeth Gilroy nee Bramley   14
Empire State Building   183, 188
English Trade   54
enormous gun barrel   179
Eperco Advertising Agency   32
Epstein, the great sculptor   30
Ernest Saunders   3, 19
Esme Jeudwine   13, 28
Evening Standard   25
Evening Star newspaper   28

F

Farmer carrying a flock of sheep   118
farmer with a giant scythe   75
Farmleigh   6
Fellow of the Royal Society of Arts   10
Fenham Barracks   9
Ferdinand Porsche   173
Ferrari 250 GTE   6
Festival Clocks of 1951   214
Fifty years of German car invention   172
Fine Art Society in Bond Street   27
Fiona Gilroy nee Keville   18
Fisherman catching a giant fish   119

INDEX

fisherman in an overloaded boat   125
Five million Guinness   82
Fleet Street   39, 55
Flora Line   27
flying toucan   131, 164
footballers   202
Ford   150
Foreign Stout   183, 244
France   9, 40, 76, 191
Francis Bacon   40
Francis Ogilvy   41, 45
190. Frank Hodge   27
Frank Reynolds   25
Frank Reynolds the editor of Punch Magazine   27
Frederick Gore,   40
Freeman of the City of London   16
French Navy   40

G

Gallup   45
Garrick Club   15, 16, 17, 19, 22, 26, 59, 60, 66, 245
General Younger   30
George Formby   9
George Hotel Vancouver   28
George Robey   9
George Wrigglesworth   59
Germany   27, 86, 167, 170
Giant Bottle as bridge support   83
Gilbert & George   40
Gilbert Hughes   45
Gilroy animal Guinness Festival clocks   59
Ginger Ale   32
Giraffe   102
girder man   48, 81, 160, 176, 179
Gleneagles   217
gnu   48, 49
Goering   174
Golden eagle   110
Golden gate Bridge   184, 187
Golf Courses   218
gondoliers in Venice   192
gorilla   94
Grace Morritt   26
Graf Zeppelin Airship   169
Great Depression   44
Green Room Club for Actors, Dover Street   25
Greenwich Naval College   32
Greenwich Village artists   27
Greta Bridge   12, 26, 27
Guinness and Oysters   214
Guinness display service   52
Guinness family   5, 55, 86
Guinness for Christmas   54
Guinness for Strength campaigns   12
Guinness Time   14, 43, 54, 62, 214, 220, 234
Guinness Time   4, 89, 102, 199, 214, 215, 232
Guinness Time clock in Piccadilly   59
Guinness Time magazine   31, 54, 61, 62, 63
Gwendoline Peri Short   10

H

H M The Queen Elizabeth   18
Half Track   169
Harold Paton   40
Harp Lager Company   3, 60
Harp magazine   63

Harry Carpenter, the boxer   26
Harry Houdini   9
Headlines   12
Heaton Park Road Upper School   9
Henry Birks   28
Henry Carr   10
Henry Moore   10
Hewitt, Ogilvy, Benson & Mather   45
hippo   94, 102, 108
History of Advertising Trust   3, 20
Hitler   172, 173, 174, 175
HMS Ellington   40
Holland Park   7, 13, 14, 15, 18, 19, 22, 23, 30, 31
Home Secretary Lord Brooke   30
honorarium   58
horse and cart   29, 44, 59
House of Commons   164, 165
Hugh de Quetteville   3, 55
Hugh MacLennan   15
Humpty Dumpty   228
Hyde Park Road, Kew Gardens   12
Hydraulic Engineering Co.   11

I

Illingworth the cartoonist   30
Imperial Tobacco   11
Independent Export Bottlers   42
Ischia, Southern Italy   16
Isotta- Fraschini   153, 156
Israel   68, 76, 77, 79, 120, 194, 218, 244
Italy   9, 10, 16, 25, 191

J

J. H. Taylor   25
J. S. Woodfield of Liverpool   39
J Walter Thompson   45, 243
J. Walter Thompson
J.Samuel White, Cowes   40
Jacob Rothschild Investment Trust (RIT)   45, 244
Jaguar   144, 146
James Blackmore   66
James Cameron   59
James Montgomery Flagg'   190
Japan Drier   48
javelin thrower   162
Jenefer Bramley   14, 15, 19
Jim Gilroy   3, 4, 7, 245
Jim Shanklin   116
John Armstrong   40
John Dykes the lawyer   26
John Gathorne-Hardy   40
John Hatch from Lazzards   58
John Morritt Gilroy   10
John Nash   40, 41
John Ranson   116
John Waddington Ltd of Leeds   51
John William Gilroy   9
Johnnie Walker   11, 40
Johnnie Walker
Johnson, commercial artist   92, 99
Joseph Stalin   5
juggler   201

K

kangaroo   86
Keith Egleston   55

Kenneth Moore   17, 66
Kiku   13
King Victor Emmanuel   10
Kings Royal Hussars at Tidworth Barracks   30
Kingsway Hall, Kingsway   39, 45
kinkajou   107
knight in armour   220
Koala bear   89
Kremlin wall, Red Square, Moscow   193

L

Lady Constantine   19
Lady Iveagh   31
Lady Partridge   14, 15, 19
Land Rover   143
Lander   122, 220
Lazards Bank   45, 58
Leaning Tower of Pisa, Italy   191
Leighton House Gallery, London   15
Lever Brothers   45
Lewis Carroll   43, 228
Lewis Carroll
lifting a tank one handed   178
Lincoln   138
lion   12, 44, 58, 85, 95
lion and the unicorn   85
Lipton's tea   39
Lithographic printing   50
lobster   121, 122, 170
lobster and oyster at the piano   122
lobster wearing an SS helmet   170
Lobsters   4, 121, 244
London   1, 3, 4, 5, 9, 12, 16, 20, 25, 26, 27, 30, 31, 39, 40, 43, 45, 51, 54, 59, 61, 66, 70, 95, 135, 151, 159, 160, 161, 164, 245
London Scottish   9
London Underground   47, 59
Lord Alexander of Tunis   18, 28, 33
Lord and Lady Millbanks   27
Lord Brabazon   27
Lord Gordon, the Comptroller of the Queens Household   31
Lord Mayor's Show   19
Lord Mountbatten   18, 19, 32
Lord Northbourne Prize for landscape composition   9
Lowndes Square, Belgravia, London   40

M

Machen & Hudson   39
Macleans   11
mad cellist   80
Maggi Hambling   40
Major Harry Morritt   12, 25, 26
Major S E Sidwell   165
man carrying a whale   93
man digging a trench   56
man launching a ship   83
Man leading a huge bull   199
man lifting a boat   118
man lifting a car   204
man lifting a giant globe   70
Man lifting a piano   204
man lifting a tree   69
man lifting car   204
man ploughing a field without a horse   204.

254

INDEX

Man sitting on a torpedo 182
man with dog 201
Mandrill on a rock 110
Mangnall-Irving Thrust-Borer 11
Mani Ayer, former CEO of Ogilvy & Mather (India) 41
Marmite 11
Marmon 151
Marquette 139
Martin Pick 20, 54, 55, 59, 61
Mather and Crowther Agency in London 45
McGill University, Montreal 15
Mechanical Grab 219
Menagerie for the Take Home poster 105
Mercedes 173, 174
MG Morris 142
Military personnel 5
Milkman with churns 203
Mills and Rockley of Ipswich 51
Ministry of Information 12, 27, 40
Molson Brewing family 28
Monk & Glass Custard 11
380. Monument Valley, Arizona 185
Moose Jaw, Calgary, Banff, Lake Louise, Vancouver 28
Morris Minor 142
Morritt Arms 12, 27
Motor Cars 134, 135, 142, 150, 151
Mount Kilimanjaro and steam train 195
Mount Rushmore, South Dakota 244
Mountbatten 14, 18, 19, 32
Mr Furlonger 15
Mr Ingleby 40
Mrs Joffey 30
Mrs Lois Maclean 28
Murder must Advertise 39, 40
Murrough Wilson, Chairman of L.N.E.R. 27
Mussolini 10
Mustard Club, J & J Coleman 11
Myrtle Cottage in Stedham 16

N

Natalie Sieveking (née Ackenhausen) 40
National Outdoor Advertising Award 181
National Outdoor Award of the Poster Industry 15
National Portrait Gallery 5
National Stout Survey 59
Nelson's Column 165
New York 41, 45, 135, 183, 184, 187, 188, 244
Newcastle 5, 9, 16, 20, 22
Newcastle Illustrated Chronicle 9
Newcastle Theatres 9
Newcastle University 16, 22
newspapers 11, 12, 51, 52
Nigeria 195
Norman Hartnell 31
Norman Smiley, Guinness MD 61

O

octopus 123
offset press 50
Ogilvy and Mather International Inc 41
Ogilvy, Benson and Mather 38, 45
old city walls of Jerusalem 194
Oliver Law 26
Olympic rings 159
Olympics in London 1948 159
orangutan 94, 244

Order of the Garter 30
Orpen 25, 27
ostrich 92, 97, 108, 235
Oswald Greene 11, 39
overloaded camel 83

P

P&O Cruises 25
Packard 137, 138, 152
Painted Hall at Greenwich 18
park keeper carrying two huge stacks of chairs 206
Park Royal 20, 45, 54, 59, 76, 169, 243
Park Royal London brewery 54, 61, 127, 164, 243
Patience Welfare 14
pelican 104
penguin 103
Peter Matthews 116
Peter Pears 40
Pheasantry Club in the Kings Road 29
Philip Benson 11
Phillip de Gylpyn Benson 39
Phoenix Park in Dublin 6
photographer 202
photolithography 50
Piccadilly neon clock, London 214
Pick's peaches 59
Pierce, commercial artist 59
Polar Bear and zookeeper 111
pole-vaulter 162
Polly Gilroy 13
Pope John XXIII 29
porter with heavy cases 65
Prince Charles 18, 32, 33
Prince Michael of Kent 18
Prince of Wales, the future Edward Vlll 12
Prince Philip, Duke of Edinburgh 17
Princess Anne 18
Princess Margaret 30, 31
Prix de Rome 10
Probyn 39
Professor Gerald Moira 10
Professor K.G. Hatten 19
Professor Kenney 19
Prohibition 183
Public Attitude Surveys 59
Punch 9, 14, 27

Q

Queen Mary 25,
Queen Mary liner 27
Queen Mother 30, 31, 33
Queen's Gate, Kensington 14, 30

R

R Clifford 135, 142
R.D. Bloomfield 40
RAF 12, 27, 32, 48, 181
RAF base and toucans 181
Randolph Churchill 40
Rasehill, Chorleywood Road, Rickmansworth 12, 27
Ray Tooby 30, 244
Raymond Erith 40
Read Brothers 39
Rhinoceros 106
Robert Bevan 11, 40, 41, 44
Robert Bevan, Captain RNVR, OBE 58

Robert McNeile, Guinness MD 58
Robert Polhill Bevan 40
Robin Bramley 14
Robin Day 17
Rokeby Hall, near Barnard Castle on the Tees 26, 27
Rolls Royce 144, 145, 152
Roman Forum 70
Ronald Barton 11
Ronald Blythe 40
Rover 143
rower and boat crew 197
Rowntree's Chocolate 39
Royal Academy 5, 9, 12, 22, 27, 66
Royal Albert Hall 25
Royal College of Art, Kensington 9
Royal Engineers 13
Royal Field Artillery 9, 10
Royal Lytham & St Annes 217
Royal Marines 32
Royal Marines, Plymouth 18
Royal Mid-Surrey Golf Club 12
Royal Naval Reserve 40
Royal Northumberland Fusiliers 9
Royal Portrait Society 31
Royal Portrush 218
Royals Ocean Racing Club 40
Royalty 5, 13
Royle family 13
Royle Publications Ltd 13
rugby scrum 116
runner 27, 161
runners 116
running toucan 130, 132
Rupert Guinness, 2nd Earl of Iveagh 6
Russia 5, 68, 79, 193
Russian Orthodox Churches, Moscow 193
Ryecroft Street, Fulham 16, 19

S

S C Allen & Co Ltd 51
Sailor loading a torpedo 176
sailor loading ordnance onto a trolley 177
Sailor returning from overseas with fruit 181
Salvador Dali 32
Samuel Herbert Benson 39
San Francisco 183, 184, 187
Sanders Phillips Ltd of London 52
Sandyford School 9
Saw Mill 203
Scarecrow 201
Schloss Neuschwanstein in Bavaria 171
Scotland Yard 30
Sculptor 29, 30, 199
sea lion 95, 96, 236
sea lion balancing a barrel 207
Seagull 200
Sebastian Earle 26
Show cards 4, 44, 55, 114, 115, 116, 118, 121, 124, 125, 204
Sidmouth, Devon 14
silk screen print 51
single skuller 197
Sir Alfred Munnings 29
Sir Archibald Sinclair, the Minister of Aviation 28
Sir Bernard Partridge 14
Sir C Aubrey Smith 25

255

INDEX

Sir Errington Keville   18
Sir Harold Gillies the surgeon   27
Sir Hugh Beaver   31, 40
Sir James Gunn RA   26
Sir James Shannon   15
Sir John Cockcroft   32
Sir John Lytham   9
Sir Lionel Heald   26
Sir Seymour Hicks, the actor   26
Sir Stanley Jackson   25
Skipper Sardines   11
Sleepers Hill, Winchester   14
Smiling Glass   208, 209, 211, 214, 238
snake   61
soldier with heavy kit   203
Speakman of Melbourne   39
Spitfire   44, 178
spitfire
squid holding glass of Guinness   123
St Helen's Church, Kensington   10
St Paul's Cathedral   163, 164
St Paul's Church, Covent Garden   19
St Pauls Churchyard, London   59
St. James' Gate Brewery in Dublin   39, 63, 167, 172
Stalin   5
Stanislawa de Karlowski   40
Stanley Darmon   55
Stanley Penn   11
Star newspaper   12, 28
Stars and stripes USA flag   189
574. Statue of Liberty New York   187, 188
steamroller   68, 78
Stech-helm   221
stone lithography   50
Stone of London   39
Stork   92, 235
stork
Straight Glass advert   44
Strongman statue   44
Stutz   155
Sunderland Public Art Gallery   12
Sunlight Soap   11
Sunningdale   14

T

T B Case the Guinness Managing Director   39
Terry Sisters   9
The Hall School   40
The Jolly Lobster   122
The Press   243
Third Reich Germany   170
Thirst lesson   213
Tommy Marks MC   3, 55, 59
Tony Anthony   60
Tony Thwaite   3, 20, 21
tortoise   98, 109, 237
toucan   117, 126
toucan opening bottles with his beak   128, 129
Toucans in the nest   130
Tower Bridge   164
Trevor Fenwick   17, 26
Tweedle Dum and Tweedle Dee   228
Two heads are better than one   211
two seals   85

U

Uncle Sam   190
United Africa Company UAC   195
United States of America   183
Unmistakable   212
Upper Grosvenor Galleries, London   16
US Naval Intelligence   40
Vesta Tilley   9
Virol   11
Vivien Pitchforth   10
Volkswagen   173

W

W. E. Phillips of Guinness   59
Walter Hill   52
Watercolours and roughs   196, 197, 198, 200, 201, 202
Waterloo Bridge   70
Waterlow & Sons Ltd   51
weathervane and toucan   244
Wedding of the Chairman, Lord Iveagh   62
Wedgewood   18
Wehrmacht Soldier   168
weight lifter   160
Wembley Empire Exhibition   59
Wembley Stadium   159
Wentworth   217
Westminster School Kings Scholar   40
Whitley Bay   9
Wilkinson (Wilks)   68
Will Hay film Convict 99   14
William Brearley   11, 53, 209, 218
Winnipeg, the prairies   28
wood chopper   44
wooden advertising boards   53
Woodpecker   89
World War II   44
World's Trade Fair in New York   135
WPP   45

Y

yacht Phryna   40

Z

Zebra   113
zinc plate   50
zookeeper carol singing   207
Zookeeper riding a camel   90
Zookeeper   87, 88, 89, 92, 93, 100, 108, 162, 235

256

First published in 2013 by
Liberties Press
140 Terenure Road North | Terenure | Dublin 6W
Tel: +353 (1) 405 5703
www.libertiespress.com | info@libertiespress.com

Trade enquiries to Gill & Macmillan Distribution
Hume Avenue | Park West | Dublin 12
T: +353 (1) 500 9534 | F: +353 (1) 500 9595 | E: sales@gillmacmillan.ie

Distributed in the United States by
Dufour Editions | PO Box 7 | Chester Springs | Pennsylvania | 19425

Distributed in the UK by
Turnaround Publisher Services
Unit 3 | Olympia Trading Estate | Coburg Road | London N22 6TZ
T: +44 (0) 20 8829 3000 | E: orders@turnaround-uk.com

ISBN:978-1-907593-99-4

This book and its contents are the copyright of David Hughes
© David Hughes, 2013

Cover design by Jim Gilroy
Internal design by Ros Murphy
Printed by Hussar

This book is sold subject to the condition that it shall not, by way of trade or otherwise, be lent, resold, hired out or otherwise circulated, without the publisher's prior consent, in any form other than that in which it is published and without a similar condition including this condition being imposed on the subsequent publisher. No part of this publication may be reproduced or transmitted in any form or by any means, electronic or mechanical, including photocopying, recording or storage in any information or retrieval system, without the prior permission of the publisher in writing.

A CIP catalogue record for this book is available from the British Library.
Design by The Frank Agency, Faringdon, Oxfordshire and Liberties Press.
Printing and publishing by Liberties Press Ltd, Dublin.

'The GUINNESS word and all associated logos are Trade Marks and are used under licence.'
'Any opinions set out in this book are those of the author and not of Guinness & Co. or its related entities.
This book is not endorsed or approved by Guinness & Co. or its related entities.'

THE GUINNESS® COLLECTORS CLUB

Join the Guinness Collectors Club at
www.guinnesscollectorsclub.co.uk